A New Model for Balanced Growth and Convergence

A New Model for Balanced Growth and Convergence

Achieving Economic Sustainability in CESEE Countries

Edited by

Ewald Nowotny

Governor of the Oesterreichische Nationalbank, Austria

Peter Mooslechner

Member of the Governing Board of the Oesterreichische Nationalbank, Austria

Doris Ritzberger-Grünwald

Director of the Economic Analysis and Research Department at the Oesterreichische Nationalbank, Austria

PUBLISHED IN ASSOCIATION WITH THE OESTERREICHISCHE NATIONALBANK

Edward Elgar

Cheltenham, UK • Northampton, MA, USA

Published by
Edward Elgar Publishing Limited
The Lypiatts
15 Lansdown Road
Cheltenham
Glos GL50 2JA
UK

Edward Elgar Publishing, Inc.
William Pratt House
9 Dewey Court
Northampton
Massachusetts 01060
USA

A catalogue record for this book
is available from the British Library

Library of Congress Control Number: 2013938072

This book is available electronically in the ElgarOnline.com
Economics Subject Collection, E-ISBN 978 1 78254 817 1

ISBN 978 1 78254 816 4

Typeset by Servis Filmsetting Ltd, Stockport, Cheshire
Printed and bound in Great Britain by T.J. International Ltd, Padstow

Contents

List of contributors   vii
Preface   ix

PART I   FRAMING THE DISCUSSION ON BALANCED
          GROWTH IN EUROPE

1   The necessity of sustainable growth and continued income
     convergence in Europe   3
     Ewald Nowotny

2   Changes in banking in the run-up to the crisis   12
     Erkki Liikanen

3   Restarting growth in Europe after the Great Recession: CEE
     versus other countries   19
     Seppo Honkapohja and Iikka Korhonen

4   The European debt crisis and a stable design of EMU   36
     Klaas Knot and Silvie Verkaart

PART II   STOP AND GO OF CAPITAL FLOWS AND
          DELEVERAGING

5   Managing stop–go capital flows in Asian emerging markets:
     lessons for the CESEE economies   49
     Andrew Filardo

6   CESEE banks deleveraging or rebalancing? Lessons from the
     EIB bank lending survey   60
     Luca Gattini and Debora Revoltella

7   Managing capital flows in a globalized economy   92
     Marek Dabrowski

PART III   GROWTH STRATEGIES OF EU
           NEIGHBOURING COUNTRIES: RUSSIA AND
           TURKEY

 8   Russia in 2012: the challenge of reforming the economy
     without a political reform   113
     Konstantin Sonin

 9   Sustaining growth in emerging markets: the role of structural
     and monetary policies   122
     Ahmet Faruk Aysan, Mustafa Haluk Güler and Cüneyt Orman

PART IV   SMALL-COUNTRY EXPERIENCES IN
          ECONOMIC ADJUSTMENT

10   Business cycle convergence or decoupling? Economic
     adjustment of CESEE countries during the crisis   147
     *Martin Gächter, Aleksandra Riedl and
     Doris Ritzberger-Grünwald*

11   South-Eastern Europe: impacts from the crisis, vulnerabilities
     and adjustments   170
     Dimitar Bogov and Aneta Krstevska

12   Economic adjustment in the Baltic countries   190
     Ardo Hansson and Martti Randveer

PART V   A PRACTITIONER'S VIEW

13   Basel III from a practitioner's perspective   209
     Esa Tuomi and Eriks Plato

14   Banks' challenges in Central and Eastern Europe   222
     Radovan Jelašić

15   Banking in CEE: less growth, more balance   226
     Gianfranco Bisagni, Matteo Ferrazzi and Pia Pumberger

Index   241

Contributors

Ahmet Faruk Aysan, Member of the Board, Central Bank of the Republic of Turkey.

Gianfranco Bisagni, Head of Corporate and Investment Banking – Central Eastern Europe and Deputy Head of Central Eastern Europe Division, Bank Austria, UniCredit.

Dimitar Bogov, Governor, National Bank of the Republic of Macedonia.

Marek Dabrowski, Fellow, CASE – Center for Social and Economic Research.

Matteo Ferrazzi, Bank Austria, UniCredit.

Andrew Filardo, Head of Economics for Asia and the Pacific, Bank for International Settlements.

Martin Gächter, Foreign Research Division, Oesterreichische Nationalbank.

Luca Gattini, Economics Department, European Investment Bank.

Mustafa Haluk Güler, Expert, Markets Department, Central Bank of the Republic of Turkey.

Ardo Hansson, Governor, Eesti Pank.

Seppo Honkapohja, Member of the Board, Suomen Pankki.

Radovan Jelašić, Chief Executive Officer, Erste Bank Hungary.

Klaas Knot, President, De Nederlandsche Bank.

Iikka Korhonen, Head of BOFIT, Suomen Pankki.

Aneta Krstevska, Chief Economist, National Bank of the Republic of Macedonia.

Erkki Liikanen, Governor, Suomen Pankki.

Ewald Nowotny, Governor, Oesterreichische Nationalbank.

Cüneyt Orman, Deputy Executive Director, Communication and

International Relations Department, Central Bank of the Republic of Turkey.

Eriks Plato, Nordea Bank.

Pia Pumberger, Bank Austria, UniCredit.

Martti Randveer, Head of the Economics and Research Department, Eesti Pank.

Debora Revoltella, Director, European Investment Bank.

Aleksandra Riedl, Foreign Research Division, Oesterreichische Nationalbank.

Doris Ritzberger-Grünwald, Director of the Economic Analysis and Research Department, Oesterreichische Nationalbank.

Konstantin Sonin, SUEK Professor of Economics, New Economic School, Moscow.

Esa Tuomi, Senior Vice President, Head of Corporate and Institutional Banking, Poland and Baltic Countries, Nordea Bank.

Silvie Verkaart, Head of Treasury and Monitoring, Financial Markets Division, De Nederlandsche Bank.

Current account deficit (2007)

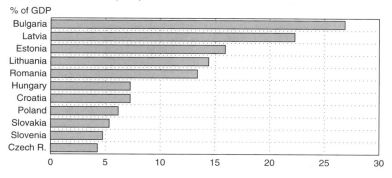

Average annual growth in house prices (2004–2007)

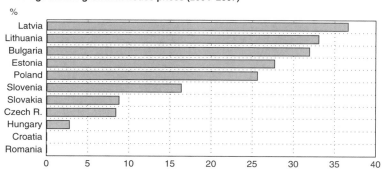

Figure 1.1 (continued)

robust performance of Poland. OeNB simulations show that a growth differential, which remains persistently below two percentage points, requires a considerably longer time period for the CESEE region to reach the income level of the euro area than expected before the crisis (see Ritzberger-Grünwald and Wörz, 2009). Also, the catching-up is less smooth due to large swings in CESEE cycles, particularly for small countries, as emphasized by Gächter, Riedl and Ritzberger-Grünwald in this volume (chapter 10).

A delayed catching-up process poses serious challenges to further economic and institutional reforms in CESEE and might affect the people's support for European integration. A continuous reduction of regional inequalities in Europe is also in the interest of Western Europe, given that several cross-country studies have shown that a more unequal income distribution is associated – at least up to a certain degree – with lower

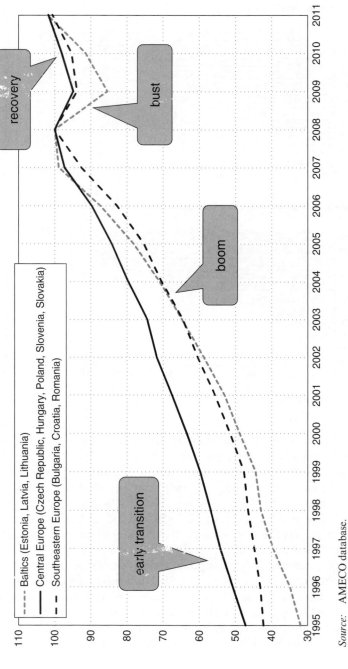

Source: AMECO database.

Figure 1.2 Real GDP growth per capita in the long run (average growth in purchasing power parity, 2008 = 100)

8

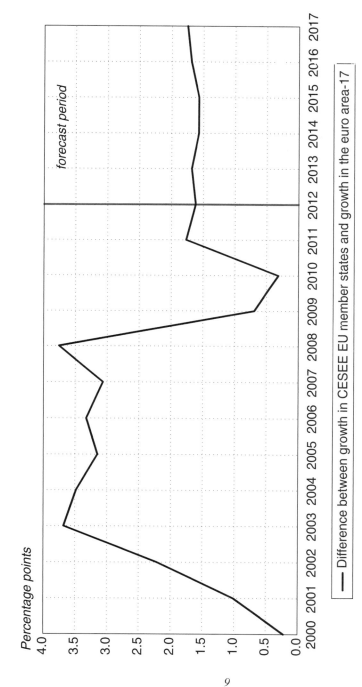

Note: Estonia, Slovakia and Slovenia are included in both the euro area aggregate and the aggregate of the CESEE EU member states.

Sources: Eurostat and IMF (World Economic Outlook, October 2012).

Figure 1.3 Growth differential of EU member states vis-à-vis the euro area (in percentage points)

long-run economic growth (see Banerjee and Duflo, 2003; Voitchovsky, 2005; or Halter and Oechslin, 2010).

1.5 CONCLUSION

Pronounced boom–bust cycles not only lead to high output volatility but also hurt the long-term growth prospects of an economy. This is especially valid for the CESEE economies that experienced a sharp output decline in 2009, and – according to the OeNB-BOF[2] projections as of November 2012 – there might even be a second recession phase in the wings in several countries of the region. The main lesson from the 2008–2009 crisis is that the foreign capital inflow-based growth model is not sustainable in the long run and cross-country contagion via trade and financial channels from Western to Eastern Europe can be quick and substantial.

Many countries have undertaken severe restructuring programmes during the last few years which aimed at reducing their public and private sector indebtedness and increasing their external competitiveness. We will have to watch the success of these programmes very closely in the upcoming years.

We also saw that the economic adjustment costs caused by high output volatility are substantial, as they have a direct impact on the speed of the catching-up of Eastern European income levels to those in Western Europe. A considerable delay in the convergence process cannot be in our interest. Therefore, we have to find new growth models that prove to be sustainable and crisis-resilient and continue to promote the convergence process in Europe.

NOTES

1. Markus Eller and Isabella Moder, of the Oesterreichische Nationalbank's staff, contributed to these remarks.
2. OeNB = Oesterreichische Nationalbank; BOF = Bank of Finland.

REFERENCES

Bakker, B. and C. Klingen (eds) (2012), 'How emerging Europe came through the 2008/09 crisis – an account by the staff of the IMF's European Department', Washington, DC: International Monetary Fund.
Banerjee, A.V. and E. Duflo (2003), 'Inequality and growth: what can the data say?', *Journal of Economic Growth*, **8** (3), 267–99.

EBRD (2009), 'Transition Report 2009 – Transition in crisis?', London: European Bank for Reconstruction and Development.

Halter, D. and M. Oechslin (2010), 'Inequality and growth: the neglected time dimension', CEPR Discussion Papers No. 8033, September.

Ritzberger-Grünwald, D. and J. Wörz (2009), 'Macroconvergence in CESEE', in OeNB (ed.), *Twenty Years of East–West Integration: Hopes and Achievements, Focus on European Economic Integration – Special Issue 2009*, pp. 56–65.

Voitchovsky, S. (2005), 'Does the profile of income inequality matter for economic growth?', *Journal of Economic Growth*, **10** (3), 273–96.

2. Changes in banking in the run-up to the crisis

Erkki Liikanen

2.1 INTRODUCTION

In the years preceding the global financial crisis that started in 2007, the landscape of banking had undergone major changes. Global financial institutions had grown ever bigger in size and scope and their organizational complexity had increased, adding to their opacity. They had become strongly interconnected via increasingly long chains of claims as well as correlated risk exposures, arising from increasingly similar investment strategies. Their leverage had strongly increased and the average maturity of their own funding had shortened.

Behind these trends were forces that intensified competition in banking; technological development and deregulation. Advances in information technology as well as in investment theory and practice meant that commercial banks faced increasing competition on both the liability side and the asset side.[1]

New savings alternatives to bank deposits, such as money market mutual funds, proliferated and new opportunities for borrowing, in addition to bank loans, emerged. In fact, an entire shadow banking sector developed, comprising a chain of non-bank institutions which were able to provide similar financial intermediary services as traditional banks.

In this environment, deregulation was partly a response to the aforementioned changes and enabled banks to cope with the increasing pressure from non-bank competitors. In the United States, the gradual unwinding and the ultimate repeal of the Glass–Steagall Act in the late 1990s made it possible to reunite investment banking and commercial banking, which had been separated since the crisis of the 1930s.[2]

In Europe, the universal banking model already had a longer history of combining commercial banking and investment banking under the same roof. However, there was a trend before the crisis, among the biggest European banking institutions, to strengthen their focus on investment

systemic crises. Hence, almost by definition, tail risks are difficult to model and measure. Separation of the riskiest trading activities from deposit banking is a key to limiting the impact of these risks. Other measures available are robust capital requirements which do not heavily rely on models, and limits on risk concentrations and counterparty exposures.

In this respect, the European High-Level Expert Group on reforming the structure of the EU banking sector acknowledges the important work in reviewing the trading book capital requirements conducted by the Basel Committee on Banking Supervision. The Group recommends that the European Commission should carry out an evaluation of whether the resultant amendments, in terms of robust capital requirements and limits on risk concentrations and counterparty exposures, would be sufficient at the EU level. The Group recommends that the Commission should also evaluate the sufficiency of the current capital requirements on real estate-related lending which has been the major source of losses in many financial crises, including the most recent one.

2.5 COMPARISON WITH OTHER STRUCTURAL PROPOSALS

An important objective of the mandatory separation, proposed by the Group, is simplicity and unambiguity. These facilitate implementation at the EU level. Furthermore, banking activities which naturally belong together should be conducted within the same legal entity.

To promote these aims the proposed mandatory separation includes both proprietary trading and market making, as differentiating these activities from one another would be challenging[5] and, if placed in different legal entities within the same banking group, some natural synergies might be lost. In this respect, the proposal defines deposit banks somewhat more narrowly than the Volcker Rule in the United States. However, an important difference is that the proposed mandatory separation in the EU can take place within a banking group, whereas the Volcker Rule prohibits proprietary trading for the entire banking group. Further, deposit banks are allowed to extend all types of corporate loans because differentiating among corporate loans according to customer size would be equally challenging at the EU level, and important scale economies in corporate lending might be lost as a result. This implies that, as regards corporate lending, deposit banks would be somewhat broader than under the proposal made by the Independent Commission on Banking headed by former Bank of England chief economist John Vickers.

2.6 THE ROLE OF BANKS IN FINANCING THE EUROPEAN ECONOMY

Banks have a pivotal role in providing finance to households and firms. This is particularly so in Europe where banks have traditionally had a large role in corporate finance. Banks' role in corporate finance is central, especially for small and medium-sized enterprises (SMEs). The continuous and smooth supply of banking services to SMEs is also essential for large corporations because SMEs are often subcontractors to them. It is of the utmost importance that regulatory reforms as a whole support and strengthen the banking sector's ability to continue to provide these socially vital financial services efficiently and in a stable manner.

NOTES

1. See, for example, Hoenig and Morris (2011).
2. See, for example, Pennacchi (2012).
3. See, for example, Adrian and Shin (2010).
4. See, for example, Haldane (2010).
5. See, for example, Duffie (2012).

REFERENCES

Adrian, T. and H.S. Shin (2010), 'The changing nature of financial intermediation and the financial crisis of 2007–09', New York Federal Reserve Bank Staff Report No. 439.

Duffie, D. (2012), 'Market making under the proposed Volcker rule', Rock Center for Corporate Governance at Stanford University Working Paper No. 106, available at http://papers.ssrn.com/sol3/papers.cfm?abstract_id=1990472.

Haldane, A.G. (2010), 'The $100 billion question', mimeo.

High-level Expert Group on reforming the structure of the EU banking sector (2012), 'Final report', 22 January, available at http://ec.europa.eu/internal_market/bank/group_of_experts/index_en.htm.

Hoenig, T.M. and C.S. Morris (2011), 'Restructuring the banking system to improve safety and soundness', mimeo, Kansas City Fed.

Pennacchi, G. (2012), 'Narrow banking', *Annual Review of Financial Economics*, **4**, 141–59.

3. Restarting growth in Europe after the Great Recession: CEE versus other countries

Seppo Honkapohja and Iikka Korhonen

3.1 INTRODUCTION

Our objective is to provide an overview of key issues related to economic growth in Central and Eastern European (CEE) countries following the recent economic downturn. The discussion mainly relies on comparisons with European Union (EU) and euro area countries, sometimes also at a more disaggregated level. We thus assume the perspective of comparative macroeconomics.

We first look back in time and consider the question of convergence in living standards. In particular, did EU membership facilitate convergence by speeding up economic growth in the CEE countries? Are per capita gross domestic product (GDP) levels converging to the EU average, in line with the convergence hypothesis? The broad and quick answer to both questions is yes.

Next we look at other variables. One set of issues and variables concerns the behaviour and measurement of macroeconomic balances; these will enable us to check on whether the convergence process is sustainable. In other words, have there been major imbalances in the economic developments? The current account and public sector balances in the CEE countries are commonly applied metrics of macroeconomic balance. We also look at private sector indebtedness.

Another variable of interest is unemployment, since it is an indicator of the degree of balance in the labour markets and success in structural adjustment. A related issue is the extent of labour and product market regulation.

Secondly, we consider the impact of the financial crisis which emerged in 2008 on growth performance in the CEE countries. The CEE countries were of course hit by the global financial crisis and the ensuing Great Recession. How deep was the resulting decline in GDP? How well did the

CEE countries adjust to the recession, as compared to other EU and euro area countries? What accounts for the differences in adjustment within the group of CEE countries?

Thirdly, we look at the most recent years, that is to say the period since 2009. How successfully did the CEE countries come out of the recession, and were they able to resume economic growth? Because the CEE countries are open economies, their future performance is critically dependent on their success in external trade. In the last part of the chapter we also consider the performance of the CEE countries in terms of recent export dynamics.

3.2   CONVERGENCE AND GROWTH

Figure 3.1 shows the CEE countries' ratios of per capita GDP to EU average (purchasing power parity adjusted) in the period from 1995 to 2011. We can see that nearly all CEE countries moved onto positive growth paths in the second half of the 1990s, following the output decline in connection with the transition from a socialist economy to a

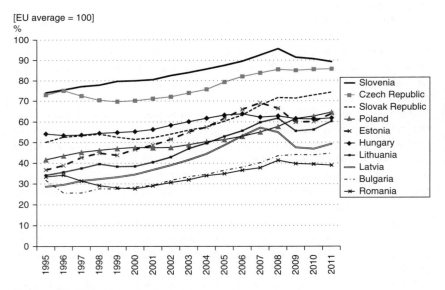

Source: World Bank.

Figure 3.1   GDP per capita at purchasing power parity in relation to the EU average

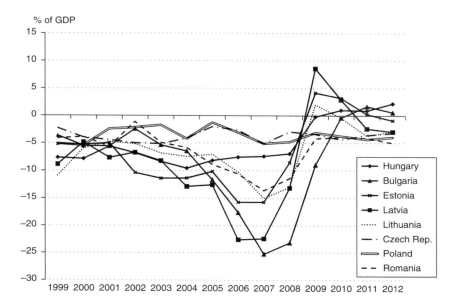

% of GDP

Sources: European Commission, ECB and Bank of Finland.

Figure 3.5 *Current account balances in the CEE countries (in per cent of GDP)*

capital inflows, which in turn led to higher demand for non-tradable goods, increases in their prices, and a consequent loss of competitiveness. This course of events is most obvious for the Baltic countries, and it resulted in current account deficits of almost 25 per cent of GDP in 2006 and 2007 in the worst cases.

When the Great Recession hit, a sudden stop of capital inflows led to swift improvements in external balances. Current account deficits are now generally in the 0 to 5 per cent range for most CEE countries. Since the recession, Bulgaria and Romania have actually managed to post small current account surpluses.

Figure 3.6 shows current account developments in the euro area. As is well known, the euro area as a whole has been in a position of near zero external balance since 2000, and movements in the balance have been miniscule. The GIIPS countries posted current account deficits before the boom years 2005 to 2008, and these deficits increased during the boom period. Current accounts started to improve with the onset of the recession, and in 2013 the GIIPS countries are moving toward external balance. For the high-ranked euro area countries, the behaviour of the

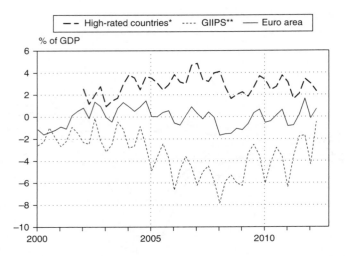

Figure 3.6   Current account balances in the euro area (% of GDP)

current account balance has been different: they have on average recorded surpluses.

Next, we consider the fiscal balances of CEE and EU countries. In Figure 3.7 the CEE countries are divided into two groups: countries with floating exchange rates and those with firmly fixed exchange rates (Baltic countries and Bulgaria). One key observation from Figure 3.7 is that public sector balances move broadly in tandem in the three groups: the EU and floating-rate and fixed-rate CEE countries. We note that both the EU countries on the average and the floating-rate CEE countries recorded clear public deficits in the first half of the 2000s. Moreover, the deficits for the latter group were relatively large. In contrast, the fixed-rate CEE countries had either small public deficits or surpluses. Therefore, we can say that the chosen exchange rate regimes in the Baltic countries and Bulgaria did operate as intended: they had a significant impact on the conduct of fiscal policy. The deficits of EU and floating-rate CEE countries shrank during the boom years from 2005 to 2007. In 2008 the public deficits began to expand for all three groups, and in the recession year 2009 they worsened significantly. But there were improvements during the recovery period of 2010 and 2011. Nonetheless public deficits were still prevalent in 2011, running in the 2 to 4.5 percent range.

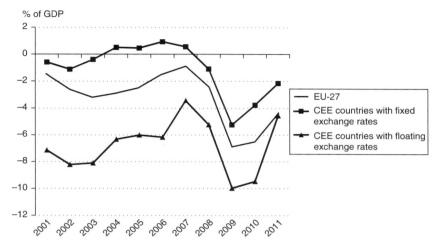

% of GDP

Source: European Commission and Bank of Finland.

Figure 3.7 Public sector balances (% of GDP)

Before looking at private sector imbalances, it is worth recalling that, especially in the boom years, the current account deficits – shown in Figures 3.5 and 3.6 – reflected high levels of private consumption and investment.[6] Figure 3.8 displays developments in private sector imbalances in the CEE and euro area countries. The figure also shows the private debt data separately for the high-rated and GIIPS countries in the euro area. Our initial observation is that starting in 2000 private sector debt in the euro area has increased from 130 per cent to 170 per cent of GDP. As can been seen, a part of the overall increase is the rapid enlargement of private indebtedness in the GIIPS countries, but private indebtedness also increased in the high-rated euro area countries.

Looking at the CEE countries,[7] we first note that the level of private indebtedness in the CEE countries is clearly below that of the 'old' EU countries. However, the CEE countries have also been faced with rising private debt–GDP ratios, from 70 per cent to 100 per cent. Figure 3.8 only displays aggregate data for the CEE countries. It should be pointed out that the differences in private indebtedness between the CEE countries are large. In Hungary and Bulgaria the private debt–GDP ratio is almost twice as high (about 150 per cent) as in the Czech Republic and Poland (about 80 per cent). Therefore it is probably true that the CEE countries' higher indebtedness increased the vulnerability of the private sector to negative income shocks.

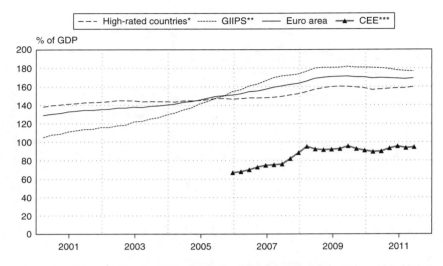

Note: * = Germany, France, Netherlands, Austria and Finland; ** = Greece, Ireland, Italy, Portugal and Spain; *** = Bulgaria, Czech Republic, Hungary and Poland.

Source: European Central Bank.

Figure 3.8   Private sector indebtedness (% of GDP)

3.5   UNEMPLOYMENT AND STRUCTURAL ASPECTS

As is well known, and apparent from Figure 3.9, the CEE countries had relatively high rates of unemployment in the early years of the 2000s. (In Figure 3.9 the group of CEE countries consists of Bulgaria, the Czech Republic, Hungary, Poland and Romania.) We note that unemployment was clearly higher in this group of CEE countries than average unemployment in the GIIPS countries of the euro area.[8] The higher unemployment rate can be partly explained by the legacy of economic transition from socialism to a more market-based economy. In almost every transition economy, this process was marked by severe imbalances in the labour markets, as many workers found that their old education and work experience had depreciated in value in the new environment. It took many years for this legacy of the transition era to fade away. Figure 3.9 also distinguishes between the high-rated countries, the GIIPS countries and the euro area average.

Unemployment in these CEE countries at first moved up slightly, but

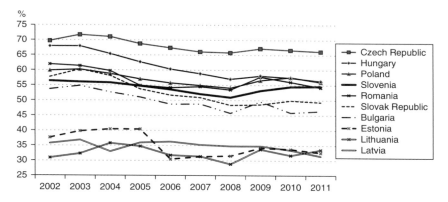

Source: IMF (Direction of Trade database).

Figure 3.13   Share of exports going to the euro area

generally been trending downward. The 2009 recession was an exceptional time, but the trend has reappeared.

It turns out that the broad picture is somewhat different when one looks at exports of CEE countries to the EU as a whole.[10] Here there are clear differences between countries. For some CEE countries, the share of exports to the EU has increased, whereas for other countries (the Czech Republic, Hungary, Latvia, Lithuania) it is possible to discern a decreasing trend. We did not have the opportunity to look at the destinations in great detail, but note that the role of trade with Russia has been increasing for most CEE countries, with Slovakia and Slovenia being exceptions here. It is also noteworthy that the share of China in CEE exports has been increasing, albeit it is still quite small, usually between 1 and 2 per cent of the total value of exports.

A further aspect of trade integration is the evolution in the quality of exports. Janský (2010) assesses the unit value of exports in the ten CEE countries that joined the EU in 2004 and 2007. He finds that unit prices have risen for all countries, signifying increased sophistication of exports. This export upgrading has occurred both within product categories and by moving into higher-value-added products.

3.7   CONCLUSIONS

Given the rocky road that the Western world has experienced since 2008, it is comforting to see that the CEE countries have generally been able to resume growth after the Great Recession. The global financial crisis has caused significant damage, but it could have been worse. It seems that the latter countries were able to make the necessary adjustments so as to improve competitiveness and reduce imbalances, and this had the result that the adverse consequences of the recession remained fairly moderate.

One important feature that has facilitated the adjustment is the relatively high flexibility of the labour and product markets. Moreover, the levels of private and public indebtedness were lower than in many other European countries, especially the GIIPS countries.

As regards the future, we would emphasize that maintaining openness and positive attitudes toward economic integration are crucial.[11] They are major building blocks in the continuous success in foreign trade. We note here that the export performance shows an improvement as the economies have been climbing out of the 2009 recession. The share of exports to the euro area is currently declining, which perhaps signals a gradual increase in export diversity. Increased diversity is likely to be beneficial, given that future prospects for different parts of the world are liable to shift, so that the outlook is quite uncertain.

To conclude this overview, the performance of most CEE countries during the turbulent years since 2005 suggests that the outlook for them is at least modestly promising. A reasonably successful performance is, however, by no means self-evident. Very determined action is required to maintain and improve competitiveness of the economy. This is in our view the key challenge facing the CEE countries.

NOTES

1. It should be emphasized that Figure 3.2 shows group averages weighted by GDP shares. It does not necessarily follow that each group member's GDP has surpassed its pre-recession peak.
2. Cuaresma and Feldkircher (2012) study other aspects of the adjustment of emerging European countries in the recession of 2008–2009.
3. See Benkovskis and Wörz (2012) for a detailed study of measures of competitiveness.
4. Goodhart and Lee (2012) compare adjustments in Latvia and Spain to Arizona and other US states. They find that Latvia's wage adjustment has been larger than usually observed in the United States. Also movement of labour across borders has made Latvia's adjustment easier.
5. Note that the rate of increase in Polish unit labour costs before the boom was exceptionally low compared to the other countries shown in Figure 3.4.
6. It may be recalled that the current account measures the deficit or surplus in the overall – both private and public – balance of savings minus investments of an economy.
7. The data for the CEE countries are available only from 2007 onward.
8. It should be noted that Poland, being a large country, dominates the data to some extent.

9. This average figure hides some differences between the GIIPS countries. Ireland is the most open of these countries, with exports exceeding 100 per cent of GDP in some years. Also Spain and Portugal have become more open relative to pre-crisis levels.
10. We omit the details for brevity.
11. The roles of openness and integration are of course commonly emphasized. For example, see Honkapohja (2011), McMorrow and Röger (2011) and Rosati (2011).

REFERENCES

Benkovskis, K. and J. Wörz (2012), 'Non-price competitiveness gains of Central, Eastern and Southeastern European countries in the EU market', *Focus on European Integration*, **Q3**, 27–47.
Cuaresma, J.C. and M. Feldkircher (2012), 'Drivers of output loss during the 2008–09 crisis: a focus on emerging Europe', *Focus on European Integration*, **Q2**, 46–64.
European Bank for Reconstruction and Development (2012), 'Transition report 2012', London: European Bank for Reconstruction and Development.
Goodhart, C. and J. Lee (2012), 'Adjustment mechanisms in a currency area', Centre for Economic Policy Research Discussion Paper 9226.
Honkapohja, S. (2011), 'Re-establishing growth after the crisis – lessons from the nordic countries', in E. Nowotny, P. Mooslechner and D. Ritzberger-Grünwald (eds), *Post-Crisis Growth and Integration in Europe, Catching-Up Strategies in CESEE Economies*, Cheltenham, UK and Northampton, MA, USA: Edward Elgar, pp. 19–31.
Janský, P. (2010), 'Rising unit values of Central and Eastern European exports: rising quality in transition?', *International Journal of Economic Policy in Emerging Economies*, **3** (2), 147–57.
McMorrow, K. and W. Röger (2011), 'Catching-up prospects after the crisis for the EUs CESEE Region', in E. Nowotny, P. Mooslechner and D. Ritzberger-Grünwald (eds), *Post-Crisis Growth and Integration in Europe, Catching-Up Strategies in CESEE economies*, Cheltenham, UK and Northampton, MA, USA: Edward Elgar, pp. 32–44.
Rosati, D.K. (2011), 'Growth prospects in the EU-10 member states after the crisis', in E. Nowotny, P. Mooslechner and D. Ritzberger-Grünwald (eds), *Post-Crisis Growth and Integration in Europe: Catching-Up Strategies in CESEE Economies*, Cheltenham, UK and Northampton, MA, USA: Edward Elgar, pp. 45–62.

4. The European debt crisis and a stable design of EMU

Klaas Knot and Silvie Verkaart

The European debt crisis confronts us with a number of questions. What went wrong? Why were we so late in spotting what went wrong? What can be done about it? The central thesis of this contribution is that the rules governing the economic and monetary union (EMU) focused too much on fiscal positions and excessive deficits. However, fiscal profligacy was not the root cause of the crisis, but mainly a manifest of much deeper-rooted macroeconomic and financial imbalances, such as asset price bubbles and loss of competitiveness. In the future design of EMU, these underlying causes will have to be addressed.

Before the start of EMU, several economists doubted whether rules for national governments were necessary at all (for an overview of the discussion, see Eichengreen and Wyplosz, 1998). Some of them were convinced that financial markets would enforce policy discipline. Markets were expected to restrain profligate governments by charging them higher interest rates and, thus, forcing them to change their ways. However, during the first ten years of EMU, the market charged euro area governments practically the same interest rate, regardless of the underlying fiscal position (Figure 4.1). This did not help to discipline governments. When the debt crisis hit in 2009, market discipline returned with a vengeance.

Although market discipline is now imposing necessary corrections, a stable monetary union cannot be based on such an 'on/off' mechanism. So what about the rules governing EMU? As is clear from Figure 4.2, the prospect of EMU entry disciplined governments, but once inside EMU, most countries relaxed fiscal discipline somewhat. We should not forget, however, that this was facilitated by some of the core countries of EMU. When it became clear that fiscal policies in France and Germany would not be able to meet the rules of the Stability and Growth Pact, it was not the policies that were changed but the Pact. This was clearly a mistake.

More in general, due to its political enforcement, the Stability and Growth Pact did not achieve fiscal discipline in good times (DNB, 2010). This resulted in procyclical fiscal policies and too-high debt levels.

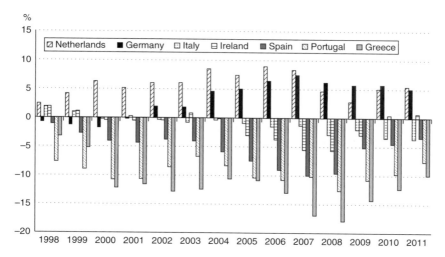

Source: Eurostat.

Figure 4.6 *Current account balances of selected euro area countries (% of GDP)*

indicators also point to competitiveness problems in most of the countries concerned. The Global Competitiveness Index of the World Economic Forum, ranking 142 countries based on policy areas such as the quality of institutions and the efficiency of the labour market, places Spain, Italy, Portugal and Greece in positions 36, 42, 49 and 96, respectively. For comparison, Finland, the Netherlands and Germany are in positions 3, 5 and 6. In the former countries, product and labour markets did not function properly, and although certain adjustments have been made, a lot still needs to be done. Markets are overregulated and labour markets are highly inflexible (Jaumotte and Morsy, 2012). By addressing these problems, labour productivity can increase, thereby lowering unit labour costs. This will not be easy, of course, but such steps are necessary for EMU to function properly (DNB, 2012a).

As Figure 4.6 shows, the competitiveness problems were reflected in the current account. Before the crisis, most Southern European countries, and to a lesser extent Ireland, experienced high and steadily increasing current account deficits, while the current account surpluses of Germany and the Netherlands improved further. For many years it was thought that in a monetary union, the current account balances of individual countries were no longer relevant; it was only the balance of payments of the euro area as a whole that mattered. We know better now.

The macroeconomic and financial imbalances had a big impact on government finances (DNB, 2012b). In the build-up phase, they boosted governments' tax income. In the bust phase, they caused a large drop in tax income, leading to an unexpected sharp increase in budget deficits and public debt. In EMU as a whole, the fiscal deficit in 2009 increased by some 5 per cent of gross domestic product (GDP) on average compared to the pre-crisis expected deficit, while public debt increased by 15 per cent of GDP. Countries with large imbalances saw their fiscal deficit rise by 10 per cent of GDP on average, and public debt by a stunning 45 per cent of GDP. This mainly reflected a drop in government income, while the costs of bank rescues and economic stimulus packages played a much smaller role (DNB, 2012b).

The imbalances and high current account deficits also implied that banks in Southern European countries and Ireland attracted a lot of private foreign financing. This fostered financial integration and interconnectedness within EMU, bringing economic benefits but also increasing the risk of contagion. Furthermore, it made Southern European and Irish banks vulnerable to capital flight. When the sustainability of their public finances, current account deficits, house prices and the underlying growth prospects was suddenly questioned by the markets, this is exactly what happened.

This process is illustrated in Figure 4.7, which shows the switch from private to European Central Bank (ECB) financing flows for banks in the countries most hit by the crisis. Before the banking crisis, the liquidity positions of the national banking sectors vis-à-vis the European Central Bank were more or less balanced (left panel). Then, banks in Greece, Portugal and Ireland ran into trouble (middle panel), followed by Spain and Italy in 2011 (right panel). Foreign banks pulled back their loans, forcing banks in these crisis countries to turn to the ECB.

To sum up, the crisis has taught us some important lessons. Firstly, it is better to prevent imbalances than to correct them. This is especially true in a monetary union, as the high degree of financial interconnectedness implies that contagion is likely and devaluation as a corrective instrument is no longer available. Secondly, preventing fiscal imbalances is impossible without also preventing macroeconomic and financial imbalances. After all, when the bubble bursts, the impact on government finances can be devastating. Finally, market discipline is not very good at preventing imbalances. Rather than responding proactively at an early stage, markets tend to enforce discipline in a corrective, costly and socially painful way. A stable monetary union cannot be based on this mechanism. It has to be based on rules instead. When it comes to enforcing these rules, the experience with the Stability and Growth Pact has shown that not only markets,

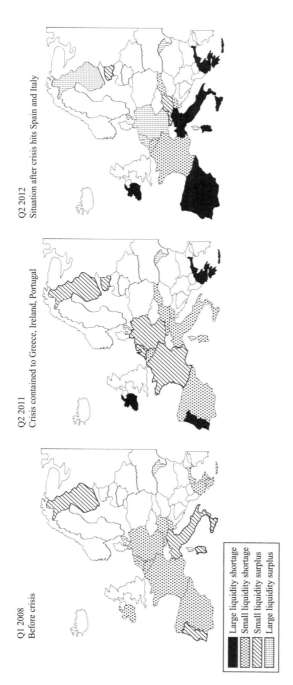

Q1 2008
Before crisis

Q2 2011
Crisis contained to Greece, Ireland, Portugal

Q2 2012
Situation after crisis hits Spain and Italy

Large liquidity shortage
Small liquidity shortage
Small liquidity surplus
Large liquidity surplus

Note: Banking sectors with surplus liquidity deposit excess liquidity with the ECB. Banking sectors with a liquidity shortage are dependent on ECB liquidity providing operations.

Source: European Central Bank.

Figure 4.7 Crisis-induced financial market fragmentation in the euro area

but also politicians have trouble in enforcing discipline in a preventive way. Due to its weak political enforcement, the Pact did not counter the deficit bias in good times, resulting in procyclical fiscal policies and too-high debt levels in many countries.

What does all of this mean for a stable design of EMU? Firstly, national governments have to restore their buffers, by bringing debt levels below 60 per cent of GDP. As the pre-crisis experience with the Pact suggests, this requires that European governments continue on the road of more politically independent enforcement of the fiscal rules. Reversed qualified majority voting has already been introduced in the corrective arm of the Pact. Useful further steps would include the extension of reversed qualified majority voting to the preventive arm of the Pact and to the debt rule. This would strengthen the role of the European Commission vis-à-vis the European Council in enforcing fiscal discipline in a preventive way.

Secondly, EMU countries have to strengthen their growth potential and competitiveness. Some euro area countries have not fully adapted to the fact that they lost the option of devaluation in order to restore competitiveness. They need to increase their flexibility and growth potential by reforming their labour and product markets (Biroli et al., 2010). Given the spillover effects of postponed structural reforms on the functioning of EMU, these reforms cannot be the sole responsibility of the governments concerned, but should also have a 'European' dimension. This can take different forms.

For instance, the country-specific reform contracts with the European Commission, as proposed by Van Rompuy (2012), could be useful in increasing the national ownership of necessary structural reforms. As these contracts still lack proper enforcement, they could be complemented by strengthening the Macroeconomic Imbalances Procedure. Extending reversed qualitative majority voting from the corrective phase to all phases of this procedure would be useful here. Last but not least, macroprudential policy can help to prevent national imbalances, by influencing banks' credit policies.

Thirdly, a banking union would increase the stability of EMU, by breaking the negative feedback loop between banks and governments. The European Council has taken a major step towards creating a European banking union and has reached agreement about banking supervision at a European level. In order for European supervision to be truly effective, it is important that a European resolution mechanism is introduced simultaneously with the implementation of European supervision. This mechanism should ensure that bank failures are settled in an orderly fashion (DNB, 2013).

Finally, some form of insurance mechanism for economic shocks might be useful as a capstone of EMU. In order to avoid such risk-sharing turning into quasi-permanent fiscal transfers, the currently vulnerable countries need a much higher level of competitiveness, growth potential and economic resilience. Therefore, the enhanced institutional features of EMU will first have to prove effective in substantially diminishing national structural weaknesses. Once economic shocks are truly evenly distributed and short-lived, for instance an EMU budget for economic stabilization purposes could limit the budgetary impact of asymmetric shocks. Alternatively, Eurobonds could prevent a liquidity problem in one euro area country from needlessly transforming into a solvency problem and provide a fire wall against the danger of contagion (DNB, 2011). Such forms of risk-sharing require more political integration and acceptability. This is probably hard to achieve without substantially lower and more converged public debt levels among participating sovereigns. But it is important to realize that with risk-sharing, national fiscal buffers can be lower than if every EMU country has to be able to absorb economic shocks by itself. In other words, defending national sovereignty as a goal in itself comes at a cost.

NOTE

1. In all of these countries, except for Germany, house prices had already risen substantially before the start of EMU. House prices peaked 250 per cent above their 1990 level in Spain, 275 per cent in the Netherlands and 450 per cent in Ireland.

REFERENCES

Biroli, P., G. Mourre and A. Turrini (2010), 'Adjustment in the euro area and regulation of product and labour markets: an empirical assessment', CEPR discussion paper, No. 8010, September.
DNB (2010), 'Reinforcing fiscal discipline in the euro area', *DNB Quarterly Bulletin*, June.
DNB (2011), 'Euro bonds as capstone of EMU', *DNBulletin*, October.
DNB (2012a), 'Catch-up effort required from lagging euro countries', *DNBulletin*, January.
DNB (2012b), 'Europe's future: from instability to stability', *Annual Report 2011*, March, pp. 27–34.
DNB (2013), 'Banking supervision to Europe – outcome of euro summit', *DNBulletin*, January.
Eichengreen, B. and C. Wyplosz (1998), 'The Stability Pact: more than a minor nuisance?', *Economics Policy*, **13** (26), 65–113.

Jaumotte, F. and H. Morsy (2012), 'Determinants of inflation in the euro area: the role of labor and product market institutions', IMF working paper, No. 12/37, January.

Pisani-Ferry, J. (2012), 'The euro crisis and the new impossible trinity', Bruegel policy contribution 2012/01, January.

Van Rompuy, H. (2012), 'Towards a genuine economic and monetary union', December.

PART II

Stop and Go of Capital Flows and Deleveraging

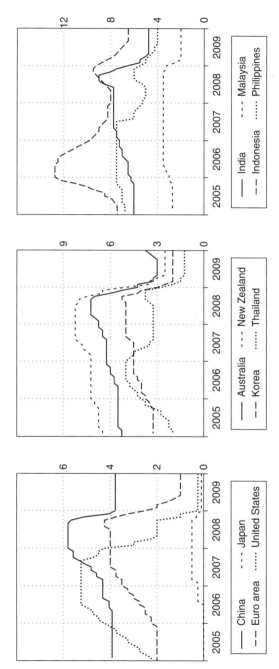

Note: For Australia, RBA cash target rate; for China, average of the one-year household saving deposits and the one-year best lending rate; for euro area, ECB main refinancing repo rate; for India, reverse repo rate; for Indonesia, one-month SBI rate; for Japan, uncollateralized overnight call rate; for Korea, overnight call rate; for Malaysia, overnight policy rate; for New Zealand, official cash daily rate; for Philippines, overnight reserve repo rate; for Thailand, 14-day repo rate before 17 January 2007; overnight repo rate thereafter; for US, Fed funds rate.

Sources: Bloomberg, Datastream, BIS, national data.

Figure 5.1   Policy response: monetary policy rates (%)

51

Table 5.1   Other people's central bank balance sheets and Asia:
quantitative easing spillovers from US quantitative easing to
Asian financial markets[1]

	Announce-ment period	Total amounts (billions)	Gov't 2-year yields (bps)	Gov't 10-year yields (bps)	Corp bond yields[2] (bps)	Sov'gn CDS premia[3] (bps)	Equity prices (%)	FX against USD[4] (%)
US QE1	Nov 08 to Nov 09	$1400	−45.37	−79.70	−52.90	−46.92	10.75	4.49
QE2	Aug 10 to Nov 10	$600	−9.06	−9.16	−14.84	−4.80	1.53	−0.36

Notes:
1. Simple average of China, Hong Kong, India, Indonesia, Korea, the Philippines, Singapore and Thailand.
2. Excluding Indonesia.
3. Excluding India and Singapore.
4. A positive change indicates an appreciation against the USA dollar.

Source: Chen et al. (2012).

targeted use of loan-to-value regulations has been implemented. The lasting effectiveness of macro-prudential tools to address macroeconomic imbalances in the region is still an open question (Filardo, 2012).

At the same time, greater efforts have been made to intensify the surveillance and monitoring of the various types of capital flows. Given the strong short- and medium-term fundamentals in Asian emerging markets, some of the capital flows such as foreign direct investment have been welcomed and are generally considered to be welfare enhancing. However, some of the flows – especially those labelled as hot money flows – add volatility without obvious economic and financial benefits. The ability to distinguish between good and bad capital flows is critical for those using capital controls. As has been discussed elsewhere, there appears to be a renewed interest in targeted capital controls as a broader strategy of capital flow management. As with the use of macro-prudential tools, the jury is still out on their effectiveness over time and their net benefits in addressing fundamentally macroeconomic imbalances.

Finally, no discussion of the capital flow issue in Asian emerging markets is complete without highlighting the institutional development of the Chiang Mai Initiative. Association of Southeast Asian Nations (ASEAN)+3 countries have pooled their resources (US$120 billion) to offer the region a multilateral foreign exchange (FX) backstop. This pooling arrangement not only provides a war chest of reserves to deploy in

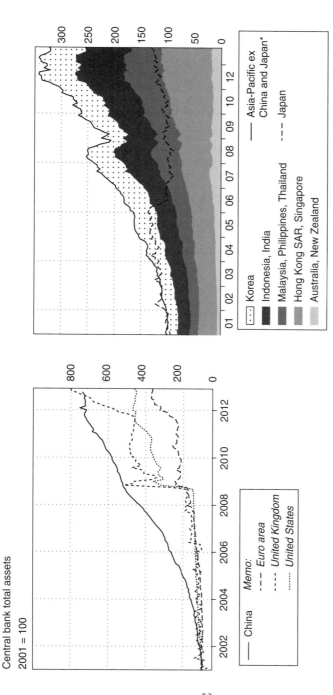

Central bank total assets
2001 = 100

Note: *Sum of listed economies.

Sources: IMF, International Financial Statistics, Datastream, BIS, national data.

Figure 5.2 Limits from soaring central bank balance sheets: central bank total assets (2001 = 100)

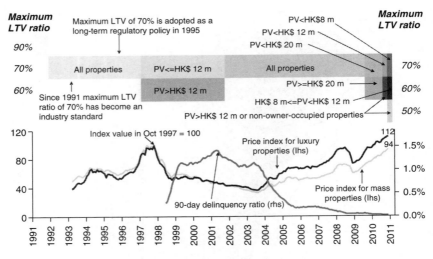

Note: LTV = loan to value; PV = property value; lhs = left-hand scale; rhs = right-hand scale.

Source: Hong Kong Monetary Association (HKMA) in BIS Papers no. 57, October 2011.

Figure 5.3   LTV policy, property prices and mortgage delinquency ratio in Hong Kong SAR

the case of destabilizing exchange rate dynamics associated with stop–go capital flows but also signals the regional commitment to each other in the case that one or several economies find themselves in difficult conditions. The benefits of this institutional development, along with the interest in developing more resilient and effective FX swap arrangements during crises, all underscore the overall regional approach to managing the risks of stop–go capital flows.

5.3   RISKS AND POLICY SPACE

Despite these developments locally and regionally, questions still remain about whether relying on these tools can provide lasting relief or whether they simply buy time. One view is that they can buy time to allow the metaphorical storm to pass, or can buy time while other more effective policy measures can be deployed to address the underlying economic and financial forces at work. In these respects, it is important that the bought time be prudently used to strengthen the economic, fiscal and financial system fundamentals. In the fullness of time, we will be in a better position to evaluate the effectiveness of these measures. So far, so good.

The putative success in managing the risks of stop–go capital flows in Asian emerging markets also raises the question of whether the risks were initially overestimated. We will never have a definitive answer but there are good reasons to suggest that the region benefited from some good luck during this period: capital flows in the region were challenging at times but never amounted to the fear from 'the mother of all carry trades'. One reason this worst-case scenario was avoided can be traced back to the rolling crises casting a pall over sentiment about the global economy. Since 2007, economic and financial turmoil in various corners of the globe have had significant spillover effects that sapped confidence. The intensification of the international financial crisis in late 2008 and early 2009 and then the European sovereign debt crisis were two of the more important shocks to the global financial system that had far-reaching effects.

For Asian emerging markets, the muted confidence had important consequences for capital flow dynamics. Figure 5.4 illustrates the negative relationship between risk perceptions as captured by credit-default swap (CDS) spreads and the strength of capital flows. Higher CDS spreads reflect greater generalized risk aversion amongst international investors. This, in turn, kept a lid on risky capital flows to Asian emerging markets. Looking forward, however, one cannot rule out the possibility that, as the prospects of a global recovery brightens and pessimism shifts to optimism, the risks of stop–go capital flows could materialize. In other words, the good luck story for the capital flow pressure issue could come to an end and a new, less benign chapter in management of stop–go capital flows could begin.

This perspective takes on even greater importance now with the policy space in Asian emerging markets shrinking. Low policy rates for the past few years have helped to support a recovery in Asian emerging markets but these rates are increasing the odds of overheating and of credit-asset price boom scenarios (see Figure 5.5). Moreover, the modest widening of interest rate spreads between domestic interest rates in Asian emerging markets and US dollar interest rates is already encouraging a pickup in cross-border US dollar lending inside the region – which not only helps to reduce the effectiveness of domestic monetary policy and boosts asset prices but also creates potential currency mismatches. These mismatches can show up on the balance sheets of banks or of the private sector, or both. All told, the accommodative monetary policies that have helped to discourage capital inflows may become a less attractive option going forward.

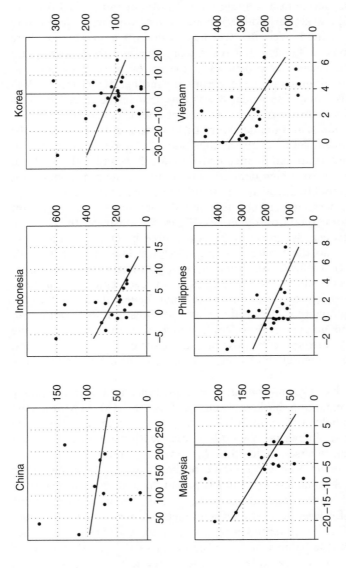

Note: Horizontal axis is net capital flows to the economy (positive/negative indicates net inflows/outflows), in billions of USD; vertical axis represents 5-year on-the-run sovereign CDS spreads, in basis points.

Sources: IMF *International Financial Statistics*; CEIC; Markit.

Figure 5.4 CDS spreads and net capital flows in Asia (Q1 2007 – latest)

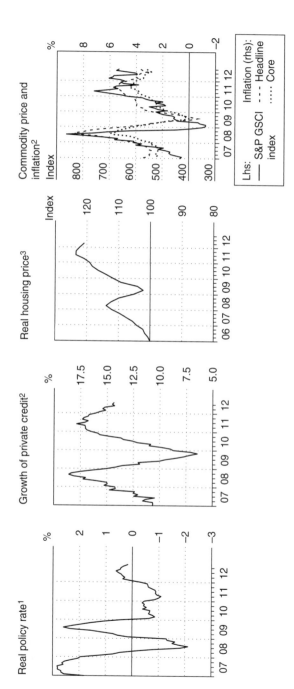

Real policy rate[1]

Growth of private credit[2]

Real housing price[3]

Commodity price and inflation[2]

Figure 5.5   Monetary policy, credit growth, housing prices and inflation in Asia

Notes:
1. Policy target rates or their proxies corrected by forward- and backward-looking inflation components (equally weighted 12-month backward-looking CPI inflation and 12-month forward-looking consensus expectations); average of China, Hong Kong SAR, India, Indonesia, Korea, Malaysia, the Philippines and Thailand.
2. Annual change; average of China, Hong Kong SAR, India, Indonesia, Korea, Malaysia, the Philippines, Singapore and Thailand.
3. End 2005 = 100; average of China (three tier-one cities), Hong Kong SAR, Indonesia, Korea, Malaysia and Singapore.

Sources: IMF, *International Financial Statistics*; Bloomberg; CEIC; national data.

At the same time, the policy room for manoeuvre on the exchange rate front is also shrinking. The central banks of Asian emerging markets have accumulated large foreign reserve positions. The carrying costs of these reserves are high and rising. As pointed out by Filardo and Yetman (2012) the foreign reserve asset accumulation poses a number of financial stability risks. The primary risks come from the ways in which the central banks sterilize FX intervention. In emerging-market economies, banks have seen their reserves held at the central bank and their holdings of central bank securities rising. In the short run, the increase in the holdings of central bank securities tends to crowd out private sector investment. So, any cessation in the trend of ever-increasing foreign exchange reserves that need to be sterilized would by itself add to the stimulative lending environment. In addition, banks' holding of an increasing amount of low interest rate assets ('lazy' assets) could provide incentives for banks to fuel future lending booms (Filardo and Grenville, 2012).

5.4   LESSONS

For emerging markets in Asia, destabilizing capital flow risks remain a fact of life. As financial prospectuses emphasize, past performance does not guarantee future returns. Shifts in global risk aversion are likely to be a critical determinant of the size and scope of stop–go capital flows in Asian emerging markets and elsewhere. So far, risk aversion has remained high due in large part to the rolling international crises. But when the worst of the crisis risks abate, the big question is: what will be the implication?

For the global economy as a whole, a robust recovery would be a good development. However, for individual economies, the policy environment could become quite challenging. In the case of Asian emerging markets, the low policy rates and bloated central bank balance sheets are creating their own set of complications. And while there is renewed interest in capital controls and macro-prudential tools as substitutes for more traditional reliance on realignments of interest rates and exchange rates, the jury is still out on their lasting macroeconomic effectiveness.

So what are the lessons for CESEE economies? My reading of the situation suggests that there is no single silver bullet that will ensure non-inflationary stable growth. No new tool is available to fundamentally change the calculus of the policy challenges. Yes, the experience of Asian emerging markets suggests that new tools can buy more time than we might have thought was possible a few years ago. But, capital flow volatility will continue to be a challenge for emerging-market economies. And, in the end, getting the policy mix right is the key to successful management of the risks. Central banks need to ensure price stability. Adopting new international regulatory reforms is necessary to enhance financial system resilience. Fiscal positions need to be sound and free from concerns of fiscal dominance. And, central banks and finance ministries should be wary of persistent one-sided exchange rate intervention. While these principles are certainly not new, they are tried, true, and form the strongest basis for future success.

REFERENCES

BIS (2010), 'The international financial crisis and policy challenges in Asia and the Pacific', BIS Papers no. 52, July.

Chen, Q., A. Filardo, D. He and F. Zhu (2012), 'International spillovers of central bank balance sheet policies', BIS Papers no. 66, October.

Filardo, A. (2012), 'Ensuring price stability in post-crisis Asia: lessons from the recovery', BIS Working Paper no. 378, April.

Filardo, A. and S. Grenville (2012), 'Central bank balance sheets and foreign exchange rate regimes: understanding the nexus in Asia', BIS Papers no. 66, October.

Filardo, Andrew and James Yetman (2012), 'Key facts on central bank balance sheets in Asia and the Pacific', BIS Papers no. 66, October.

6. CESEE banks deleveraging or rebalancing? Lessons from the EIB bank lending survey

Luca Gattini and Debora Revoltella

6.1 INTRODUCTION

Following a boom–bust cycle, lending growth has been stalling in the Central, Eastern and South-Eastern Europe (CESEE) region. This represents a potential drag on economic recovery. Consequently, understanding the determinants of credit growth becomes key to the definition of effective policy actions. The last fifteen years since the mid-1990s have seen an impressive development of the banking market in the CESEE region. Starting from the mid-1990s, a process of deep transformation allowed banks to gradually become real intermediaries of resources, with access to finance substantially increased in both the retail and the corporate sector. A privatization process allowed several international players to enter the region and to engage in regional growth strategies. These large players became market leaders in almost all countries of the region, carrying fresh capital and new banking practices. Lending was growing fast before the 2008–2009 crisis. Large market potential and banks' access to funding from parents fuelled growth, supported by a general underestimation of risks. In turn internal demand started to accelerate, with both consumption and investment growing fast. The 2008–2009 crisis changed the picture. External demand collapsed and the correction of capital inflows was rather sharp, leading to negative economic growth all over the region. Concerns about potential spill-overs, via the parent–subsidiary channel, from the international financial crisis to the region increased. Against this background, the so-called Vienna Initiative (see below) has functioned as an anchor, strengthening confidence in the financial markets and preserving banking activities. The European Commission and the International Monetary Fund (IMF) provided financial support to countries in need, while the international banks active in the region committed to remain supportive to their subsidiaries, providing capital and funding. International financial institutions engaged in a Joint Action Plan. The initiative strategically contributed to preserving financial stability in the overall CESEE region. Indeed tail risks disappeared and fully fledged bank runs were avoided.

Following a recovery in 2010, growth has slowed down again at the international and regional level and recessionary signals have appeared in some countries. The higher the pre-crisis imbalances were, the longer economic activity is taking to recover. Potential growth for the region has been reassessed and it has been linked more closely to the underlying country fundamentals – that is, productivity and export performance capacity. At the same time, the euro area sovereign debt crisis, new international regulation and a reassessment of local market opportunities are leading to a rethinking of the operational strategies for the cross-border banks active in the CESEE region. The strategic commitment to the region does not seem to be at stake, albeit a progressive reduction of parent–subsidiary funding. In cumulated terms, the reduction in cross-border lending to banks reached some 4 per cent of regional GDP[1] in the Q3 2011 – Q2 2012 period, with some countries hit harder. In other words, the banking model is changing. A focus on sustainability is becoming a fundamental drive in global banks' strategic decisions. Global banks are calling for their subsidiaries to adopt a more self-sustained model, with lending financed mostly via domestic funding – for example deposits. At the same time, weak economic growth affects demand for lending, while non-performing loans (NPL) are weighing on banks' portfolios. Lending growth has been stalling in most of the countries in the region, representing a drag to recovery. In such a context a proper assessment of the current situation is key to the design of effective policy actions.

In October 2012, under the umbrella of the revived Vienna Initiative 2,[2] the European Investment Bank (EIB) designed a bank lending survey for the CESEE region, to disentangle demand and supply factors as well as the underlying domestic and international components affecting lending activity in the region. This chapter presents and discusses the results of the survey. The chapter is structured as follows. Following this introduction, section 6.2 presents some facts on the banking markets in CESEE today. Section 6.3 explains the background for the survey. Section 6.4 presents the results at the parent banks' level, while section 6.5 focuses on results at the subsidiary level. Section 6.6 includes a simple analysis to test the reliability of the survey results against recent macroeconomic developments. Section 6.7 concludes.

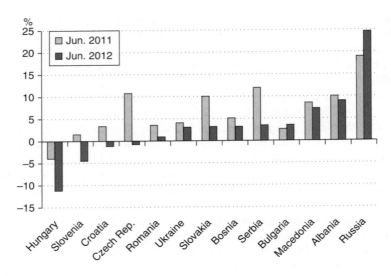

Source: IMF.

Figure 6.1   Nominal year-on-year credit growth

6.2   MAIN FACTS: BANKING IN CESEE

Following a boom–bust cycle, lending growth has been stalling in CESEE, representing a drag to recovery. The latest figures for foreign exchange (FX)-adjusted nominal year-on-year credit growth (see Figure 6.1) show that growth stalled in some countries and turned negative for few other countries. Understanding the causes of weak lending activity is key to the design of proper policy actions.

From a more structural standpoint, the CESEE has still a penetration gap which makes the overall region attractive from a banking perspective. The loan to gross domestic product (GDP) ratios were around 60 percentage points and the deposit to GDP ratios were on average around 50 percentage points in the majority of CESEE countries in 2012. This compares to average ratios of roughly 105 percentage points for the loan to GDP ratio and 85 percentage points for the deposit to GDP ratio in the euro area in 2012.[3]

The CESEE banking sector is mostly foreign owned. In the pre-crisis period booming credit activities were financed via parent–subsidiary funding. Parent banks were providing long-term funding in euros to their subsidiaries. Such funding was also fundamental to allow the matching of maturities given the lack of long-term domestic sources. Yet the euro

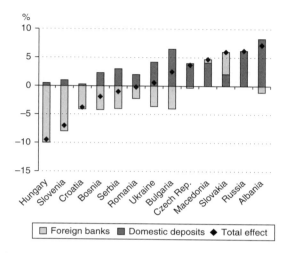

Source: BIS data, IMF and authors' calculations.

Figure 6.2 Banks' funding sources

area sovereign debt crisis, new international regulation and a reassessment of local market opportunities have been leading to a rethinking of
the operational strategies for the cross-border banks active in the CESEE
region. The strategic commitment to the region does not seem to be at
stake, despite a progressive reduction of parent–subsidiary funding. In
cumulative terms, the reduction in cross-border lending to banks reached
some 4 per cent of regional GDP in the Q3 2011 – Q2 2012 period, with
some countries hit harder. In other words, the banking model is changing. Global banks are calling for their subsidiaries to adopt a more self-
sustained model, with lending financed mostly via domestic funding (see
Figure 6.2), for example deposits. While the loan-to-deposit ratio has been
declining in most of the countries of the region, deposit growth has generally compensated parent–subsidiary funding.

In this context, the loan-to-deposit (LTD) ratio acquires an additional
signalling power as a rough indicator for the self-sustainability of the local
banking model. The new model suggests that the capacity to raise deposits
might become a constraint to lending growth. Figure 6.3 shows a cross-
country comparison of LTD ratios in 2011. With an average level slightly
higher than 100 per cent, the relative position of single countries is rather
diverse. Serbia, Ukraine and Slovenia have an LTD ratio around or close
to 150 per cent while Albania has a level of roughly 60 per cent.

NPL definitions vary among countries and cross-country comparisons

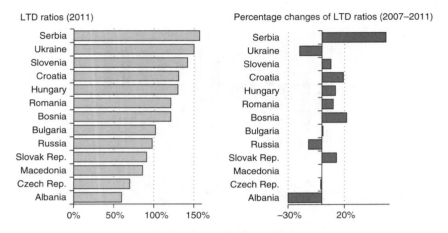

LTD ratios (2011)   Percentage changes of LTD ratios (2007–2011)

Source: National authorities and IMF; authors' calculations.

Figure 6.3   Loan-to-deposit ratio (2011 levels and percentage changes
*   between 2007 and 2011)*

are rather difficult. Non-performing loans weigh on banks' portfolios in
CESEE. As illustrated in Figure 6.4, the average NPL ratio shifted from
roughly 3 per cent in 2007 to more than 12 per cent in 2011 in selected
CESEE countries. Due to the credit boom phase, pre-crisis figures certainly masked the true credit quality of the portfolio. At the same time,
NPL levels are largely explained by the severity of the crisis combined
with a widespread presence of FX lending. Despite relatively high capital
buffers in the local banks, NPLs represent a drag on economic growth as
they constrain both credit demand and supply.

6.3   A UNIQUE BANK LENDING SURVEY IN THE CESEE REGION: BACKGROUND

In October 2012, under the umbrella of the freshly revived Vienna
Initiative 2, the EIB conducted a bank lending survey to monitor
the underlying dynamics in the banking sector of the CESEE region.
The survey aimed at understanding the constraints of lending growth
on the demand and the supply side and the links between domestic and
international determinants. The survey addressed a highly representative
group of euro area parent banks with a significant cross-border exposure
to the CESEE region and to their subsidiaries within the region. The

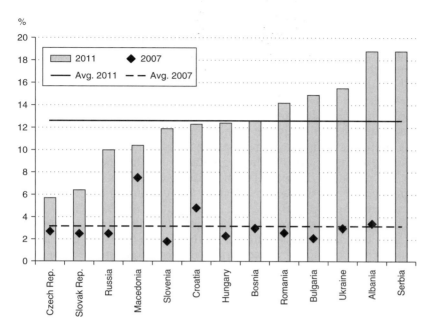

Note: Data are not fully harmonized across countries due to different recording and collection practices.

Source: World Bank and national authorities; authors' calculations.

Figure 6.4   *NPL ratios of selected CESEE countries (pre-crisis vs. post-crisis levels)*

survey included a rather large set of questions addressed to both the parent banks and the regional subsidiaries. Additionally most of the questions had a backward- and a forward-looking component. The latter dimension allowed for capturing banks' expectations along several dimensions and, by doing so, helped to anticipate a potential change of trend compared to the recent past. The survey took a conjunctural perspective since the questions mainly asked for an assessment of the past six months and six months ahead. This is very much in line with other surveys of similar nature, such as the European Central Bank (ECB) bank lending survey.[4]

As mentioned, the survey disentangled the cross-border dimension by including a detailed set of international and domestic factors affecting supply and funding conditions. In greater detail, parent banks were requested to provide information at the group level on overall market conditions, on supply conditions, on funding as well as on their strategic decisions on capital increases and restructuring. Attention was paid to group activities within the CESEE region including cross-border lending to subsidiaries. At the subsidiary level the survey was designed to disentangle the influence of international and domestic factors and to shed light on the underlying demand and supply components affecting credit developments. Detailed reporting was requested on the fundamental supply constraints, demand drivers and the factors affecting them. Several breakdowns were investigated along different dimensions, namely: client type, maturities, currency denomination, local and international factors including competition, funding conditions and non-performing loans. Last but not least, the overall market access in terms of funding, its different sources and the factors affecting the funding conditions were also investigated together with past and expected NPL developments.

The overall participation rate was high and responses were complete and detailed; however the outcome of this first round should be considered preliminary and subject to further improvements. Indeed the survey was conducted at a rather short notice and a tight time window was allocated to banks for providing answers. Not all the banks addressed were able to contribute. However the survey secured a relatively high number of responses both in terms of banks' coverage and country and regional coverage. The survey covered eight groups with operations in multiple CESEE countries and 42 subsidiaries. The responses to the survey at the subsidiary level (see section 6.5) show the aggregate outcomes for a selected set of countries with an average coverage of around 40 per cent of the market measured in terms of asset values. In particular we have included the following set of countries: Albania, Bosnia-Herzegovina, Bulgaria, Croatia, the Czech Republic, Hungary, Macedonia, Romania, Serbia, Slovakia, Slovenia and Ukraine.

6.4   MAIN RESULTS FROM THE GROUP-LEVEL SECTION OF THE SURVEY

Cross-border banking groups remain committed to the CESEE region but they are becoming more selective in their strategies at the country level (see Figure 6.5). The global financial crisis and the euro area crisis have left their mark on the cross-border banking groups active in the region. All of them have engaged, and expect to continue to engage, in various strategic operations to increase capitalization. Almost all banks have been increasing capital employing either market or non-market sources. Indeed some banks have gained access to state support. At the same time, they are deleveraging at the group level. All surveyed groups signal their continued

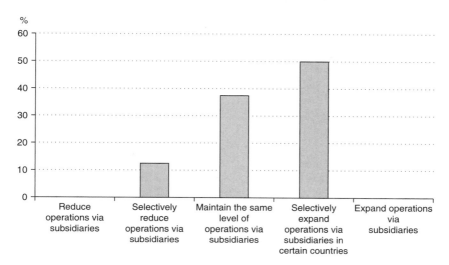

Note: Survey question: 'Longer-term strategies (beyond 12 months): looking at operations via subsidiaries in CEE-SEE, your group intends to . . .'.

Source: EIB bank survey.

Figure 6.5 Longer-term strategies of banking groups active in the CESEE region

commitment to their operations in the CESEE region. However, they are taking a more selective approach to the different local markets, and have been rebalancing their strategies toward a more self-sustained local banking model. This seems to imply a larger adjustment for those countries where market and local funding opportunities are relatively weak. All in all, the survey points to a possible marginal decrease of funding volumes and conditions to subsidiaries six months ahead. However this may be very much dependent on factors other than the parent company's own decisions, such as international as well as domestic elements – for example local demand, local supply and local funding conditions.

Almost all parent banks have undertaken some form of strategic restructuring and capital increase operations since the beginning of the crisis (see Figure 6.6). Asset sales appear to be one of the main options chosen to increase the capital ratio over the past 12 months. Looking ahead, at least 50 per cent of the banks signal the possibility of a continuation of strategic restructuring and various forms of capital increases over the next six months. Interestingly, state contribution to capital continues to play a significant role and this can be justified by the presence in our survey of some

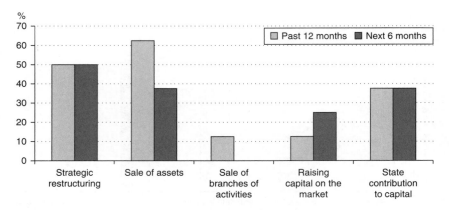

Note: Survey question: 'In the last 12 months has your group conducted strategic operations to increase the capital ratio? If yes, which type?'

Source: EIB bank survey.

Figure 6.6   Strategic operations to increase the capital ratio (% of positive responses)

Greek banks.[5] In addition it is worth stressing that fewer groups expect to increase capital selling assets and no group foresees sales of branches whilst more groups anticipate being able to raise capital on the market over the next six months. This may signal a potential normalization in the overall market conditions and a return of confidence in the market. Indeed group access to any sort of funding was tilted to the positive side and remains tilted to positive expectations looking ahead (see Figure 6.7). In general, group access to funding is considered stable or slightly improving, but positive expectations six months ahead are marginally levelled off compared to the same statistics over the past six months. Looking at the last six months, 60 per cent of the parent banks considered access to funding to be stable, while roughly 40 per cent signalled improvements. When asked for expectations for the next six months, the share of those with a positive view declines to 20 per cent. All in all a more conservative attitude prevails. The aggregate picture hides a reshuffling across respondents. Most of those groups signalling an increase over the past moved to a stable expectation, whilst some of those indicating a stable situation over the past shifted to positive expectations. Overall this highlights a potentially improved market access over the next six months compared to the past.

Against this background, parent banks expect some deleveraging to continue in the next six months, with declines in the loan-to-deposit ratio

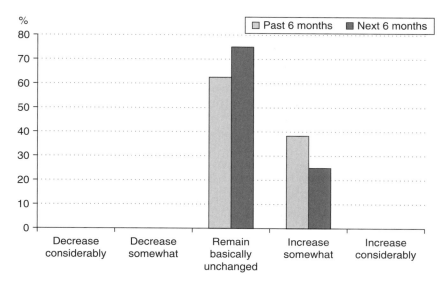

Note: Survey question: 'In terms of funding: has your group's access to the capital/ wholesale/retail funding market changed over the past six months, or are you expecting it to change over the next six months?'

Source: EIB bank survey.

Figure 6.7 Group access to funding

at the group level (see Figure 6.8). This indicates that a process of adjustment in banks' balance sheets is still ongoing. Group credit standards and credit conditions were described as generally unchanged and somewhat tilted to the negative side over the past six months, whereas expectations are more positive with a share of respondents turning from tightening to unchanged conditions. A significant subcategory of groups' lending activity relates to cross-border lending operations. A question in the survey tried to address this point. In terms of cross-border lending, almost 80 per cent of the banks expect to maintain the same level of operations and a little more than 20 per cent to reduce them. Direct lending to corporate and retail clients is seen more positive whilst most of the contraction is expected in funding to subsidiaries. However a category is missing in this question which relates to equity commitments in the region. Groups may expect a reduction of cross-border lending whilst maintaining or selectively increasing their equity exposure in the region. Indeed banks' intensions on overall long-term strategies provide more expansionary than contractionary signals (see Figure 6.9). Last but not least, lower cross-border lending

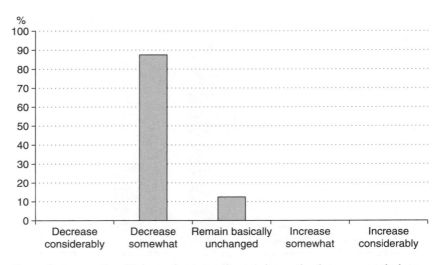

Note: Survey question: 'Deleveraging – over the next six months, do you expect the loan-to-deposit ratio of your group to . . .'.

Source: EIB bank survey.

Figure 6.8   Deleveraging: expectations of the group's loan-to-deposit ratio

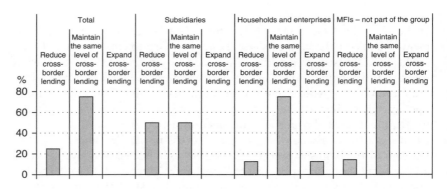

Note: Survey question: 'Concerning cross-border lending operations to CEE-SEE countries and its breakdown by receiver entity, your group intends to . . .'.

Source: EIB bank survey.

Figure 6.9   Cross-border lending operations in the CESEE region (group-level intentions)

is also a function of local market conditions (at the subsidiary level) which can influence domestic demand and supply conditions. These are factors investigated in the section of the survey addressed to the subsidiaries and analysed in section 6.3.

6.5 MAIN RESULTS FROM THE SUBSIDIARY LEVEL SECTION OF THE SURVEY

The results of the survey addressed to subsidiaries in CESEE have been primarily analysed looking at the net percentage difference of the responses – that is, the percentage of positives minus negatives (excluding the unchanged responses). This is an often-cited indicator which has a barometer function. It helps to detect potential drifts and tendencies in the panel of respondents, for instance with regard to the development of credit supply and demand conditions (see Figure 6.10).

Banks report that, in addition to subdued credit demand, domestic

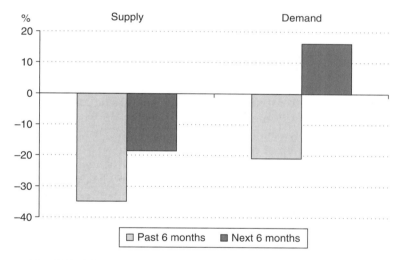

Note: 'Supply' is defined as subsidiary's credit standards (credit supply) as applied to the approval of loans or credit lines to enterprises and households; 'demand' is defined as demand for loans or credit lines to enterprises and households. Negative (positive) supply-side values indicate tightening (easing) of credit standards; negative (positive) demand-side values indicate demand decrease (increase).

Source: EIB bank survey.

Figure 6.10   Development of credit conditions (in net %)

and international supply-side factors are also responsible for sluggish credit growth. With cross-border banking groups pushing for a more self-sustained local banking model and weak local market conditions, CESEE subsidiaries have generally been experiencing a period of both soft credit demand and tight credit supply. On the demand side, the list of negative factors is long: low consumer confidence, unfavourable housing price prospects, subdued merger and acquisitions activities, and weak fixed investment dynamics. As to the international determinants of credit supply, the global market outlook, group funding conditions, group capital constraints, and group-level non-performing loans were all quoted as having had a clear negative influence on local credit standards over the past six months.

As to the local determinants of credit supply, the local market outlook, local regulation, compliance with often high local capital requirements, and non-performing loans at the subsidiary level were the key constraining factors over the last six months. Local bank funding on the other hand was increasingly seen as improving, thereby making a contribution toward less tight supply conditions. Indeed, as the shift toward more self-sustained local banking model proceeds, improved access to local funding becomes pivotal for restarting credit growth.

Going forward, banks expect a pick-up of credit demand, continued tight international supply conditions, and somewhat easier domestic supply conditions. International factors will continue to contribute to credit standard tightening, whereas subsidiaries' access to domestic funding is expected to contribute positively. Supply-side constraints could thus become selectively more binding, depending on whether improvements in local supply conditions provide enough room to accommodate the prospective pick-up of credit demand.

Overall supply conditions are tilted to the downside and are expected to remain skewed toward a tightening area six months ahead. Among the supply conditions the survey allows to discern between two types of supply-side factors, namely: (1) credit standards applied to the approval of loans or credit lines; (2) conditions and terms for approving loans or credit lines. The former set of supply conditions – credit standards – are tilted significantly to the downside (see Figure 6.11). However expectations signal some improvement six months ahead. Credit standards are expected to evolve in aggregate differently across types of clients. In particular loans or credit lines to small and medium-sized enterprises (SMEs) and consumer credit are expected to have less restrictive credit standards, whilst more restrictive standards are expected on loans for house purchases. The latter supply conditions – conditions and terms for approving loans or credit lines – are also tilted to the downside (see Figure 6.12).

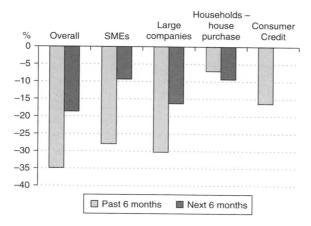

Note: Survey question: 'Bank (local subsidiary/branch)'s credit standards (credit supply) as applied to the approval of loans or credit lines to enterprises and households . . .'. Negative (positive) values indicate tightening (easing) of credit standards.

Source: EIB bank survey.

Figure 6.11   *Supply conditions (credit standards applied to the approval of loans or credit lines; in net percentages)*

Banks' margins and size of the average loan are among the two most relevant constraining factors. Contemporaneously conditions and terms seem to be more constrained for corporates – in particular SMEs – than for households.

When asked about the factors affecting credit standards, banks could select several domestic and international factors affecting loans to enterprises and loans to households. The overall messages are similar across the two different types of clients. Figure 6.13 reports the results for the enterprise segment of the market. However very similar results are available for the consumer segment.

Among the domestic factors, respondents highlighted local market outlook, local bank outlook, local regulation, local bank capital constraints and local non-performing loans. These have consistently weighed negatively on credit supply (credit standards) over the last six months. Looking ahead, there is a tendency to a rebalancing of expectations with a significant reduction of the negative views on local market and bank outlooks, whereas expectations are relatively stable and on the negative side for local regulation and capital constraints. Local bank funding weighed negatively over the past six months, whereas it is expected to exert a

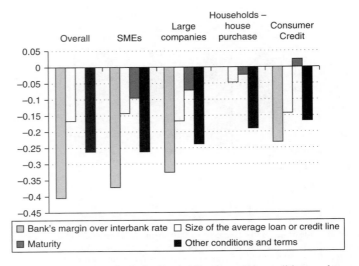

Note: Survey question: 'Have bank (local subsidiary/branch)'s conditions and terms (e.g. maturity, pricing, size of average loan, etc.) for approving loans or credit lines changed over the past six months?' Negative (positive) values indicate tightening (easing) of conditions and terms.

Source: EIB bank survey.

Figure 6.12   *Supply conditions (terms and conditions for approving loans or credit lines)*

positive contribution over the next six months. Therefore it is expected to contribute to easing credit standards.

Among the international factors, respondents stressed that the global market outlook, group funding, group capital constraints and group non-performing loans have a clear negative influence on local credit standards. Still constraining local standards, the negative views are expected to reduce over the next six months, notably for the global market outlook and group funding, but not for group capital constraints and regulation. Over the next six months and on a positive note, the group outlook seems to exert a positive effect on local credit standards as the number of positive responses outweighs the negatives.

Negative views on overall demand conditions have outweighed positive responses, looking at the past six months (see Figure 6.14). Looking forward, a remarkable turnaround is expected. Divergences emerged across different segments of the market. Over the past six months demand drifted sharply to the downside for loans to corporates and for house

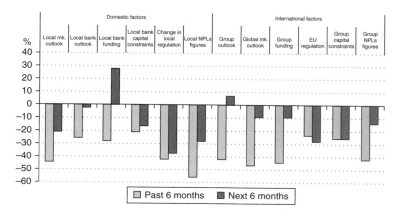

Note: Survey question: 'Factors affecting your bank's credit standards. Have the following domestic and international factors contributed to tighten (ease) your credit standards over the past six months, and do you expect them to contribute to tighten (ease) your credit standards over the next six months?' A negative percentage indicates that a factor is more constraining than easing supply conditions and vice versa.

Source: EIB bank survey.

Figure 6.13   Factors affecting supply conditions (credit standards; in net percentages)

purchase, whilst it was more mildly negative for loans to SMEs and consumer credit. In other words, demand was more subdued in those segments where large loans are usually demanded. Expectations on demand are turning positive in almost all segments. However discrepancies in expectations persist. Demand for loans to SMEs is expected to pick up, whilst only a marginal positive improvement is anticipated on loans for house purchases. These features can be related to the underlying factors influencing demand conditions (see Figure 6.15). The questions in the survey can discern between factors affecting demand for credit to enterprises and loans to households. Over the past six months household demand for loans was negatively impacted upon by all factors including housing market prospects, confidence and subdued private consumption. The main drag on corporates' demand for loans was the lack of fixed investments. To the contrary, debt restructuring was mentioned as the only factor positively affecting corporate demand for credit.

Banks continue to have a negative perception in terms of non-performing loan trends. After the 2009 crisis, CESEE countries have been strongly affected by the surge in NPLs. Indeed the answers to the question on NPLs reached a very high consensus among respondents

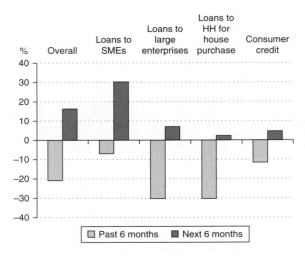

Note: Survey question: 'Demand for loans or credit lines to enterprises and households
(to your local subsidiary/branch)'. Negative (positive) values indicate demand decrease
(increase).

Source: EIB bank survey.

Figure 6.14   *Demand conditions (in net percentages)*

(see Figure 6.16). Seventy per cent of respondents in net percentage
terms report total NPL ratios to have been positioned on a deteriorating
trend over the past six months. When asked about their expectations,
local banks signal further deterioration to come albeit with slightly less
negative responses compared to their views over the previous six months.
Usually, high NPL ratios reduce profitability, affect liquidity conditions
and reduce banks' willingness to lend. Indeed non-performing loans have
been mentioned as one of the main factors that constrain supply (see
Figure 6.13).

Rather interesting information can be drawn from the question on local
funding conditions at the subsidiary level. Overall funding conditions are
described as balanced over the past six months and are expected to remain
balanced over the next six months (see Figure 6.17). However, divergences become apparent when we look at the detailed funding sources.
Expectations are for an improvement in local funding, with the majority
of banks expecting an expansion in retail funding and to a large extent
also in corporate funding. International financial institutions' funding
conditions are also expected to improve over the next six months. To the
contrary, the majority of banks still expect access to intra-group funding

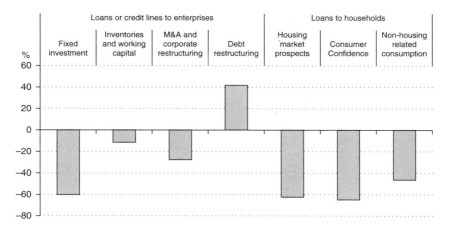

Note: Survey question: 'How have the following factors (in your local subsidiary/branch) affected clients' demand for loans and credit lines over the past six months?' A negative percentage indicates that a factor is weighting more negatively than positively and vice versa.

Source: EIB bank survey.

Figure 6.15 Factors affecting client demand (in net percentages)

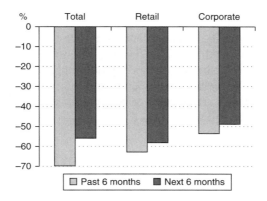

Note: Survey question: 'Gross non-performing loans ratio in your local subsidiary/branch (excluding extraordinary operations) . . .'. A negative percentage indicates that the NPL ratio is increasing.

Source: EIB bank survey.

Figure 6.16 NPL ratio (in net percentages)

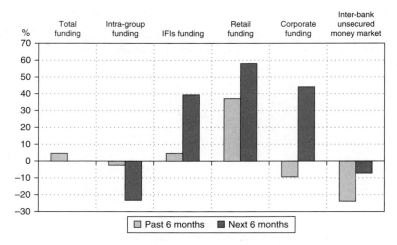

Note: Survey question: 'In terms of funding: has the market access of your local subsidiary/branch changed over the past six months, or do you expect it to change over the next six months?' Positive values indicate more favourable funding conditions.

Source: EIB bank survey.

Figure 6.17   Funding conditions (in net percentages)

and the interbank unsecured money market to deteriorate, with negative responses outweighing more visibly the positives in comparison to the past six months. Such trends are consistent with a rebalancing of the banking model in the region, with domestic funding potentially asked to take over other funding gaps, including intra-group funding. All in all, indirect (and not direct) sovereign exposures, credit lines from parent companies and the rating of the group are detected as latent limiting factors affecting subsidiaries' funding conditions.

6.6   A SIMPLE STATISTICAL EXERCISE USING THE RESULTS OF THE BANK LENDING SURVEY

To test the validity of the survey results, we investigated the interrelations across responses within the survey. To do so we constructed a cross-correlation matrix of the answers to the questions addressed to subsidiaries. We also correlated these answers with the answers of the first part of the survey directed to the groups operating in the CESEE region. The full set of results is reported in the Appendix. We tested the significance of zero pair-wise correlation, and the tables in the Appendix report only the statistically significant coefficients with threshold p-values being below or equal to 10 per cent. The reported coefficients have the expected sign. This validates further the internal coherence of the responses. Furthermore, it is allows to expand the investigation in the attempt to relate some of the survey findings to country-specific and banking group-specific macroeconomic and financial variables.

To start our analysis we primarily looked at the overall demand and supply (credit standards) conditions as referred to in section 6.5 and Figure 6.10. Specifically we took up the answers on overall developments in demand for loans and credit lines by households and enterprises and on the overall conditions of credit standards (supply side) as applied to the approval of loans and credit lines to enterprises and households over the last six months. Our ultimate goal is to construct a binary model relating the ordered answers to a subset of macroeconomic and financial indicators potentially influencing demand and supply conditions. In detail we will use a simple probit model for our investigation.[6]

As a first step we transformed the ordered responses to the survey into binary variables taking value of 1 if demand (supply) was significantly or somewhat decreasing (tightening) and 0 otherwise. We collected a set of explanatory variables at country and group level reflecting country net external position, domestic growth, banking exposure, country-wide financial weaknesses and domestic banking sector returns. All variables refer to 2011. We considered NPL ratios at the country level as a measure of the overall quality of bank loans. This variable is relevant for domestic financial stability considerations as high ratios may impact negatively on profitability thereby reducing banks' willingness to lend. We also integrated return on equity (ROE) at the domestic banking system level into the model. ROE is a measure of the overall attractiveness of the banking sector and its performance in a given fiscal year. A loan-to-deposit ratio was also included. These are group-level ratios tracking loans and deposits specifically for the banking group activities in the CESEE region. This is a commonly used statistic for assessing bank liquidity. The less liquid a certain market is, the more problematic an increase in lending activities can be. GDP growth rates were also introduced to capture the overall macroeconomic condition of a country in a given year. This can be intended as a proxy for income developments potentially affecting demand for credit. Last but not least, we included the net current account position to capture external imbalances leading to net inflows or outflows of money and investments.

The results of our statistical analysis are reported in Table 6.1. Primarily we found that overall negative demand conditions for loans and credit

Table 6.1   Probit models for credit determinants

	Demand: Pr(demand = 1) if decreasing	Supply: Pr(supply = 1) if tightening
NPL ratio – country	−0.062	−0.146
	(−0.51)	*(−1.56)*
Return on equity	−0.074	0.049
	(−1.42)	*(−1.43)*
LTD ratio – Group	−0.073	**0.016**
exposure in CESEE	*(−1.33)*	***(1.82)***
GDP growth	**−0.655**	0.051
	(−2.29)	*(0.28)*
Current account	0.000	**−0.119**
	(0.00)	***(−1.77)***
C	**9.905**	0.782
	(1.66)	*(−0.63)*
Pseudo R^2	0.25	0.14

Note: t-statistics are based on robust standard errors correcting for small sample; in bold results with a p-values less or equal to 10%; the values of the RHS variables refer to 2011 annual levels or growth rates; LTD stands for loan-to-deposit ratio of a certain group and covers loans and deposits of all units in the CESEE region; NPL ratio stands for non-performing loan over total loans; 'demand' is derived from the bank lending survey and is a dummy variable which takes value of 1 when respondents indicated an overall decreasing demand over the last six months and value 0 when respondents indicated an increasing or stable demand over the last six months; 'supply' is derived from the bank lending survey and is a dummy variable which takes value of 1 when respondents indicated a tightening supply (credit standards) over the last 6 months and value 0 when respondents indicated an easing or stable supply over the last 6 months.

Source: EIB bank survey.

lines have been negatively correlated to GDP growth. In other words a positive GDP growth is more likely to trigger a more positive demand for loans or credit lines. Supply conditions seem to be mainly related to the overall banking group liquidity as proxied by the LTD ratio in the CESEE region and to the overall country net external position. Indeed a higher LTD ratio increases the likelihood of more restrictive credit supply conditions as banks are more exposed to potential liquidity shortages and need to safeguard themselves taking into account their overall funding composition and potential alternative funding sources. The model suggests a reversed relation between the net current account position and supply conditions. This is not surprising if one considers that the pre-crisis boom cycle generated large current account deficits and was fuelled by lending growth financed from abroad.

6.7   CONCLUDING REMARKS

This chapter focuses on the determinants of credit growth, looking at the fundamental economic factors affecting the stall in growth and credit activities in the CESEE region. The chapter presents the results of a unique bank lending survey, conducted by the EIB in the context of the Vienna Initiative 2. The survey investigates the determinants of lending activities in the region over the second half of 2012 as well as the near-term expectations.

The results confirm the strategic commitment of international banks to the region, despite a progressive reduction of intra-group funding to their subsidiaries. In cumulative terms, reduction in cross-border lending to banks has reached some 4 per cent of regional GDP in the Q3 2011 – Q2 2012 period according to Bank for International Settlements (BIS) data, with some countries hit harder. International banks are becoming more selective in their strategies at country level, differentiating according to the perceived long-term growth potential of each local market. Regional subsidiaries report that sluggish credit growth is a consequence of both demand and supply factors. In a scenario of contracting demand over the past six months, the only positive contribution came from debt restructuring. This is a signal of rather poor market conditions. Interestingly, looking at the supply side, domestic factors play a role, as well as international factors. Domestic factors include local market potential growth, availability of local funding, NPLs and local regulation. International factors reflect the request from parent banks for more self-financed growth of local subsidiaries. This trend is also fostered by constraints affecting parent banks themselves including poor global outlook, restricted access to long-term funding, capital constraints and regulatory issues.

All in all, the survey provides supportive information for defining policy actions. On the one hand, results confirm the hypothesis of a rebalancing in the banking model for the CESEE region. Local market conditions as well as international constraints represent a drag to lending growth. Addressing those factors – the weight of NPLs or the lack of long-term domestic funding – should be one of the priorities. On the other hand, results also highlight the challenge of defining an optimal level of parent–subsidiary support, to allow the region to continue to benefit from financial integration as a driver for economic convergence. A reliance only on local funding sources to finance domestic credit growth would translate into a much slower financial sector deepening and sluggish overall economic activity.

NOTES

1. Statistics based on Bank for International Settlements (BIS) data and referred to in the Vienna Initiative 2 deleveraging monitor (Vienna Initiative, 2012).
2. The two main areas of interest for the Vienna Initiative 2 are: (1) cross-border bank deleveraging in Central Eastern and South-Eastern Europe (CESEE); and (2) home–host coordination on cross-border banking activities in CESEE. The Vienna Initiative was established at the height of the global financial crisis of 2008–2009 as a private–public sector platform to secure adequate capital and liquidity support by Western banking groups for their affiliates in CESEE. The initiative was relaunched as 'Vienna 2' in January 2012 in response to renewed risks for the region from the euro area crisis. Its focus is now on fostering home and host authority coordination in support of stable cross-border banking and guarding against disorderly deleveraging. Western banking groups continue to play an important role in the Initiative, both by supporting the coordination efforts and doing their own part to avoid disorderly deleveraging. For more details on the Initiative see http://ec.europa.eu/economy_finance/articles/governance/2012-07-20-vienna-2_en.htm.
3. Few countries are present in both regions (e.g. Slovakia, Czech Republic and Slovenia).
4. The Eurosystem has developed a survey of bank lending in the euro area. It is designed to provide information on supply and demand conditions in the euro area credit markets and the lending policies of euro area banks. The survey addresses issues such as credit standards for approving loans as well as credit terms and conditions applied to enterprises and households. It also asks for an assessment of the conditions affecting credit demand. For more details see http://www.ecb.int/stats/money/surveys/lend/html/inde6.en.html.
5. The Greek banking system has been fully bailed out and it is undergoing a full recapitalization process financed with a European Financial Stability Facility (EFSF) assistance facility. These amounts impact directly on the public finances of Greece. Consequently this is a fully fledged state contribution to banks.
6. The responses to the survey have been translated into ordered variables taking values from 1 to 5. The lower the value the more negative (strongly decreasing or strongly tightening) the response was. The value of 3 indicates a neutral response or no change in the previous six months or over the next six months. Given this transformation, we could have employed an ordered probit approach. However the number of observations was not deemed sufficient to obtain reliable results. Consequently we opted for a transformation of the ordered variables into binary outcomes taking up value 1 for any negative response and 0 otherwise.

BIBLIOGRAPHY

Avdjiev, S., Z. Kuti and E. Takats (2012), 'The euro area crisis and cross-border bank lending to emerging markets', *BIS Quarterly Review*, December, 37–47.

Berg, J., A. Van Rixtel, A. Ferrando, G. de Bondt and S. Scopel (2005), 'The bank lending survey for the euro area', ECB Occasional Paper No. 23, February.

European Central Bank (ECB) (2013), 'The Euro Area Bank Lending Survey January 2013', available at http://www.ecb.int/stats/pdf/blssurvey_201301.pdf?0fcdf99edcf5ba8367be036d72d000b1.

European Investment Bank (EIB) (2013), 'Banking in Central and Eastern Europe and Turkey – challenges and opportunities', available at http://www.eib.org/attachments/efs/economic_report_banking_cee_tr_en.pdf.

Institute of International Finance (2013), 'Emerging Markets Bank Lending

Conditions Survey – 2012/Q4, IIF 2013', available at http://www.iif.com/emr/global/emls/

Milesi-Ferretti, Gian-Maria and Cédric Tille (2011), 'The great retrenchment: international capital flows during the global financial crisis', *Economic Policy*, **26** (66), 285–342, available at http://www.cepr.org/meets/wkcn/9/979/papers/Milesi-Ferretti_Tille.pdf.

Vienna Initiative (2012), 'CESEE deleveraging monitor', November, available at http://ec.europa.eu/economy_finance/articles/governance/pdf/2012-11-12-deleveraging-monitor_en.pdf.

APPENDIX

Table 6A.1   Pair-wise correlations of the answers to the subsidiary section of the survey

			Overall banks credit standards	Bank's conditions and terms for approving loans or credit lines				Factors affecting your bank's credit standards – domestic and international factors			
				Bank's margin over interbank rate	Size of average loan	Maturity	Other terms and conditions	Local market outlook	Local bank outlook	Local bank funding	Local bank capital constraints
			b_01_01_0	b_02_01_0	b_02_02_0	b_02_03_0	b_02_04_0	b_03_01_0	b_03_02_0	b_03_03_0	b_03_04_0
Overall banks credit standards		b_01_01_0	1								
Bank's conditions and terms for approving loans or credit lines	Bank's margin over interbank rate	b_02_01_0	0.5881 *0.000*	1							
	Size of average loan	b_02_02_0	0.4684 *0.0015*	0.4258 *0.0044*	1						
	Maturity	b_02_03_0				1					
	Other terms and conditions	b_02_04_0	0.4716 *0.0014*	0.4159 *0.0055*	0.672 *0*	1					
Factors affecting your bank's credit standards – domestic and international factors	Local market outlook	b_03_01_0	0.5623 *0.0001*	0.4845 *0.001*	0.3604 *0.0176*	0.5854 *0*	1			
	Local bank outlook	b_03_02_0	0.7652 *0*	0.462 *0.0018*	0.3493 *0.0217*	0.3757 *0.013*	0.5352 *0.0002*	1		
	Local bank funding	b_03_03_0	0.4153 *0.0056*		0.4359 *0.0035*		0.3018 *0.0492*	0.4163 *0.0055*	1	
	Local bank capital constraints	b_03_04_0							0.4455 *0.0028*	1

					Total demand for loans or credit lines	Gross non-performing loans ratio	Funding – market access						Factors affecting funding conditions
Default figures (i.e. NPLs)	Group company outlook	Global market outlook	Group funding	Default figures (i.e. NPLs)			Total funding	Intragroup funding	Local currency funding	IFIs funding	Retail funding	Corporate funding	Direct exposure to sovereign debt
b_03_09_0	b_03_10_0	b_03_11_0	b_03_12_0	b_03_16_0	b_04_01_0	b_06_01_0	b_07_01_0	b_07_02_0	b_07_03_0	b_07_11_0	b_07_12_0	b_07_13_0	b_08_01_0

Table 6A.1   (continued)

			Overall banks credit standards	Bank's conditions and terms for approving loans or credit lines				Factors affecting your bank's credit standards – domestic and international factors			
				Bank's margin over inter-bank rate	Size of average loan	Maturity	Other terms and condi-tions	Local market outlook	Local bank outlook	Local bank funding	Local bank capital con-straints
			b_01_ 01_0	b_02_ 01_0	b_02_ 02_0	b_02_ 03_0	b_02_ 04_0	b_03_ 01_0	b_03_ 02_0	b_03_ 03_0	b_03_ 04_0
	Default figures (i.e. NPLs)	b_03_ 09_0	0.3248 *0.0336*	0.3954 *0.0087*			0.2752 *0.0741*	0.4335 *0.0037*		0.3238 *0.0342*	
	Group com-pany outlook	b_03_ 10_0	0.3353 *0.0279*	0.2544 *0.0997*	0.4435 *0.0029*		0.6194 *0*	0.3273 *0.0322*	0.3007 *0.0501*	0.5285 *0.0003*	0.5357 *0.0002*
	Global market outlook	b_03_ 11_0	0.6564 *0*	0.7282 *0*	0.3704 *0.0145*	0.2806 *0.0683*	0.5174 *0.0004*	0.7463 *0*	0.5534 *0.0001*		
	Group funding	b_03_ 12_0	0.3914 *0.0095*				0.3021 *0.049*		0.5401 *0.0002*	0.504 *0.0006*	0.5109 *0.0005*
	Default figures (i.e. NPLs)	b_03_ 16_0	0.4254 *0.0045*	0.2544 *0.0997*					0.4778 *0.0012*	0.377 *0.0127*	
Total demand for loans or credit lines		b_04_ 01_0	0.3425 *0.0246*	0.3064 *0.0457*	0.6207 *0*		0.5072 *0.0005*	0.3177 *0.0379*	0.3253 *0.0333*	0.3251 *0.0334*	
Gross non-perfor-ming loans ratio		b_06_ 01_0									
Funding – market access	Total funding	b_07_ 01_0									0.3458 *0.0231*
	Intra-group fun-ding	b_07_ 02_0				−0.3584 *0.0183*	−0.2832 *0.0657*				
	Local cur-rency funding	b_07_ 03_0					0.3041 *0.0474*			0.337 *0.0271*	0.4136 *0.0058*

	Total demand for loans or credit lines	Gross non-performing loans ratio	Funding – market access						Factors affecting funding conditions

Default figures (i.e. NPLs)	Group company outlook	Global market outlook	Group funding	Default figures (i.e. NPLs)			Total funding	Intra-group funding	Local currency funding	IFIs funding	Retail funding	Corporate funding	Direct exposure to sovereign debt
b_03_09_0	b_03_10_0	b_03_11_0	b_03_12_0	b_03_16_0	b_04_01_0	b_06_01_0	b_07_01_0	b_07_02_0	b_07_03_0	b_07_11_0	b_07_12_0	b_07_13_0	b_08_01_0
1													
0.4702 *0.0015*	1												
0.4169 *0.0054*	0.4015 *0.0076*	1											
0.3202 *0.0363*	0.6689 *0*	0.2726 *0.077*	1										
0.755 *0*	0.5222 *0.0003*		0.574 *0.0001*	1									
	0.391 *0.0095*	0.3944 *0.0089*	0.3728 *0.0138*		1								
−0.465 *0.0017*	−0.2575 *0.0955*		−0.3323 *0.0295*			1							
			−0.3041 *0.0474*				1						
							0.4623 *0.0018*	1					
0.444 *0.0029*	0.5032 *0.0006*		0.2903 *0.059*	0.3688 *0.015*			0.3226 *0.0349*		1				

Table 6A.1 (continued)

		Overall banks credit standards	Bank's conditions and terms for approving loans or credit lines				Factors affecting your bank's credit standards – domestic and international factors			
			Bank's margin over inter-bank rate	Size of average loan	Maturity	Other terms and conditions	Local market outlook	Local bank outlook	Local bank funding	Local bank capital constraints
		b_01_ 01_0	b_02_ 01_0	b_02_ 02_0	b_02_ 03_0	b_02_ 04_0	b_03_ 01_0	b_03_ 02_0	b_03_ 03_0	b_03_ 04_0
Factors affecting funding conditions	IFIs funding b_07_ 11_0								0.3101 *0.043*	
	Retail funding b_07_ 12_0		0.3681 *0.0152*	0.5017 *0.0006*			0.3893 *0.0099*	0.3773 *0.0126*	0.2975 *0.0527*	
	Corporate funding b_07_ 13_0				0.2978 *0.0524*				0.5801 *0*	
	Direct exposure to sovereign debt b_08_ 01_0	0.294 *0.0556*	0.3557 *0.0192*							

Source: EIB bank survey.

Default figures (i.e. NPLs)	Group company outlook	Global market outlook	Group funding	Default figures (i.e. NPLs)	Total demand for loans or credit lines	Gross non-performing loans ratio	Total funding	Intra-group funding	Local currency funding	IFIs funding	Retail funding	Corporate funding	Direct exposure to sovereign debt
b_03_09_0	b_03_10_0	b_03_11_0	b_03_12_0	b_03_16_0	b_04_01_0	b_06_01_0	b_07_01_0	b_07_02_0	b_07_03_0	b_07_11_0	b_07_12_0	b_07_13_0	b_08_01_0
							0.3283 *0.0316*	0.3008 *0.05*		1			
		0.2542 *0.1*			0.3129 *0.041*			−0.262 *0.0897*	0.2763 *0.0729*		1		
0.3254 *0.0332*	0.416 *0.0055*							−0.4637 *0.0017*	0.417 *0.0054*			1	
		0.3195 *0.0368*					0.3099 *0.0432*						1

Table 6A.2 *Pair-wise correlations between the answers to the subsidiary section (x-axis) and the answers to the parent section (y-axis) of the survey*

			b_01_ 01_0	b_02_ 01_0	b_02_ 02_0	b_02_ 03_0	b_02_ 04_0	b_03_ 01_0	b_03_ 02_0	b_03_ 03_0	b_03_ 04_0
Group strategic opera-	Strategic restruc- turing	a_02_ 01_0	0.5368 *0.0002*	0.6189 *0.000*	0.3092 *0.0436*	0.3057 *0.0462*	0.2763 *0.0729*	0.413 *0.0059*	0.4277 *0.0042*		
tions to increase	Sale of assets	a_02_ 02_0		0.3218 *0.0353*		0.3254 *0.0332*					
the capital ratio over the last 12 months	Sale of branches of activities	a_02_ 03_0									
	Raising capital on the market	a_02_ 04_0	0.2891 *0.0601*		0.3284 *0.0315*	0.3495 *0.0216*		0.2616 *0.0902*		0.2629 *0.0885*	0.2665 *0.0841*
	State con- tribuion to capital	a_02_ 05_0			−0.5141 *0.0004*		−0.3171 *0.0383*		−0.5343 *0.0002*		
Group's access to capital/ wholesale/retail funding		a_04_ 01_0			0.4035 *0.0073*		0.2763 *0.0729*		0.406 *0.0069*		
Longer term strategies (beyond 12 months) on operations in CESEE		a_05_ 01_0	0.4963 *0.0007*	0.4644 *0.0017*	0.4399 *0.0032*		0.4453 *0.0028*	0.3496 *0.0216*	0.4072 *0.0067*	0.5243 *0.0003*	
Total cross-border lending operations to CESEE		a_06_ 01_0		−0.3806 *0.0118*							0.3869 *0.0104*
Deleveraging – expected loan-to-deposit ratio		a_07_ 01_0							0.3031 *0.0482*		

Source: EIB bank survey.

b_03_ 09_0	b_03_ 10_0	b_03_ 11_0	b_03_ 12_0	b_03_ 16_0	b_04_ 01_0	b_06_ 01_0	b_07_ 01_0	b_07_ 02_0	b_07_ 03_0	b_07_ 11_0	b_07_ 12_0	b_07_ 13_0	b_08_ 01_0
		0.4889									0.2769		
		0.0009									*0.0722*		
−0.2812	−0.2878			−0.2878				0.332	−0.2797			−0.3768	
0.0677	*0.0613*			*0.0613*				*0.0297*	*0.0693*			*0.0128*	
			0.285	0.2717									
			0.064	*0.0779*									
	0.2814									−0.3122			
	0.0675									*0.0415*			
−0.4547	−0.5659		−0.4296	−0.4669				0.2975	−0.3413			−0.447	
0.0022	*0.0001*		*0.004*	*0.0016*				*0.0527*	*0.0251*			*0.0027*	
0.2664	0.4374							−0.2941	0.2798			0.401	
0.0842	*0.0034*							*0.0556*	*0.0692*			*0.0077*	
0.4519	0.5915	0.3946	0.4766	0.5247		−0.2884							
0.0024	*0*	*0.0088*	*0.0012*	*0.0003*		*0.0607*							
	0.2587	−0.3352							0.3051			0.3556	
	0.0939	*0.028*							*0.0467*			*0.0193*	
							−0.3033						
							0.0481						

7. Managing capital flows in a globalized economy

Marek Dabrowski[1]

7.1 INTRODUCTION

The purpose of this chapter is to analyse the phenomenon of the increasing size and volatility of private capital flows since the 1990s and to assess the underlying causes and resulting consequences for macroeconomic policy-making at both a national and a global level. Special attention will be devoted to emerging-market economies of Central and Eastern Europe and the former USSR, but most of our findings and conclusions also apply to other emerging regions. After a brief analysis of the dynamics of capital flows in the 1990s and 2000s and the determining factors we will turn to two important and sensitive areas of macroeconomic management: balance of payments (BoP) policy and monetary policy. Free capital mobility has dramatically narrowed the room for manoeuvre of national policies in both areas, especially in small open economies, which is not always well understood by both policy-makers and analysts. This makes a strong case for supranational macroeconomic policy coordination, especially in the area of monetary policy. However, such coordination seems to be still a distant prospect, as several conceptual questions and political obstacles need to be solved first.

7.2 LIVING IN A WORLD OF FREE AND TURBULENT CAPITAL FLOWS

Most of the twentieth century (from the Great Depression in the early 1930s until the 1980s) was characterized by far-reaching trade protectionism and capital movement restrictions. Under these circumstances the assumptions that a particular national economy functions in at least partial isolation from the rest of the world, and that the national government is fully sovereign in many important economic policy areas, seemed to be accurate.

This changed dramatically in the 1990s and 2000s with the dismantling of many trade barriers (unilaterally, bilaterally and multilaterally) and the rapid integration of financial markets. The latter has been the result of advancing current and capital account liberalization across the world, the liberalization of the banking sector and other financial markets segments (through the elimination of various forms of financial repression), the transnational expansion of large banks and non-bank financial institutions to emerging-market and developing economies,[2] the privatization of banks and other financial institutions in the latter, and finally the rapid progress in telecommunication and information technologies (ICT) and financial innovations (facilitated, in turn, by a combination of legal innovations and new ICT tools). All these factors have eliminated institutional, legal and technical barriers to unrestricted capital movement, especially private financial flows, across the globe, substantially reduced transaction costs and helped to integrate national financial markets into a single global market.

The increasing financial integration and opening has affected, in particular, emerging-market economies, that is middle- and low-income countries which did not participate, for various reasons, in cross-border private capital flows before the 1990s. Some of them (countries of the former Soviet bloc, China, Vietnam) followed the communist model of predominantly state-owned and centrally planned economies. On the other hand, many developing countries in Asia, Africa and Latin America, even if representing a sort of market economy with dominant private ownership, followed protectionist trade and investment practices, had inconvertible currencies and underdeveloped and heavily repressed financial sectors, and suffered from high inflation and periodic BoP crises, and so on. Those countries started to benefit from private capital flows only after comprehensive policy reforms at the end of the 1980s and 1990s, which led to disinflation, a reduction in barriers to trade and foreign investments, large-scale privatization, and the opening of the financial sectors and capital accounts.

Figure 7.1 illustrates the rapid but highly volatile growth of net private capital flows[3] to emerging-market and developing economies in the 1990s and 2000s. After a more than fourfold increase in the first half of the 1990s (from US$42.2 billion in 1990 to US$190.7 billion in 1995) net capital flows collapsed to below the 1990 level (US$38.8 billion in 1999), following a series of emerging-market financial crises.[4] Net private flows recovered from 2003 onward, increasing even more rapidly than in the first half of the 1990s and peaked at US$694.4 billion in 2007. In 2008 the first stage of the global financial crisis reduced net private flows almost three times to US$264.5 billion but they recovered quickly, reaching a level of US$604.7 billion in 2010. The year 2011 and, most likely, 2012 saw another contraction.

USD billion

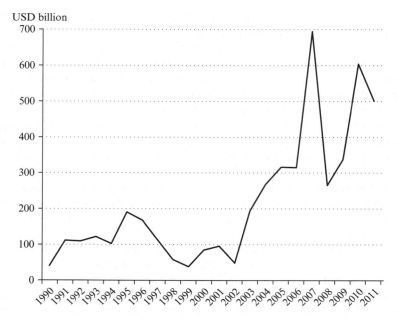

Source: IMF (2012b).

Figure 7.1 Net private financial flows to emerging-market and developing economies, 1990–2011 (USD billion)

A disaggregation of net private financial flows between major regions (Figure 7.2) gives us a picture of even greater volatility than in the case of the global figures. In the 1990s most net flows went to countries of developing Asia and Latin America and the Caribbean, although the former experienced short-lasting net capital outflows in the aftermath of the Asian crisis (1998–2000). In the mid-2000s boom, Central and Eastern Europe (CEE), the Commonwealth of Independent States (CIS), developing Asia, Latin America and the Caribbean, and the Middle East and North Africa experienced large private capital inflows. When the global financial crisis started in 2008 private flows to the CIS countries and CEE dramatically collapsed (or even became negative in the CIS) but continued or even intensified (especially in 2010–2011) to developing Asia and Latin America and the Caribbean.

The Middle East and North Africa experienced only short periods of larger net inflows (in the early 1990s and the latter 2000s). The CIS countries suffered from net capital outflows through most of the two decades analysed here apart from a short boom period from 2005 to 2007. Finally,

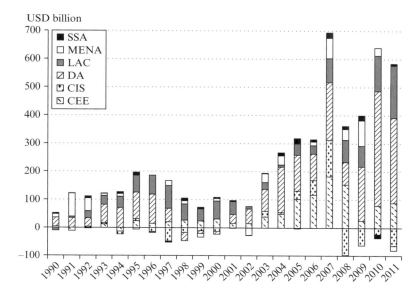

Note: SSA – Sub-Saharan Africa, MENA – Middle East and North Africa, LAC – Latin America and Caribbean, DA – Developing Asia, CIS – Commonwealth of Independent States, CEE – Central and Eastern Europe.

Source: IMF (2012a).

Figure 7.2 Net private financial flows by major emerging-market regions, 1990–2011 (USD billion)

net flows to sub-Saharan Africa oscillated around zero in the 1990s and have increased somewhat since 2004, peaking at US$19.0 billion in 2007. Figure 7.3 demonstrates a few selected cases of high volatility in CEE and the CIS region in 2002–2011. These countries experienced changes in size of net private financial flows by several percentage points of gross domestic product (GDP) during just a few years.[5]

Bulgaria represents the most extreme case: net financial inflows increased from approximately 9 per cent of its GDP in 2003–2005 to 23.9 per cent in 2006 and 28.7 per cent in 2007, and then collapsed to a level of 1.1 per cent in 2010. Georgia, Macedonia, Moldova and Ukraine exhibited similar, but slightly less volatile patterns. In the examined period Estonia experienced three short periods of large net inflows (2003–2004, 2007–2008 and since 2010) interrupted by two periods of net outflows (2005–2006 and 2009). Slovenia turned from a net capital exporter in 2003–2007 into a large importer (2009–2011).

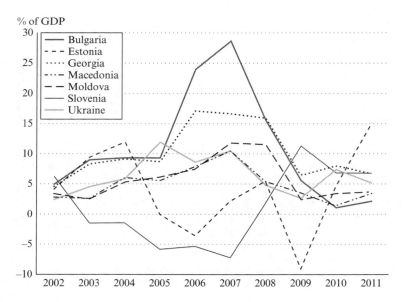

Source: IMF (Balance of Payment Statistics).

*Figure 7.3   Net private capital flows to selected emerging-market
economies in Europe, 2002–2011 (% of GDP)*

Looking for the causes of such volatility one can find several country-specific (pull) factors, for example: large-scale privatization transactions (which usually have a one-off character), large green-field direct foreign investment (frequent phenomena in commodity-producing countries), changes in fiscal and monetary policies (which increase/decrease supply and the attractiveness of fixed-income financial instruments), changes in market perception of a country's macroeconomic and microeconomic fundamentals and associated risk.

Nevertheless, the presence of regional and global booms and busts suggests the importance of factors that are beyond the control of national policies. They may reflect changing sentiments and 'herding' behaviour of financial market participants in the short term (sometimes referred to as the contagion effect), but this seems to be insufficient explanation.

Changes in global monetary conditions (push factor) are among the key suspects. In the absence of a single conceptual definition and without statistics on global money supply or liquidity (I will return to this issue at the end of my analysis) changes in United States (US) money supply

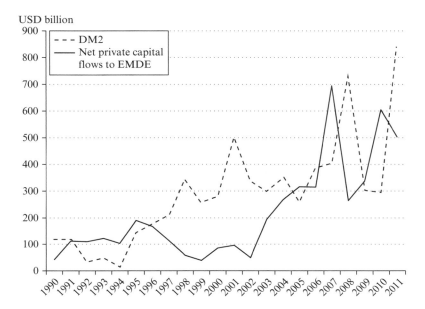

Source: US Federal Reserve Board (H.6 Statistical Release for 20 December 2012). http://www.federalreserve.gov/datadownload/LoadChart.aspx?rel=H6&series=de0d7f93074e32 cae3e619735d9cc5ce&filetype=spreadsheetml&label=include&layout=seriesrow&from= 01/01/1990&to=11/30/2012 (accessed 10 January 2013); IMF (World Economic Outlook, October 2012).

Figure 7.4   Annual increase in US money supply (DM2) and net private financial flows to emerging-market and developing economies, 1990–2011 (USD billion)

may provide some indication in this respect, taking into consideration the role of the US dollar as the most important global reserve and transaction currency. Figure 7.4 plots the net annual private financial flows to emerging-market and developing economies against the annual increase in US money supply (M2 aggregate). Although no close correlation can be detected from Figure 7.4 until the mid-2000s, the situation seemed to change after this date. There is a visible co-movement in fluctuation of both variables.[6]

Changes in international financial sector regulations may be another factor which explains fluctuations in the size of cross-country capital flows. Below I will concentrate on discussing consequences of volatility in capital flows for macroeconomic policy-making in individual countries rather than analysing in detail the causes of volatility.

7.3 CAPITAL FLOWS AND CHANGES IN CURRENT ACCOUNT BALANCE

The management of a country's balance of payments is the area of macroeconomic policy where unrestricted capital mobility brought the biggest, if not revolutionary, changes. The 'traditional' approach to BoP analysis was based on realities of largely closed (or only partly open) economies with a limited role of cross-border private capital flows and the ability of national governments to influence saving and investment decisions of domestic economic agents. Such an analysis usually started from domestic factors of competitiveness, in the first instance labour unit costs denominated in foreign currency. These factors determined the trade and current account balance. Capital account transactions had to counterbalance the current account. If a country ran a current account deficit it needed, for example, foreign credit (private or official), foreign direct investment (FDI) or other kinds of capital inflow to finance that deficit. If it ran a current account surplus this surplus had to be absorbed in the form of capital account transactions with the opposite sign, that is, through various forms of capital exports or outflows, or increasing official reserves (which is also a form of capital export).

If the current account balance was considered unsustainable, given difficulties in conducting counterbalancing capital account transactions, policy adjustment was needed. The adjustment might be implemented through the instruments of exchange rate policy (devaluation or revaluation of domestic currency), trade policy, monetary and fiscal policies (which determined the level of domestic absorption), and others.

Summing up, in a world of restricted capital mobility the current account balance determined capital account flows. In a world of free capital mobility, however, the reverse causality dominates. In a small open economy, net capital flows (at least their private component) have a largely exogenous character and the current account balance must adapt to changes in the capital account (through changes in real exchange rates).

Figures 7.5 and 7.6 illustrate the mirror character of changes in net private financial flows and current account balances in two emerging market regions – CEE, and Latin America and the Caribbean – which are dominated by small open economies with largely open capital accounts. Their experience in the 1990s and 2000s confirms the phenomenon of limited control of national macroeconomic policy over current account balances and real exchange rates in a world of unrestricted capital movement. Even if a country's monetary authority controls its nominal exchange rate through some sort of currency peg or managed float,

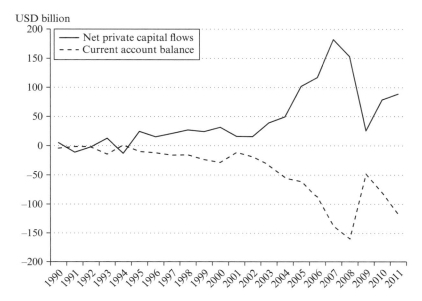

Source: IMF (2012a).

Figure 7.5 *Net private capital flows and current account balance in CEE countries, 1990–2011 (USD billion)*

the real exchange rate adjusts to the BoP equilibrium through inflation differentials.

Other regions than CEE and Latin America and the Caribbean do not represent so clear a mirror pattern of changes in net private financial flows and current account balances due to the impact of other factors, such as the role of official development aid (sub-Saharan Africa), or changes in the official reserves (both international reserves of monetary authority and sovereign wealth funds) in the case of developing Asia, the Middle East and North Africa, and the CIS economies.

7.4 FREE CAPITAL MOVEMENT AND CURRENT ACCOUNT IMBALANCES

Living in a world of largely unrestricted capital movement requires a new attitude to current account imbalances. The 'traditional' analytical framework for the balance of payments mentioned in the previous section was based on the explicit or implicit assumption that today's current

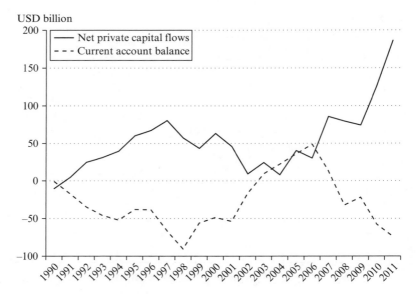

Source: IMF (2012a).

Figure 7.6   Net private capital flows and current account balance in Latin American and Caribbean countries, 1990–2011 (USD billion)

account deficit must be compensated by future current account surpluses (i.e., a current account must be balanced at least over the long term). This was related to another implicit (not clearly articulated and not always well recognized) assumption that capital ownership residency has a fixed character.[7] This means that capital invested in country A, financed by savings coming from country B, will 'belong' to the latter, including its right to repatriate factor income (interest or dividend) and, eventually, the invested capital stock. Such assumptions might be justified in a world of restricted capital movement which, in turn, was reflected in the empirical phenomenon of the 'home country bias' in investing gross national saving as described by Feldstein and Horioka (1980).

Following the 'traditional' analytical framework, each kind of net capital inflows (including FDI) leads to the accumulation of a country's external liabilities, which: (1) cannot grow indefinitely; (2) must be repaid at some point; and (3) the higher they are, the more vulnerable the country's external position is. Consequently, various numerical criteria (e.g., a current account deficit exceeding 4 or 5 per cent of GDP – see Summers, 1996) were applied both by international financial institutions and private investors in the late 1990s and early 2000s to identify countries considered as potential candidates for a BoP crisis.

This often led to paradoxical conclusions when countries considered by international investors as business friendly, and therefore attracting large amounts of private investment (and consequently running high current account deficits), were assessed as conducing unsustainable policies and 'overheated'. On the contrary, countries characterized by a poor business climate which were not able to attract net private capital inflows or even suffered from net capital outflows (of both residents and non-residents) recorded either balanced or positive current accounts and were considered as macroeconomically 'healthy' under the '5 per cent doctrine'.

More recently, in the 2000s the problem of large current account imbalances between major world economies and regions has become the subject of hot policy debates. Many authors (e.g., Roubini and Setser, 2005) predicted that such imbalances would lead to a global BoP crisis unless they were reduced in a gradual and orderly manner. However, the 2007–2009 global crisis was caused by the collapse of housing and stock market bubbles in the United States. Current account imbalances between major economic players such as the United States, the European Union (EU), China, other Asian economies and oil-producing countries neither were the primary cause of this crisis,[8] nor became significantly corrected as a result of this crisis. Emerging-market economies suffered a sudden but short lasting stop in private capital flows (as illustrated in Figure 7.1) but this resulted from drying global liquidity after the Lehman Brothers bankruptcy rather than from country-specific factors. Among emerging-market economies a sudden stop in capital flows in 2008–2009 affected both countries with large current account deficits (Baltic countries, Bulgaria) and those with large current account surpluses (Kazakhstan, Russia).

The same kind of discussion was repeated after the European debt crisis erupted in 2010. Those who do not want to accept the most obvious diagnosis on the fiscal roots of this crisis search for other kinds of explanations, including the BoP crisis hypothesis. However, as the euro area as a whole has a broadly balanced current account (or a small surplus), advocates of the BoP crisis diagnosis point to internal current account imbalances between European Monetary Union (EMU) member countries (e.g., Mayer, 2011; Krugman, 2012; Sinn, 2012). Since 2010 the subsequent peripheral euro area countries in troubles suffered from capital outflows, but this was the consequence of the increased risk of default on sovereign debt and the associated perception of a possible collapse of the common currency project rather than the primary cause of the crisis (Dabrowski, 2012). All the above discussed shortcomings of the 'traditional' BoP analytical framework call for its substantial revision, regarding both its key assumptions and the resulting policy implications.

Firstly, in a world of largely unrestricted capital movements, major sources of capital do not have a country of origin, given the transnational character of major corporations, financial institutions and investment funds, even if they invest on behalf of residents of concrete countries. In addition, with the free movement of people, physical persons (especially wealthy ones) may easily change their country of residence (domicile), moving together with their accumulated savings.

Secondly, private investors seek the highest rate of return in their investment and reinvestment decisions, regardless of their country of residence. Each individual rate of return consists of two major components: (1) a country-related component reflecting a country's investment climate; and (2) a project-related component.

Thirdly, there is not necessarily a diminishing rate of return in relation to a country-related component. This means that country A may offer a higher rate of return than country B for similar projects for a long period of time, due to a better investment climate.

However, if the investment climate deteriorates (or investors fear such deterioration) and the expected rate of return in country A becomes lower than that of country B, the direction of capital movement may change. Such change will affect not only 'foreign' capital (that from country B) but also domestic residents (those from country A). In our new framework, country A (capital importer) is not immunized from the danger of capital outflows, but such a danger originates from changes in the country-related component of the expected rate of return (comparing to other countries) rather than from the non-resident origin of the invested capital.

Looking at the problem of cross-country current account imbalances from the 'supply-side' perspective there are countries which for various historical, demographic, institutional and other reasons are able to generate a systematically higher rate of national saving than others, in excess of their own investment needs. Unrestricted capital movement and global financial market enable moving this excess saving to countries and locations where they can be invested in the most efficient way to the benefit of both savers and investors.

However, one cannot say that current account imbalances have become totally irrelevant. As long as country A has its own currency and sovereign monetary and fiscal policies, at some point its current account deficit may start to be considered by investors as too high and its liabilities in foreign currency unsustainable. This may cause its exchange rate risk premium (devaluation risk) to increase and its expected rate of return to decrease. These developments may trigger a sudden outflow of capital (both resident and non-resident) and BoP and currency crisis. Thus the current account balance and, more generally, the balance of payments must remain a subject of interest and concern of national economic policies.

7.5 CAN COUNTRIES INFLUENCE THE SIZE AND DIRECTION OF PRIVATE CAPITAL FLOWS?

If the balance of payments and current account balances still matter, how may national governments influence the size and direction of private capital flows, the key exogenous factor determining a country's external position? As we suggested earlier, finding an instrument or set of instruments which could effectively perform such a task is not easy. Capital controls such as a ban on certain transactions, licence requirements to conduct them, and the taxation of capital flows (explicit or implicit, for example unremunerated reserve requirements) are formally unavailable for EU members and advanced candidates because such controls violate the *acquis communitaire* (one of the four Single Market basic freedoms). The non-EU countries which belong to the Organisation for Economic Co-operation and Development (OECD) are also constrained by the OECD Code of Liberalization of Capital Movements, although in a less rigorous way than in the case of the EU *acquis* (see OECD, 2012).

However, countries which are not constrained by international treaties and other formal obligations and which have tried capital controls have found those tools to be problematic. Individual instruments may have some, but rather a temporary, impact on the structure and maturity of capital flows (see Baba and Kokenyne, 2011). If a country has already reached an advanced degree of its economic openness and financial sector sophistication, capital movement restrictions could be quite easily circumvented through current account transactions, those capital account transactions which remained unrestricted, offshore markets and various kinds of derivatives. Thus the ultimate effect of capital controls is building various kinds of market distortions and decreasing transparency of capital flows rather than impacting upon their size and direction.

The effectiveness of monetary policy in terms of its influence on the size and direction of private capital flows is rather limited and depends on the underlying regime. There is no impact under a hard peg because there is no sovereign monetary policy at all. A flexible exchange rate allows for some accommodation of volatility in capital flows through either nominal appreciation or depreciation of a national currency and associated exchange rate risk premiums or adjustments of the central bank's interest rates. However, if the exogenous changes in private capital flows are strong enough (as experienced in the period of 2004–2011) a country's tolerance of exchange rate fluctuation can reach economic and political limits. In addition, in some circumstances both capital inflows and outflows may become self-accelerating under flexible exchange rates (speculation for currency appreciation or depreciation).

Adjusting interest rates in response to fluctuations in capital flows involves a risk of damaging domestic macroeconomic conditions with negative consequences for the real sector: interest rate cuts may cause the economy to overheat, whereas a radical increase in interest rates to stop capital outflow may trigger a downturn.

Hybrid monetary regimes, which target both exchange rate and interest rate or monetary aggregates, may try to sterilize both capital inflows and outflows. However, sterilization of capital inflows is usually costly and ineffective in the long term as it creates a one-way bet for the market players. In turn, sterilization of capital outflows may easily lead to a meltdown of international reserves and trigger a speculative attack against the country's currency.

Fiscal policy may have some impact on the current account as it influences net national saving (a fiscal deficit decreases net national saving and a fiscal surplus increases it). However, one should take into account the offsetting effects in terms of net private financial flows. For example, fiscal contraction, which is widely considered as one of the measures to diminish current account imbalances, may not necessarily bring the expected results due to 'crowding-in' effects (Rostowski, 2001). Successful fiscal adjustment is usually perceived by investors as a factor decreasing country risk (i.e., increasing the expected rate of return) and boosts private capital inflows, thus leading to higher account deficits.

Fiscal policy may also have some microeconomic impact through various kinds of fiscal incentives and disincentives. For example, in some countries which experienced housing market booms and busts in the 2000s, special tax incentives artificially stimulated housing investments. However, in most cases such incentives or disincentives influence the structure of capital flows rather than their total volume. The same concerns micro-prudential financial regulations. They may have a benefit of their own by increasing the robustness of a financial sector. However, their impact on capital flows may concern their structure rather than the overall volume.

Finally, macro-prudential financial regulation may have some impact on both the volume and structure of capital flows. However, this is a relatively new regulatory concept and will very much depend on its practical operationalization: what kind of financial flows and variables will be monitored, by whom and according to which criteria, and what kind of preventive and corrective instruments can be adopted (see Macroprudential, 2011). Its early record looks mixed. In some countries it serves as a new label for the old practices of capital control.[9] In others the debate on the concept, the analytical and institutional framework, and the instruments of macroprudential regulation is still in a relatively infant stage. It seems that more time and practical experience is required to assess its regulatory potential and effectiveness, including its impact on cross-border financial flows.

The above picture confirms, once again, my earlier view on the limited potential of national policies in small open economies to regulate the balance of payments, current account balances and the real exchange rate in a world of unrestricted capital movement. This means that prudent macroeconomic (especially fiscal) and regulatory policies at the national level may increase a country's financial safety and its ability to withstand various exogenous BoP shocks but do not guarantee its full immunity against external turbulence and BoP crisis.

7.6 CAPITAL MOBILITY AND MONETARY POLICY

There are similar limits to national sovereignty with regard to monetary policy. In a small open economy, money supply is at least partly exogenous as a result of unrestricted financial flows. Even under a freely floating exchange rate and inflation-targeting, the room for manoeuvre of national monetary policy is limited and determined by political and economic tolerance of exchange rate fluctuations. 'Leaning against the winds' of international financial markets usually leads to either appreciation or depreciation of the domestic currency. Excessive appreciation deteriorates the competitiveness of domestic producers while excessive depreciation may have negative pass-through effects on inflation, increase the domestic currency value of foreign-currency-denominated liabilities, and may trigger a flight from the domestic currency, especially in countries with fresh memories of high inflation or hyperinflation, insufficiently credible national monetary policy and high actual dollarization or euroization. To respect these limitations the central bank's interest rate decisions must take into account international financial market trends and cannot deviate too much from them.

On the other hand, changes in interest rates on international financial markets are determined by the monetary policy decisions of central banks of major advanced economies, in particular the US Federal Reserve Board (Fed). The global integration of financial markets and the role of the US dollar as the number one international reserve and transaction currency leads to a situation when the Fed's monetary policy decisions have an economic impact far beyond its formal jurisdiction (see Ghosh et al., 2012). To a lesser extent, this also relates to the euro and the Japanese yen.

In the 2000s the Fed's monetary policy went through two large-scale easing cycles: in the early 2000s, following the dot.com recession and the 9/11 terrorist attack; and since summer 2007 when the subprime mortgage crisis erupted. Monetary easing was determined by the Fed's perception of US domestic economic conditions and remained in line with its formal legal mandate. However, in both instances monetary easing contributed to a huge expansion of international liquidity and net private financial flows to emerging-market and developing economies, and their subsequent volatility as demonstrated in Figure 7.1.

Monetary policy decisions in major advanced economies put other central banks, including those in emerging-market and developing economies, in an uneasy position. Because of their limited ability to 'lean against the wind' (see above) they must follow decisions of major players even if macroeconomic conditions in their own countries differ substantially. Very often what is perceived by central banks of smaller countries as external shocks (increase in commodity prices or sudden changes in country risk perception) is a by-product of monetary decisions of major central banks.

Solving this conflict would require broadening the actual mandate and goal function of the Fed and other central banks which issue international reserve currencies. They should pay more attention to international spillovers of their monetary policy decisions (see Ostry et al., 2012 on source-country policies). This is not a matter of policy altruism but a well-recognized interest of their own economies. In many instances negative externalities will come back, as a boomerang, to a given monetary authority, even if this happens with a certain time lag. They may have a form of higher commodity prices, financial bubbles and BoP crises in other economies but affect the home country's financial sector, and so on.

More generally, systematic global monetary policy coordination would help to decrease a one-way dependence of smaller central banks in respect to key players. However, this is not an easy goal to achieve, at least not soon, for at least two fundamental reasons.

Firstly, any attempt at collective action at a supranational level compromises national sovereignty. In the case of monetary policy coordination the differences in the legal mandates of individual central banks, some of them being exclusively responsible for price stability (the European Central Bank, ECB), others (such as the Fed) also obliged to follow output or employment goals and specific guarantees of their independence anchored in national legal systems, may create an additional obstacle.

Secondly, even if the political and legal obstacles were overcome, the attempt at global monetary policy coordination would face a shortage of macroeconomic theory providing conceptual and analytical tools for such coordination. For the time being there is no conceptual clarity on how to define and measure global money supply or global liquidity (see Chen et al., 2012 for an attempt to measure global liquidity), which factors and mechanisms determine changes in global money supply (however defined), what is the role of cross-country money multipliers under various exchange rate regimes, and so on. All the theoretical models of monetary policy (such as the Taylor rule) analyse its determinants, tools and consequences within a single national economy. There is no global monetary model, nor are there even sufficient external spillovers in national models.

Practical attempts at global macroeconomic policy coordination undertaken so far within the Multilateral Consultation framework of the International Monetary Fund (IMF) (see IMF, 2007b) and G-20 (see G-20, 2012, paragraph 7) have focused mainly on current account imbalances and their reduction through greater nominal exchange rate flexibility. As explained above, such an approach is based on an analytical framework and a set of assumptions typical for economies with restricted capital accounts, and targets secondary symptoms of macroeconomic distortions rather than their primary causes.

7.7 CONCLUSIONS

The global integration of financial markets seems irreversible under the current circumstances and, most likely, will further progress in the next ten years or so. The two biggest emerging-market economies, China and India, are expected to fully open their capital accounts and liberalize their financial sectors at some point. This creates a necessity to adjust economic theory and policy at the national as well as the global level to unrestricted capital movements, rather than the reinvention of capital controls and the isolation of individual countries from the turbulence of international markets. This is a task for academia, market analysts, policy-makers and international institutions.

Economic theory must undertake an effort to elaborate a global monetary model which will offer more than the sum of national monetary conditions (e.g., including cross-border monetary and fiscal multipliers and spillovers). Consequently, this should create a conceptual ground for understanding mechanisms and instruments which determine global liquidity as the precondition to any successful attempts to regulate it. Researchers, analysts and policy-makers should come to an understanding of all the consequences of unrestricted capital movement for macroeconomic analyses and policies. This concerns, in particular, the largely exogenous character of changes in capital and current account balances (with the former determining the latter), the real exchange rate, the limited sovereignty in the area of monetary policy, and so on. Instead of mechanically seeking a return to balanced current accounts within national boundaries as the proof of macroeconomic health, it is more desirable to analyse in-depth factors which determine the actual BoP position and flows, try to assess their sustainability, and design policies which make countries more immune to sudden and excessive fluctuation in global capital flows.

There is no single instrument which would allow accomplishing this goal. Rather, a package of various macro and micro policies is required to increase a country's macroeconomic safety and ensure sustainable growth prospects. However, such a package should not include a return to capital controls, as they are largely ineffective and breach the international obligations of many countries.

Still, even the best-designed national policy mix in a small open economy cannot guarantee complete immunity from external shocks triggered by policy decisions of other countries, especially the biggest players. This is the price which must be paid for numerous benefits stemming from the globalization process and free capital movement. However, the realization of this risk as well as of the limited room for decision-making at the country level (due to constraints imposed by international markets) should encourage national policy-makers to seek greater international cooperation and coordination in macroeconomic, particularly monetary, policies.

This is a formidable task and there is a long way to go, but it is worth a try. It requires overcoming various political constraints, building new legal and institutional frameworks, and developing a theoretical background and analytical tools for global coordination and decision-making. Smaller countries have an obvious incentive to participate in such an effort: they have already lost a substantial part of their sovereignty in macroeconomic management. However, the big players should also understand and accept the advantages of a collaborative approach and of sharing their policy-making sovereignty; even the largest economies are not isolated from the rest of the world. If their authorities are concentrated too much on narrow domestic agendas they risk exporting problems and distortions to others (beggar-thy-neighbour policies) with the probability that the external damage done will affect them sooner or later. The role of an economic superpower, including the issuance of a global reserve currency, does not only come with extra privileges, it also comes with responsibilities.

NOTES

1. This chapter was prepared during my visiting research fellowship at the Bank of Finland Institute for Economies in Transition (BOFIT) between November 2012 and February 2013. I would like to acknowledge the supporting role of the Bank of Finland, which provided me with excellent opportunities to work on this topic. However, the chapter reflects my personal views and opinions and not necessarily those of the Bank of Finland or the Center for Social and Economic Research (CASE), and I accept the sole responsibility for its content and quality.
2. For a list of emerging-market and developing economies and their regional breakdown, see IMF (2012a, Table E, pp. 182–3), and IMF (2007a).
3. Net private capital flows include net direct investment, net private portfolio investment and other (long- and short-term) net private investment flows.
4. It involved, among others, Mexico in 1994–1995 and the subsequent 'Tequila' crisis in Latin America, then the Asian crisis of 1997–1998, the Russian and CIS crisis of 1998–1999, Brazil in 1999, Argentina in 1999–2001, and Turkey in 2000–2001. There were also some smaller-scale episodes of macroeconomic and financial turmoil such as in Bulgaria in 1996–1997 and the devaluation of the Czech crown in 1997.
5. See Ghosh et al. (2012) for a more complete list of episodes of large private capital inflows to emerging market and developing economies (called 'surges' by the authors) in the period 1980–2009.
6. See also IMF (2012c, pp. 22–4) on the role of monetary policy and financial sector regulations in the major advanced economies in determining the size of capital flows to emerging market and developing economies, and Ghosh et al. (2012) on the role of US interest rates.
7. This section draws on Dabrowski (2008) where the shortcomings of the 'traditional' balance of payments analytical framework and search for an alternative framework are discussed in a more comprehensive way.
8. Rather, they could be considered as secondary symptoms of other macroeconomic excesses (soft monetary policy in the United States and other advanced economies) or regulatory distortions (related to the financial sector, housing market etc.).
9. See IMF (2012c, Box 2) on the differences between capital flow management instruments and macroprudential measures and their potential overlaps.

REFERENCES

Baba, C. and A. Kokenyne (2011), 'Effectiveness of capital controls in selected emerging markets in the 2000s', IMF Working Paper, WP/11/281, 1 December.

Chen, S., P. Liu, A. Maechler, C. Marsh, S. Saksonovs and H.S. Shin (2012), 'Exploring the dynamics of global liquidity', IMF Working Paper, WP/12/246, 11 October.

Dabrowski, Marek (2008), 'Rethinking balance of payments constraints in a globalized world', in Anders Aslund and Marek Dabrowski (eds), *Challenges of Globalization: Imbalances and Growth*, Washington, DC: Peter G. Peterson Institute for International Economics.

Dabrowski, M. (2012), 'Fiscal and monetary policy determinants of the Eurozone crisis and its resolution', CASE Network Studies and Analyses, 443.

Feldstein, M. and C. Horioka (1980), 'Domestic saving and international capital flows', *Economic Journal*, **90**, 314–29.

G-20 (2012), 'Communiqué of Ministers of Finance and Central Bank Governors of the G20', Mexico City, available at http://www.g20mexico.org/index.php/es/comunicados-de-prensa/537-final-communique; 4–5 November.

Ghosh, A.R., J.I. Kim, M.S. Qureshi and J. Zalduendo (2012), 'Surges', IMF Working Paper, WP/12/22, January.

IMF (2007a), *World Economic Outlook: Spillovers and Cycles in the Global Economy*, Washington, DC: International Monetary Fund, April.

IMF (2007b), 'Staff Report on the multilateral consultation on global imbalances with China, the euro area, Japan, Saudi Arabia, and the United States', available at http://www.imf.org/external/np/pp/2007/eng/062907.pdf.

IMF (2012a), *World Economic Outlook: Coping with High Debt and Sluggish Growth*, Washington, DC: International Monetary Fund, October.

IMF (2012b), *World Economic Outlook Database*, October, Washington, DC: International Monetary Fund.

IMF (2012c), 'The liberalization and management of capital flows: an institutional view', IMF Policy Paper, 14 November, available at http://www.imf.org/external/np/pp/eng/2012/111412.pdf.

Krugman, P. (2012), 'European crisis realities', *New York Times*, 25 February, available at http://krugman.blogs.nytimes.com/2012/02/25/european-crisis-realities/.

Macroprudential (2011), 'Macroprudential policy tools and frameworks: Progress report to G20', Joint Paper of the Financial Stability Board, International Monetary Fund and Bank for International Settlements, available at http://www.imf.org/external/np/g20/pdf/102711.pdf.

Mayer, T. (2011), 'Euroland's hidden balance-of-payments crisis', Deutsche Bank Research, 26 October.

OECD (2012), 'OECD Code of Liberalization of Capital Movements', available at http://www.oecd.org/daf/inv/investment-policy/codes.htm.

Ostry, J., A.R. Ghosh and A. Korinek (2012), 'Multilateral aspects of managing the capital account', IMF Staff Discussion Note, SDN/12/10, 7 September.

Rostowski, Jacek (2001), 'The approach to EU and EMU membership: the implication for macroeconomic policy in the applicant countries', in Marek Dabrowski and Jacek Rostowski (eds), *The Eastern Enlargement of the EU*, Boston, MA, USA; Dordrecht Netherlands and London, UK: Kluwer Academic Publishers, pp. 35–51.

Roubini, N. and B. Setser (2005), 'Will the Bretton Woods 2 regime unravel soon? The risk of a hard landing in 2005–2006', Federal Reserve Bank of San Francisco, February, available at http://www.frbsf.org/economics/conferences/0502/Roubini.pdf.

Sinn, H.-W. (2012), 'The European balance of payments crisis: an introduction', *CESifo Forum*, Special Issue, available at http://www.cesifo-group.de/portal/pls/portal/docs/1/1213636.PDF.

Summers, Lawrence H. (1996), 'Commentary', in Ricardo Hausmann and Liliana Rojas-Suarez (eds), *Volatile Capital Flows*, Washington, DC: Inter-American Development Bank, pp. 53–7.

PART III

Growth Strategies of EU Neighbouring
Countries: Russia and Turkey

8. Russia in 2012: the challenge of reforming the economy without a political reform

Konstantin Sonin

The intention behind this chapter is to provide some regional flavour to the broader macroeconomic issues of this book. I start with the short-term outlook. The Russian economy has been growing quite fast since 2010. That is to say, it has been growing fast compared to Europe and fast compared to the United States, but it has been growing slowly compared to Russia's peers among the BRIC countries (Brazil, Russia, India, China) (see Figure 8.1) and also low compared to what we had in the 2000s.

The same 3 to 4 per cent growth is also the consensus forecast for 2012 and the next couple of years. If one compares this with what has been

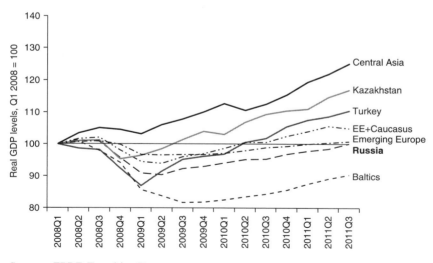

Source: EBRD Transition Report.

Figure 8.1 Russia vs. its neighbours

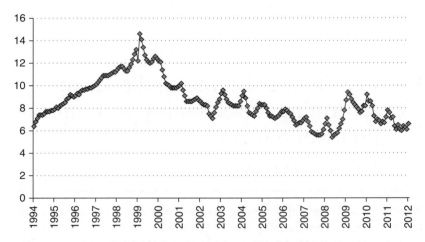

Source: Goskomstat, CEFIR (Center for Economic and Financial Research – Russia).

Figure 8.2   Unemployment in Russia

going on in Russia since the world financial crisis that hit Russia in 2008, it is actually not bad, but it is also not that great. Russia has experienced one of the worst consequences of the economic crisis. We had the largest drop in gross domestic product (GDP) per capita, we have one of the highest unemployment spikes as a result of the crisis, yet the country is recovering, not as fast as Turkey, not as fast as Kazakhstan, but it is still doing much better than the Baltics. Compared to other emerging economies, Russia's performance during the crisis was significantly worse, yet at the time of writing in early 2013 the growth rates are lower, and the forecasts are also quite modest.

Looking at the unemployment data (see Figure 8.2), the first thing to note is that unemployment is not a Russian problem. Normally, we have a shortage of labour supply and so, we have very low unemployment in a normal state and even during the crisis we had, by European standards, a low unemployment rate. Also, unemployment has been declining recently.

Inflation (see Figure 8.3) is another matter. Historically, we have had high inflation rates, but as of this writing, thanks to the slowing growth rates and thanks to what is going on in the euro area and in the United States, we have inflation that is falling.

Access to credit also looks optimistic: the percentage of firms that answer that they have normal access to credit (access to average credit rates) is now the same as during the high-growth years. The consequences of the collapse of Lehman Brothers and of the economic crisis are evident

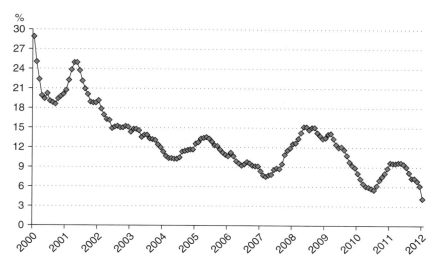

Source: Goskomstat, CEFIR.

Figure 8.3 Inflation

in Figure 8.4, but in mid–2011, access to credit was back to pre-crisis levels.

Let me also add some more information on the consequences of crisis, although this is not exactly macroeconomics. In terms of consumption, the consequences of the crisis were huge. If one compares the reduction in food consumption in Russia to countries in Western Europe (see Figure 8.5), then while in Western Europe 11 per cent of households have had to cut down their food consumption during the crisis, in Russia 35 per cent of the households reported that they cut down their food consumption. This is true on aggregate, and this is true when subdividing data by goods category. The only respect in which we are ahead of Western Europe is in consumption of alcohol. As a reaction to the crisis, Russians did not reduce their consumption of alcohol as much as Western European households.

Turning to the long-term perspective and politics, the question arises as to whether Russia may be turning into the next South Korea, as posed by my colleagues Guriev and Zhuravskaya (2010) (see Figure 8.6). In this figure one line represents Russia and the other Korea, and Korean data are 11 years earlier. The kinks in the data represent the 1997 Asian crisis for Korea, and the 2008–2009 crisis for Russia. It is remarkable how close these lines are. However, there is a kind of a cheat in this picture. And the cheat is, of course, that for Russia, the four last points were projections in

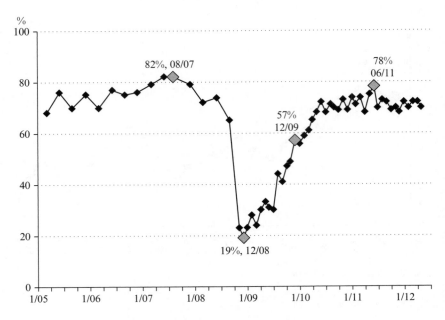

Source: Gaidar Institute for Economic Policy (firm survey).

Figure 8.4   Percentage of firms with normal access to credit

2009. In reality, the growth rates were half of the Korean post-1998 crisis growth. The question is: was it reasonable in 2009 to expect Russia to be the next Korea, another kind of growth miracle?

There are a couple of reasons why emerging market countries could grow faster than developed ones. One is a major long-term macroeconomic reason, let us call it the 'Solow reason': the countries that do not have enough capital could grow faster because they accumulate capital on their way to the steady state. The developed countries are already in the steady state and cannot grow by investing more, but the emerging markets do.

The second reason why the emerging countries could grow faster than the developed countries is that there is the advantage of backwardness (Gershenkron, 1962); we do not need to spend money on developing new technology, we could just adopt technology on the path to the technology frontier. If you come to Moscow, if you look around, everything new is a copy of something that was invented somewhere else before. If you go to a coffee shop, this will be a Starbucks clone, obviously. Starbucks has actually had a very hard time competing with its clones in Moscow.

But of course, if this were true, the emerging countries would be growing

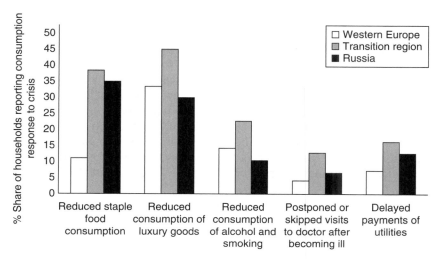

Source: EBRD.

Figure 8.5 Consumption change

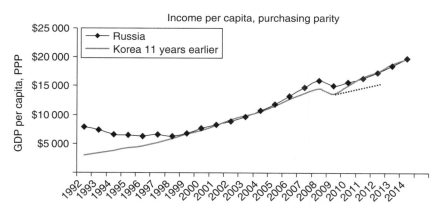

Source: Guriev and Zhuravskaya (2010) based on data from the IMF's *World Economic Outlook*, October 2009.

Figure 8.6 The next South Korea?

much faster than developed countries. In actual fact there are obstacles to fast growth and the main obstacle is that if institutions are weak, then this weakness increases the cost of investment and these advantages no longer play a role (North, 1981; Acemoglu and Robinson, 2006).

How do institutions help in understanding the Russian situation? In Russia we need to have major improvements in several critical institutions. We need courts that are politically independent, that is, courts that make decisions with no regard to calls from the presidential administration. We need efficient law enforcement, that is, a non-corrupt police force; and we need to have non-corrupt regulators. Even reducing top-level, cabinet-level corruption would be major progress. And if you look at institutions in Russia and in South Korea, then the observation that Russia is not going the way of South Korea, that this is too optimistic a comparison, starts to make a lot of sense. Basically, all the institutional parameters are much worse in Russia than they were in South Korea.

Looking at cross-country corruption data, Russia's corruption level is surprising. There is nothing surprising about a developing country being corrupt; this is a standard feature of developing countries. But Russia is much more corrupt than it should be for its level of development and for its level of education. In econometric terms, controlling for everything, Russia is much more corrupt than it should be. In a sense, this is good news. If I were talking to investors I would say that there is huge potential to combat corruption. We could make jokes at the expense of investors here, right?

Looking at the data on start-up opportunities, Russia is at a very low level compared to its peers. In the Hermitage Foundation index of economic freedom, Russia is near the bottom of economic freedom. In the World Bank Doing Business index, Russia is ranked 111th in 2012.

Since President Putin promised, during his last election campaign, that we are going to be number 20 in the Doing Business ranking by the end of his next term (2018), government working groups have been installed for each parameter in this ranking and they are working hard how to change either the country or the perception. I think it was a good promise, and it was a good idea to set up these working groups to make some progress here. But then, we need to take a step back and look at where institutions come from, where the police and courts and non-corrupt regulations come from.

Basically, what we economists know is that good institutions might be based politically on two things. One is mature democratic institutions. This is normal and familiar, and I am not going to talk about this. Yet there is another model – and many researchers and commentators make a strong argument that this makes sense – that good institutions might be politically based on something else. In this alternative model, there is a strong yet non-democratic political authority. One example of such a regime is what we would call the 'institutionalized ruling party'. This is a party which has control over its leadership, but there is no democratic election in the sense that the party does not allow outsiders to change what is going on inside the party. Mexico had this kind of system for 70 years, and there were a lot of Communist regimes of this type in Eastern Europe, in the Soviet Union and in East Asia. China now is an example of this institutionalized ruling party regime.

Also, there are personalistic non-democratic regimes, which are very different from the institutionalized ruling party. This is the kind of situation where the leader controls the government mechanism, not vice versa. These days, this type of regime is well represented in the former Soviet Union countries.

In Russia, we have a highly personalized yet weak autocratic regime: people have a lot of freedom but very little political power. To give a personal example, I can write in my newspaper column whatever I want; there are no restrictions whatsoever. I remember writing a column saying that Putin was no longer a good leader for the country and we needed change, and then discovered that this column had been posted on Putin's official website; for some reason, it was there for two years. Some people think that if there is a dictatorship, then this means a brutal regime like that of Stalin or Pol Pot. No, in Russia today we can say everything that we want, but when we vote, my vote – and the vote of those who vote like me, against Putin and his party – counts less than votes of those who vote for Putin and his party.

A paper of mine published in the *Proceedings of the National Academy of Sciences*, one of the leading scientific journals, demonstrates, based on a field experiment, that the parliamentary elections of December 2011 were subject to massive electoral fraud (Enikolopov et al., 2013). In actual fact, Putin's party got about 25 to 25 per cent of the Moscow vote, while the official vote count was given as 47 per cent. We know much less about Putin's election numbers in the March 2012 elections: we could be sure that he got around 50 per cent of the vote if the votes had been counted properly, and we also know that the runner-up got no more than 20 per cent. This is clear evidence that Putin would have beaten any opponent one to one (at least, given the controlled selection of opponents). Also, despite having had a year of very large protests (by Russian standards, and we Russians are very patient), we do not have any kind of well-organized opposition. For now, it seems that Putin will stay in power forever; he has been in power since 2000 and there does not appear to be any viable succession path.

So, now that I have classified Russia, what is known about the sustainability of this alternative model? On the institutionalized ruling party regime, the jury is still out. The Mexican example was successful in terms of growth rate, in terms of consolidation of the country, and the ultimate transfer to democracy was extremely smooth. It was so smooth that many people did not notice that they somehow transferred from a real dictatorship to a real competitive democracy.

The Communist regimes example was a catastrophe, an economic collapse of Herculean proportions. Then there is the example of China: the majority of experts think that it will see a successful continuation of growth and, eventually, a successful transition to democracy. Yet what we know for sure about personalistic non-democratic regimes is that there are very, very few examples of sustainable development in this mode. Still, there is the example of Spain, which transitioned very smoothly from a personalistic military dictatorship to democracy, although the Spaniards actually had as much experience of democracy before 1975 as Russia had before 1991. For Russia, this analysis predicts that there will be not much progress in improving institutions under the current political regime, but it does not exclude the possibility of transitioning to a regime which will be more conducive to growth.

Taking a less 'historical' view, Russia needs to have another growth model, so before concluding I would like to address key reforms: what we need and what we have. What we certainly need is privatization. One result of both the crisis of 2008–2009 and the pre-crisis political developments was a huge expansion of the government involvement in the economy. There are two competing tendencies: one tendency was that there has been a huge nationalization drive, and the other that during the crisis a large part of the economy was effectively nationalized as a result of massive bailout operations. Both work in the same direction. Therefore, we now need to privatize large enterprises and to deregulate.

Yet privatization is actually going in another direction right now. At the time of writing, there is a huge nationalization operation, the buyout of TNK-BP, a major oil company, by Rosneft, a state-owned giant. This is one of the largest nationalizations in history, and certainly the largest in which the former owners have not been expropriated, but are actually getting market price.

With regard to other major reforms, Russia has made significant progress on the World Trade Organization (WTO) frontier. Since Russia became a WTO member, we have retreated a couple of steps, but still the accession was a significant achievement. With regard to inflation targeting and the floating rouble, it is not clear what is going on, as the Russian Central Bank is murky about its strategy, but a lot of work in the right direction has been done since the crisis. On the other hand, the pension reform has clearly stalled.

REFERENCES

Acemoglu, Daron and James Robinson (2006), *Political Origins of Dictatorship and Democracy*, Cambridge, MA: MIT Press.

Enikolopov, Ruben, Vasily Korovkin, Maria Petrova, Konstantin Sonin and Alexei Zakharov (2013), 'Field experiment estimate of electoral fraud in Russian parliamentary elections', *Proceedings of the National Academy of Sciences*, **110** (2), 448–52.

Gerschenkron, Alexander (1962), *Economic Backwardness in Historical Perspective: A Book of Essays*, Cambridge, MA: Belknap Press of Harvard University Press.

Guriev, Sergei and Ekaterina Zhuravskaya (2010), 'Why Russia is not South Korea', *Journal of International Affairs*, **63** (2), 125–79.

North, Douglass (1981), *Structure and Change in Economic History*, New York: W.W. Norton.

9. Sustaining growth in emerging markets: the role of structural and monetary policies

Ahmet Faruk Aysan, Mustafa Haluk Güler and Cüneyt Orman

9.1 INTRODUCTION

The contribution of emerging market economies to world output increased significantly in the 2000s. According to an HSBC report (Ward, 2012), emerging market economies now account for roughly 50 per cent of world output, up from about 35 per cent in 2000. While the global financial crisis of 2008 sharply reduced economic growth rates worldwide, the slowdown in emerging market economies has been substantially less than that observed in advanced economies, and the emerging market economies have also been the main drivers of growth in the subsequent recovery (see Figure 9.1). The most recent Organisation for Economic Co-operation and Development (OECD) 'Going for Growth' report projects that the emerging market economies will continue to be the drivers of global growth until 2060, with major consequences for the composition of the world economy.[1]

Despite their perceived favourable growth prospects and increasing importance in the global economic landscape, however, emerging market economies face a number of institutional and structural challenges that may pose risks to the sustainability of their high growth performance. Some of the institutional difficulties have historically been, and to varying degrees for different countries, continue to be, the presence of weak democracies, opaque government policies, and populist cycles aiming to maximize short-term objectives. The main structural challenges, on the other hand, have typically been the unsustainably high levels of public debt, high and chronic inflation, and shallow and under-regulated financial sectors. Fortunately, there has been tremendous progress in several emerging market economies along both dimensions in the recent decades, with desirable outcomes. Nevertheless, the emerging market economies

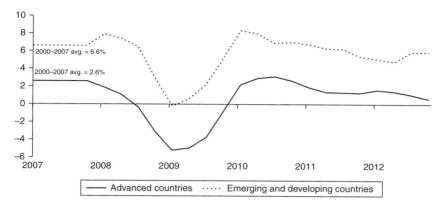

Source: Bloomberg.

Figure 9.1 Global growth rates (annual change, %)

still have a long way to go in ensuring that the recent progress can be carried into the future. In particular, the ability of the emerging market economies to sustain the high levels of growth rates they have attained in the recent past is closely linked with their ability to deal ably with the above-mentioned institutional and structural challenges.

This chapter aims to portray the experience of Turkey in addressing these institutional and structural changes since the 1990s. To this end, section 9.2 provides a detailed account of Turkey's experience in recent years. Section 9.3 then compares and contrasts the recent experience of Turkey with the experiences of peer emerging market economies in the Central, Eastern and South-Eastern Europe (CESEE) region to assess the relative performance of Turkey. Section 9.4 provides our concluding remarks.

9.2 ASSESSING THE GROWTH EXPERIENCE OF TURKEY

In order to get a better understanding of the growth experience of Turkey, it is important to look at its macroeconomic background and identify its major economic and institutional set-ups. In the 1990s, economic growth in Turkey was low and volatile, with three major recessions, the last one being the most severe (see Figure 9.2). By all accounts, the 1990s was a lost decade for Turkey. The severity of the 2001 crisis made it a turning point in the sense that it sparked a political momentum to engage in widespread

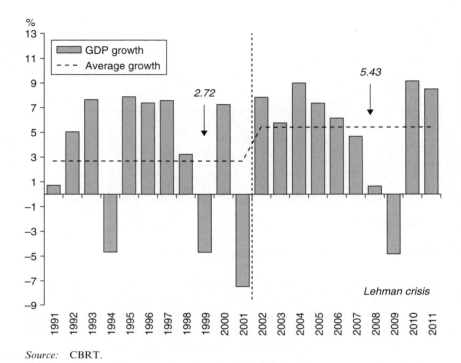

Source: CBRT.

Figure 9.2   GDP growth (annual change, %)

institutional and structural reforms. This laid the foundations for a new
era in which the Turkish economy has undergone a set of fundamental
changes that resulted in an unprecedented growth performance. In particular, for the first time in half a century, the Turkish economy grew at an
average annual rate of nearly 7 per cent between 2002 and 2007. In order
to understand the factors that contribute to this dramatic change, we now
analyse the pre- and post-2001 crisis periods in detail.

9.2.1   Before the 2001 Crisis

Before the 2001 crisis, there were a number of structural problems in
the Turkish economy regarding the institutional and economic set-up.
A weak democratic system with fragile coalitions and weak governments was among the main institutional factors that retarded economic
performance.[2] Prior to the crisis, multi-party coalition governments had
been the norm and the average life of these coalition governments was

only 16 months, compared to 60 months during the 2001–2012 period. Predictably, such a democracy tended to suffer from myopic electoral concerns, was hostage to populist policies, and failed to recognize the importance of fiscal discipline.

Government policies in the pre-crisis period were also opaque and unaccountable. State-owned banks financed the discretionary political spending of the ruling government and as a result encountered large duty losses, which were conveniently concealed thanks to the non-transparent accounting procedures.[3] These losses were compensated from the public budget. High and persistent budget deficits increased the influence of politics on the economy at large.

Another major institutional problem before 2001 was the lack of an independent central bank. The lack of an independent monetary authority was in fact a huge convenience for the government since the rapidly growing government debt could be 'repaid' through an equally rapid monetary expansion. Unsurprisingly, this resulted in a highly inflationary economic environment that was at the same time fraught with uncertainty.

A final factor contributing to the 2001 crisis was the heightened level of risk in financial markets, which increased the vulnerability of the banking system. In a system of pegged exchange rates and a significantly under-regulated banking system, most Turkish banks took excessive risk. In financing the high public sector deficit, banks were heavily involved in short-term borrowing in foreign currency from abroad. The size of bank open currency positions grew larger over time. In addition, the maturity of capital inflows remained short due to the uncertainty produced by the highly inflationary environment. This, coupled with the large 'duty losses' of state-owned banks financing discretionary political spending (see below), inevitably increased the vulnerability of the system. This consequent upward pressure on real interest rates worked to harm the potential growth rate.

In such a vulnerable financial environment, three major economic crises occurred in 1994, 1998 and 2001. Unlike the 1994 and 1998 crises, the 2001 crisis brought about unprecedented changes in Turkey's political and economic landscape and paved the way for the introduction of significant structural and institutional reform packages.

9.2.2 After the 2001 Crisis

On 19 February 2001, at a time of extremely weak economic fundamentals, Turkey's last coalition government faced a severe political crisis when a public dispute between Turkey's President and Prime Minister about corruption escalated. This political tension caused panic in financial markets and triggered a financial crisis. With the run on foreign currency, the Central Bank of the Republic of Turkey (CBRT) lost a large share of its reserves, and the payment system was frozen as the Turkish lira liquidity shrank rapidly, and the public banks with high daily liquidity needs faced a severe liquidity crisis. Due to the pressures in financial markets, the exchange rate-targeting strategy was abandoned and the Turkish lira was allowed to float freely against foreign currencies on 22 February 2001. In that year, the economy experienced a 9.5 per cent contraction.

Following this sharp contraction, the so-called 'Strengthening the Turkish Economy' economic reform programme was introduced. With the implementation of structural reforms and programmes after the crisis, the economy started to grow rapidly, the political influence on markets dissipated, and the economy gained more stability.[4] Since the reform programmes brought about a drastic transformation of the Turkish economy and created an environment that is conducive to stronger and stable growth, it is worthwhile to give an overview of these reforms and analyse their impact on the economy.

One of the most important reform areas was central bank independence. The independence of the CBRT ended the institutional relationship between the government and the monetary authority (see Figure 9.3), meaning that the government could no longer rely on the central bank to inflate away the debt burden of the government.

In addition to central bank independence, there were new laws and regulations on the restructuring of the banking sector. First, a domestic debt swap was launched in order to ensure easy liquidity for the Treasury and to lower the risk of banks by closing banks' open currency positions. These steps taken to strengthen the fiscal environment were combined with the introduction of legislative and operational regulations on the transparency and the effective supervision of the system. In this context, the Banking Regulation and Supervision Agency (BRSA), which was established not long before the crisis, was authorized as the sole regulator and supervisor in the banking sector. Under the new system, regulations were launched to closely monitor the banks for excessive risk-taking and their open currency positions. Reforms also covered the state banks, and the practice of assigning loss-creating duties to state banks, resulting in corresponding 'duty losses', was ended; such political spending is now covered by the governmental budget. Moreover, some state banks merged and others were liquidated. These changes helped weaken the political influence on the economy significantly, and as a result, reduced economic uncertainty.

Concurrently with the above-mentioned steps, tight monetary policy and fiscal policy were implemented. The CBRT began implementing first an implicit and then an explicit inflation-targeting policy, as a result of

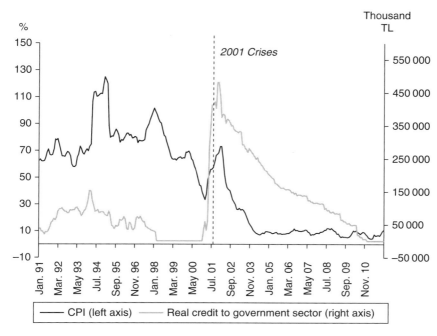

Source: CBRT.

Figure 9.3 CBRT monetization and inflation

which the effectiveness of the monetary transmission mechanism increased dramatically. At the same time, very high primary surplus targets were announced by the government and, in order to achieve the targets, regulations were introduced in various taxation and public spending domains (see Figure 9.4). With tight fiscal measures, interest payments and the debt stock began to decrease. Specifically, the public debt stock went down from over 70 per cent of gross domestic product (GDP) in 2001 to less than 40 per cent in 2011 (see Figure 9.5). In addition, the maturity of government borrowing improved significantly after 2001. In particular, the average maturity of borrowing increased from 410 days in 2000 to 1170 days in 2011.

The economic reform programme after the 2001 crisis was extremely fruitful. The inflation rate, which was about 60 per cent before the crisis, declined rapidly and by 2004 single-digit inflation was achieved for the first time in decades. With the confidence in the Turkish lira reconstructed, the currency reform of dropping six zeros from the lira was introduced in 2005. As a result of increased macroeconomic and financial stability combined with the renewed confidence in the government, the improved

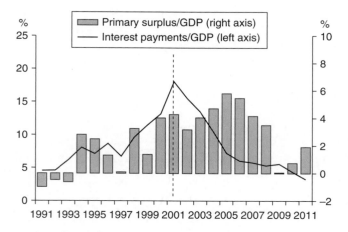

Source: Undersecretariat of Treasury.

Figure 9.4   Interest payments and primary surplus

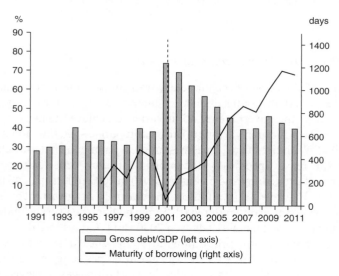

Source: Undersecretariat of Treasury.

Figure 9.5   Debt-to-GDP ratio and borrowing maturity

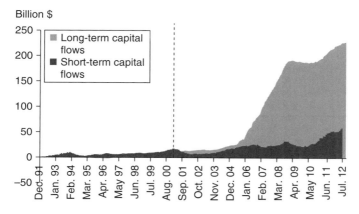

Source: CBRT.

Figure 9.6 Capital flows (cumulative)

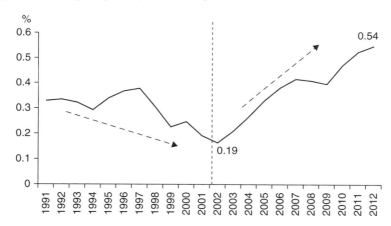

Source: CBRT.

Figure 9.7 Credits to the private sector/total assets

prospects for European Union (EU) membership and the positive international conjuncture, capital inflows soared, most of which were in the form of long-term capital (see Figure 9.6). The rise in capital inflows, in turn, enabled the banking system to offer greater resources to the private sector. While the share of private sector credit in banks' assets was as low as 19 per cent in 2001, it increased to 54 per cent in 2011, and in real terms increased by 242 per cent (see Figure 9.7).[5]

Table 9.1   Sources of growth

	Contribution		
	Employment	Capital stock	Total factor productivity
1990–2000	24.3	75.6	0.1
2002–2010	21.8	53.5	24.6

Source: Republic of Turkey Ministry of Development.

The positive economic outlook in the post-crisis period also improved political stability. Long-term policies and perspectives of governments ruling for longer periods replaced populist policies of short-term coalition governments. While the average life of government was 16 months in the 1990s, it increased to 60 months between 2002 and 2012. The EU compliance package passed by Parliament and government policies became more transparent and accountable.

All the above-mentioned developments in Turkey's economy created an enabling environment for growth. At a fundamental level, there were important changes in the dynamics of productivity, the composition of expenditures, and the role of the private sector in the economy. In particular, productivity increased considerably in the 2000s. The contribution of total factor productivity to growth increased dramatically from 0.1 per cent in the 1990s to 25 per cent after 2001 (see Table 9.1). Labour factor productivity and its contribution also increased after 2001 (see Figure 9.8).

Another significant change in the economic dynamics of Turkey took place in the composition of expenditures. Both investment and consumption expenditures increased considerably. Importantly, investment expenditures rose more than consumption expenditures, reaching 250 per cent in real terms by 2011 (see Figure 9.9). This type of change in expenditure composition is favourable since it increases the potential growth rate of an economy in the long run.

Last but not least, the private sector started to play a larger role in economic activity and became the main source of growth and employment after 2002. Government investment expenditures' contribution to growth, on the other hand, did not change significantly. As can be seen from Figure 9.10, private sector real investment expenditures increased threefold in the 2000s.

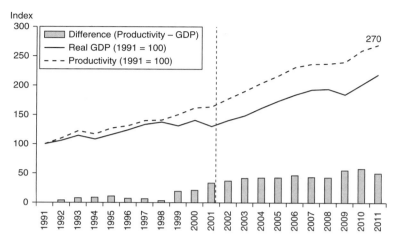

Source: CBRT.

Figure 9.8   Productivity and real GDP (1991 = 100)

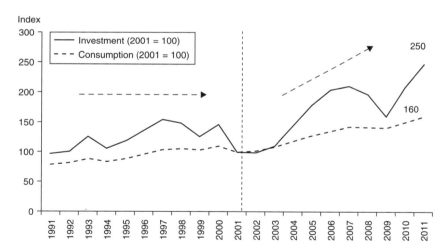

Source: CBRT.

Figure 9.9   Investment and consumption expenditures (2001 = 100)

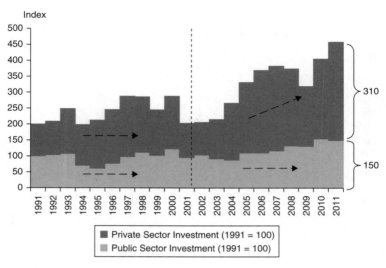

Source: CBRT.

Figure 9.10   Public and private sector investment expenditures (1991 =
100)

9.2.3   Monetary Policy Stance after the Collapse of Lehman Brothers: An Immediate Response to the Crisis

The global financial crisis of 2008 underscored the importance of a proactive central bank in protecting the environment for stable growth. Being proactive requires closely monitoring the developments in both domestic and global economies and taking the necessary precautions in a timely manner. Following the collapse of Lehman Brothers, the CBRT moved ahead of most other emerging market economies' central banks and took decisive measures to protect economic growth. In addition to the longer-term structural reform process initiated after the 2001 crisis, monetary policy measures implemented in response to the Lehman crisis and macroeconomic governance in this period eased the adverse effects of the turmoil on the economy. Some of the main policy measures taken by the CBRT are the following:

1.   The CBRT cut overnight rates by a total of 10.25 per cent from November 2008 to November 2009. This is more than any other country operating within an inflation-targeting framework.

2. The band between the borrowing and the lending rates was gradually reduced in order to limit fluctuations in overnight interest rates.
3. The CBRT used foreign exchange (FX) reserves to support the banking system. The CBRT acted as a broker in the FX market between the financial institutions to facilitate the flow of FX liquidity in the system. The maturity of foreign exchange deposits borrowed by banks from the CBRT was extended and the lending rates were reduced. Additional FX liquidity was also provided to the banking system by a 200 basis point reduction in the FX required reserves ratio.

9.2.4 Soft Landing after 2010

With the help of these measures, the initial impact of the recent global crisis on the Turkish economy remained rather limited. In fact, after a contraction in 2008 and 2009, the economy started to recover rapidly. However, from late 2009 onwards, credit growth and then the current account deficit began to grow rapidly as well. The announcement of a second round of quantitative easing (QE2) in the United States in late 2010 further fuelled this growth, starting to create serious risks for macro-financial stability.

From Q4 2009 to Q2 2011, the current account deficit and credit growth increased from 2.1 per cent and 0.4 per cent of GDP, to 9.9 per cent and 14.8 per cent of GDP, respectively. At the same time, the quality of current account deficit financing deteriorated significantly, with short-term capital flows almost completely replacing long-term flows. For Turkey, the stability (or the lack thereof) of capital flows has historically been a key factor in determining the national growth performance and macroeconomic stability (see Figure 9.11). In particular, a high current account deficit coupled with a high share of short-term capital flows in its financing has typically been associated with elevated risks for macro-financial stability. Therefore, a key objective of the CBRT's new policies and measures after QE2 has been to bring credit growth and the current account deficit to sustainable levels as well as to improve the financing of the current account deficit.

The first element in the new policy mix was a widened interest rate corridor. In particular, the overnight borrowing rate was reduced sharply while the lending rate was kept unchanged. This wide interest rate corridor allowed for significantly more volatility in short-term interest rates while leaving the average funding rate virtually unchanged. Open-market operations conducted via quantity auctions further intensified the volatility in the short-term rates (see Figure 9.12). Both of these actions worked to discourage the inflow of short-term foreign capital, thereby contributing

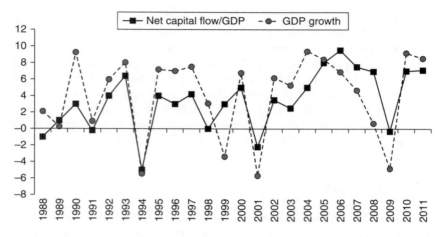

Source: CBRT.

Figure 9.11   GDP growth and net capital flows/GDP

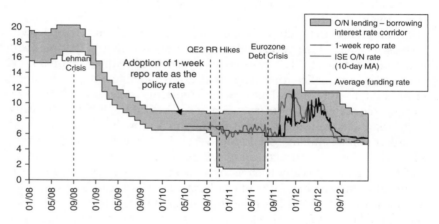

Source: CBRT.

Figure 9.12   Interest rate corridor and average funding rate

to the overall stability of capital flows. This corridor policy is used coun-
tercyclically. During good times, when the global financial markets lead to
a surge in capital inflows, the corridor is broadened; whereas during bad
times, when capital inflows are reversed or tend to follow a weaker trend,
the corridor is narrowed.

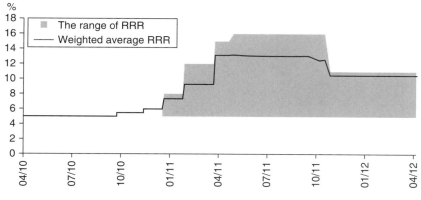

Source: CBRT.

Figure 9.13 Reserve requirements

The second important element in the new policy mix has been the Reserve Option Mechanism. Under this mechanism, banks are allowed to deposit foreign currencies or gold for their Turkish lira reserve requirements. This facility not only provides Turkish lira liquidity to banks in a more permanent way and lowers their cost, but also supports the CBRT's reserves, which in turn reduces the adverse impact of volatile capital flows on the financial system and alleviates the appreciation and depreciation pressures on the Turkish lira.

At the time the interest rate corridor was widened downwards, the CBRT took a number of accompanying measures to slow down credit growth. Specifically, the remuneration of reserves was halted, reserve requirements were increased, and the coverage of reserve requirements were increased to include repos. In addition, reserve requirements were differentiated by maturities in order to alleviate the maturity mismatch concerns (see Figure 9.13).

With the help of this new policy mix, the economy began to move in the desired direction. Specifically, the increased volatility in short-term interest rates resulted in declines in the volatility of exchange rates (see Figure 9.14), encouraging long-term capital movements. The improvement in the quality of capital inflows became visible as early as early 2011 (see Figure 9.15). This also helped reduce excessive appreciation pressures on the Turkish lira, leading to depreciation in the real exchange rates (see Figure 9.16). As a result, the composition of demand started to move in the desired direction, slowing domestic demand and speeding up foreign demand. This rebalancing in the composition of demand, in turn, helped

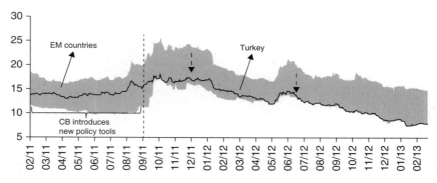

Source: Bloomberg, CBRT.

Figure 9.14 *Volatility in emerging market currencies (implied for the next 12 months, %)*

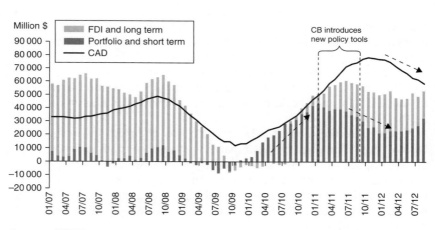

Source: CBRT.

Figure 9.15 *Current account deficit and its finance*

reduce the current account deficit to more reasonable levels. Hikes in required reserves coupled with a number of measures taken by the BRSA increased loan interest rates and began to impact on credit growth by mid-2011 (see Figure 9.17).

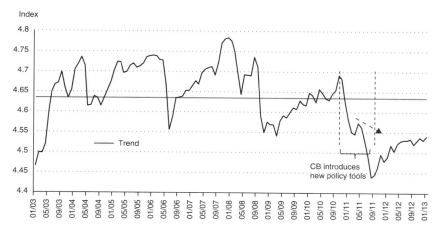

Source: Bloomberg, CBRT.

Figure 9.16   CPI-based (developing economies) real effective exchange rate (base year = 2003)

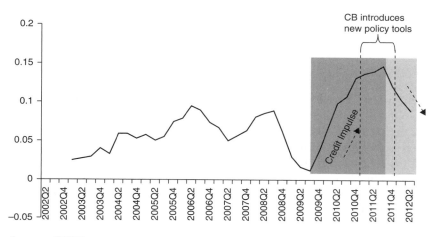

Source: CBRT.

Figure 9.17   Total credit change/GDP

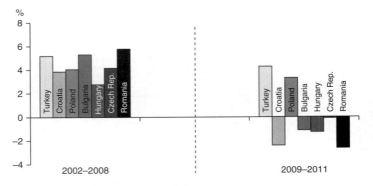

Source: World Bank (World Development Indicators (WDI) database).

Figure 9.18   Average growth rates

9.3   THE TURKISH ECONOMY VERSUS CESEE ECONOMIES

While the growth performances of Turkey and CESEE economies were quite similar during 2002–08, the growth paths decoupled significantly following the collapse of Lehman Brothers in 2008 (see Figure 9.18). Specifically, while the average growth rates were generally negative for the CESEE economies during 2009–11, Turkey and Poland enjoyed average growth rates of roughly 4 per cent and 3 per cent, respectively. Remarkably, Turkish economic growth in 2010 and 2011 was 9.2 and 8.5 per cent, respectively, among the highest growth rates in the world.

What are the factors that contributed to this strong recovery in Turkey in the past few years? Foremost among them is the tight fiscal policy, that is, low levels of public debt and budget deficit. In contrast with most of the CESEE countries, Turkey has succeeded in maintaining its tight fiscal stance after the crisis. As can be seen from Figures 9.19 and 9.20, Turkey and Hungary were the only two countries in this region to actually improve their fiscal positions during this period relative to the pre-crisis period. This provided an environment that is supportive of growth led by the private sector.

Another factor that helps to explain the Turkish growth performance is the presence of a sound banking system that was created thanks to the ambitious reforms following the 2001 crisis. Importantly, there were no bank failures in Turkey during the global crisis. In fact, the Turkish banking system has come out stronger from the global crisis. Turkish banks have one of the lowest non-performing loan ratios and one of the

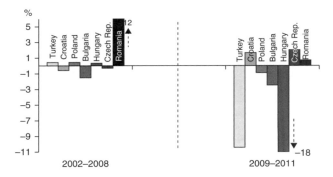

Source: World Bank (World Development Indicators, WDI, database).

Figure 9.19   *Increase in general government final consumption expenditure/GDP*

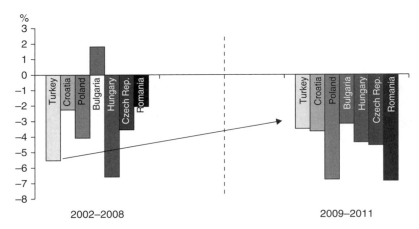

Source: World Bank (World Development Indicators, WDI, database).

Figure 9.20   *General government budget deficit (% of GDP)*

highest capital adequacy ratios both in the world and in comparison with the emerging market economies in the CESEE region (see Figures 9.21 and 9.22).

Low foreign ownership is another factor that contributes to the soundness of the Turkish banking system (see Figure 9.23). Globalization of the financial system through foreign bank ownership could internationally transmit shocks through the banking sector.[6] Thanks to low foreign ownership,

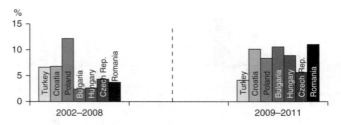

Source: World Bank (WDI database), EBRD (Transition Report).

Figure 9.21   Banks' nonperforming loans to total loans (in %)

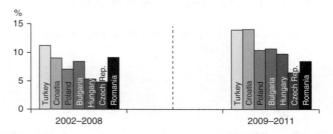

Source: World Bank (WDI database), EBRD (Transition Report).

Figure 9.22   Banks' capital to assets ratio (in %)

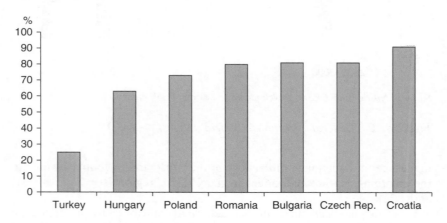

Source: WDI, EBRD (Transition Report).

Figure 9.23   Foreign ownership in the banking sector (in %)

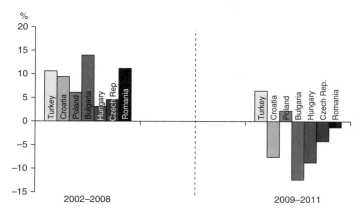

Source: World Bank (WDI database).

Figure 9.24 *Gross fixed investment of selected countries (annual growth in %, 2002–2011)*

Turkey has been affected less by the recent crisis than many other countries. Moreover, Turkish households were banned from taking out FX-denominated loans from banks in 2009. This policy measure shielded households against currency risk and also against excessive borrowing.

Besides, the imposition of loan-to-value restriction helped to alleviate credit risk in the aftermath of the crisis. On 16 December 2010, the BRSA limited residential mortgage loans to 75 per cent of the appraised value of the residential unit in order to contain credit supply and also to alleviate credit risk associated with the swings in real-estate valuations over time. According to the same resolution, mortgages on commercial real-estate properties are limited to 50 per cent of the appraised value of the real estate.

Finally, a combination of disciplined fiscal and wise monetary policies as well as a sound banking system produced an environment that is supportive of investment in Turkey. As can be seen from Figure 9.24, differently from the CESEE countries, Turkey has succeeded in sustaining its high investment profile even after the crisis.

9.4 CONCLUSION

There has been a tremendous increase in the importance of emerging market economies in the world economic landscape. They have also been quite resilient to the global financial crisis and were the main drivers of growth in the subsequent recovery. Despite their favourable economic outlook, however, the emerging market economies, both in the CESEE region and elsewhere, face a number of institutional and structural challenges which may jeopardize their recent success story. Whether they will be able to carry this success into the future depends critically on their success in dealing with various challenges, some of which we have touched upon in this chapter.

The recent experience of Turkey provides a good example. We have provided evidence that when the right institutional and structural steps are taken, the growth potential and stability can be significantly increased. A strong structural and fiscal position also provides room for monetary policy-makers to effectively navigate their economies through turbulent times such as the recent global financial crisis. The newly designed 'monetary policy mix' of the CBRT also started to produce positive results in a short period of time. The unconventional monetary policies adopted by the CBRT are also a good indication of the institutional change in Turkey. The macro-prudential policy needs of Turkey are well addressed in this new policy framework which aims at reaching the main objective of price stability without ignoring financial stability in the medium and the long run. This chapter presents the new monetary policy framework adopted in Turkey against which the dimension of institutional and structural change in Turkey may be assessed.

NOTES

1. Written by eight OECD economists, the title of the report is 'Looking to 2060: Long-term Global Growth Prospects' and was published in November 2012; see Johansson et al. (2012).
2. Öniş and Aysan (2000) and Akin et al. (2009) provide evidence that the unstable political landscape of the 1990s had a substantial adverse effect on the Turkish economy.
3. For evidence on these so-called duty losses, see IMF (1998), Al and Aysan (2006), Aysan and Ceyhan (2007), Aysan and Ceyhan (2008a, 2008b) and Abbasoglu et al. (2007).
4. The European Council at its December 2004 summit in Brussels clearly underlined the rapid pace of transformation and reform that Turkey experienced after 2001. Also see Turhan (2008), Aysan et al. (2011), Turhan and Kilinc (2011) and Kılınç et al. (2012).
5. See UNCTAD (2003) on the importance of private sector credits in generating high and sustained growth in middle-income developing countries.
6. See Cetorelli and Goldberg (2011).

REFERENCES

Abbasoglu O.F., A.F. Aysan and A. Gunes (2007), 'Concentration, competition, efficiency and profitability of the Turkish banking sector in the post-crisis period', *Banks and Bank Systems*, **2** (3), 106–15.

Akin, G.G., A.F. Aysan and L. Yildiran (2009), 'Transformation of the Turkish financial sector in the aftermath of the 2001 crisis', in Z. Onis and F. Senses (eds), *Turkish Economy in the Post-Crisis Era: the New Phase of Neo-Liberal Restructuring and Integration to the Global Economy*, London: Routledge, pp. 73–100.

Al, H. and A.F. Aysan (2006), 'Assessing the preconditions in establishing an independent regulatory and supervisory agency in globalized financial markets: the case of Turkey', *International Journal of Applied Business and Economic Research*, **4**, 125–46.

Aysan, A.F. and S.P. Ceyhan (2008a), 'Structural change and the efficiency of banking in Turkey: does ownership matter?', MPRA Paper 17849, University Library of Munich, Germany.

Aysan, A.F. and S.P. Ceyhan (2008b), 'What determines the banking sector performance in globalized financial markets? The case of Turkey', *Physica A: Statistical Mechanics and its Applications*, **387** (7), 1593–602.

Aysan, A.F., M.M. Karakaya and M. Uyanık (2011), 'Panel stochastic frontier analysis of the profitability and efficiency of the Turkish banking sector in the post-crisis era', *Journal of Business Economics and Management*, **12** (4), 629–54.

Cetorelli, N. and L. Goldberg (2011), 'Global banks and international shock transmission: evidence from the crisis', *IMF Economic Review*, **59** (1), 41–76.

IMF (1998), 'Turkey: Recent economic developments and selected issues', IMF Staff Country Report, 98/104, Washington, DC.

Johansson, A., Y. Guillemette, F. Murtin, D. Turner, G. Nicoletti, C. Maisonneuve, G. Bousquet and F. Spinelli (2012), 'Looking to 2060: Long-term global growth prospects', A Going for Growth Report, Paris: OECD.

Kılınç, M., Z. Kılınç and M.I. Turhan (2012), 'Resilience of Turkish economy during the global financial crisis of 2008', *Emerging Markets Finance and Trade*, **48** (S5), 19–34.

Öniş, Z. and A.F. Aysan (2000), 'Neoliberal globalization, the nation state and financial crisis in the semi-periphery: a comparative analysis', *Third World Quarterly*, **21** (1), 119–39.

Turhan, M.I. (2008), 'Why did it work this time? A comparative analysis of transformation of Turkish economy after 2002', *Asian-African Journal of Economics and Econometrics*, **8**, 255–80.

Turhan, M.I. and Z. Kilinc (2011), 'Turkey's response to the global economic crisis', *Insight Turkey*, **13** (1), 37–45.

UNCTAD (2003), 'Trade and development report: capital accumulation, growth and structural change', Geneva: United Nations Conference on Trade and Development.

Ward, K. (2012), 'The world in 2050: quantifying the shift in the global economy', HSBC Global Research.

PART IV

Small-country Experiences in Economic Adjustment

10. Business cycle convergence or decoupling? Economic adjustment of CESEE countries during the crisis

Martin Gächter, Aleksandra Riedl and Doris Ritzberger-Grünwald

10.1 INTRODUCTION AND MOTIVATION

The financial crisis that turned into a sovereign debt crisis in 2010 has shifted both public and academic interest towards business cycle developments within the troubled euro area, while the previously fast-growing literature on business cycle convergence of Central, Eastern and South-Eastern European (CESEE) countries has been receiving less attention. Despite the prominence of the debt crisis within the euro area, it remains interesting to know which CESEE European Union (EU) member states experienced smooth economic adjustment (i.e. synchronous cycles) as opposed to countries which diverged considerably during the crisis.

Recently, Kose et al. (2012) stressed that global emerging market economies decoupled somewhat from industrialized countries in terms of business cycle synchronization in the 1990s and 2000s, while business cycles within each of these two groups of countries converged over time.[1] From a theoretical perspective, this relationship is ambiguous. On the one hand, rising trade and financial integration might lead to a convergence of business cycles, as proposed by Frankel and Rose (1998). On the other hand, rapidly rising income levels in emerging market economies are expanding the size of the domestic market, making them less reliant on demand from advanced economies.

While the results by Kose et al. (2008, 2012) have been questioned by Wälti (2010), they also raise a question about the corresponding relationship at the European level. Since the onset of the European debt crisis, wide-ranging economic coordination measures have been decided and implemented at the EU level. The strengthening of the Stability and

Growth Pact in 2011 aims at more harmonized and coordinated fiscal policies in the EU, while the Europe 2020 growth strategy targets structural policies across member countries. Furthermore, according to the treaties of EU accession, membership in the euro area is still the long-run objective of all CESEE countries that joined the EU in 2004 or 2007. While CESEE countries are therefore increasingly linked to advanced European economies through EU membership and enhanced trade interlinkages, the opposing argument of increasing income and domestic market size also applies to emerging market economies in Europe. Clearly, this relationship might also depend on the size of the economy. As smaller countries are observed to be more open – and hence more reliant on external demand – they might experience a higher co-movement with the euro area cycle. Conversely, a higher fraction of external demand might cause more volatile cycles over time, leading to larger deviations from the euro area cycle.

Against this background, we want to shed some light on the economic adjustment experiences of European countries in recent years, especially during the financial crisis that emerged in 2008. A particular focus is put on business cycle heterogeneity as well as correlations across and between CESEE and euro area countries, with a view to analysing whether the magnitude of synchronization mirrors the size of the economy. Finally, we want to examine the development of trend growth differentials between the CESEE region and the euro area. As evidence points towards a decoupling of global emerging market economies from industrialized countries in terms of trend growth rates (Helbling et al., 2007; Kose et al., 2012), we wish to explore whether this pattern also applies to emerging market economies in Europe and whether the relationship between trend growth rates has changed significantly since the beginning of the financial crisis.

The chapter is structured as follows. Section 10.2 gives an overview of the theoretical background as well as the current literature on business cycle synchronization between the CESEE region and the euro area. Section 10.3 explains the dataset and the methodology of our study, while section 10.4 reports empirical results. Finally, section 10.5 draws some conclusions.

10.2   LITERATURE REVIEW

10.2.1   Theoretical Background: Income versus Business Cycle Convergence

In the empirical literature, two main strands of literature on convergence can be distinguished, namely studies on (i) income convergence, and on

(ii) business cycle convergence. The former concept is based on neoclassical growth models (see, e.g., Solow, 1956). According to those studies, diminishing returns to capital cause an inverse relationship between a country's per capita growth rate and its starting level of income per person. In empirical studies, this relationship is commonly tested with regressions following Barro (1991), where the average growth rate of gross domestic product (GDP) per capita is regressed on the initial level of GDP per capita and some additional control variables (e.g. human capital) in various country samples. Thus, income convergence focuses on a long-run setting, which is particularly relevant for emerging market economies. Recent studies on income convergence in Central and Eastern Europe find a pronounced catching-up process in Eastern Europe in the second half of the 1990s as well as the 2000s (Vojinovic and Próchniak, 2009), although the convergence process seems to be rather heterogeneous (Cavenaile and Dubois, 2011).

Figure 10.1 shows the bivariate relationship between initial GDP per capita levels and the cumulative growth rates from 2000–2011 for the 12 initial euro area countries as well as for the eight CESEE economies that joined the EU but not the euro area in this period, and the five EU countries that adopted the euro after the first changeover wave.[2] While the link is rather ambiguous across the advanced euro area economies, the catching-up process is quite pronounced for both the later euro area members and the CESEE EU economies: the lower the income per capita in 2000, the higher the cumulative growth rate in the following decade. As shown in the bottom panel of Figure 10.1, the extent of the catching-up process does not seem to be dependent on the size of the economy.

This chapter, however, mainly focuses on the second strand of literature, that is, business cycle convergence in the CESEE region, but also draws certain conclusions concerning the catching-up process and how it has changed during the recent crisis. The concept of business cycle convergence examines whether countries' short-run fluctuations around long-run trend GDP have become more synchronized. This analysis is particularly relevant for the establishment of a common currency area. In this context, the theory of optimum currency areas (OCA) put forward by Mundell (1961), McKinnon (1963) and Kenen (1969) has proposed a wide range of criteria for the optimality of a region for establishing a currency union, for instance wage and labour market flexibility, trade and financial integration, coordination of fiscal policies, and so on. Generally, the synchronization of business cycles across member states has been proposed to be the 'meta-criterion' for the establishment of an optimum currency area. The line of argument is simple: if two countries share the same business cycle,

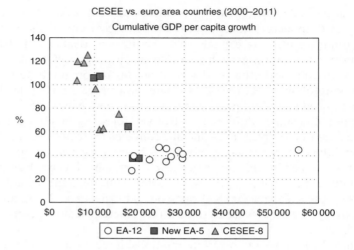

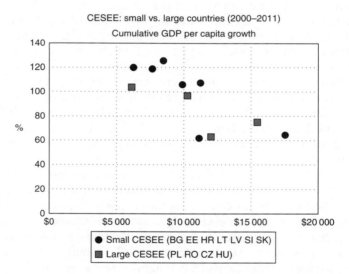

Note: BG = Bulgaria; CZ = Czech Republic; EA = Euro area; EE = Estonia; HR = Croatia; HU = Hungary; LV = Latvia; LT = Lithuania; PL = Poland; RO = Romania; SI =Slovenia; SK = Slovakia.

Source: IMF (2012), and authors' calculations.

Figure 10.1   Income convergence (GDP per capita) in the euro area and in the CESEE region

abandoning an independent monetary policy is less costly, as the same monetary stance might be optimal for both countries.

As highlighted by Fidrmuc and Korhonen (2006), the OCA theory was commonly applied after the break-down of the Bretton Woods system to assess the appropriateness of a possible fixed exchange rate for any given country. Subsequently, the OCA theory attracted renewed increased interest before the introduction of the euro, with most empirical studies assessing the correlations of business cycles between Germany and other potential member countries.[3] The EU accession by ten countries in 2004,[4] followed by the entry of Romania and Bulgaria in 2007, led to a deeper analysis of the new member states and their business cycles. In particular, the membership of several new member states in the exchange rate mechanism II (ERM II) as a required milestone on the road to the euro increased public interest in such studies. Fidrmuc and Korhonen (2006) give a comprehensive review of this literature, with most studies finding a considerably increased synchronization of CESEE countries with the euro area in the run-up to EU accession. Interestingly, the effects of the economic crisis that emerged in 2008 on business cycle synchronization in Europe (and on CESEE countries in particular) have hardly been examined so far, although the often cited heterogeneity in both monetary and fiscal policy in those countries makes a corresponding analysis very interesting.

10.2.2 Business Cycle Convergence between the CESEE Region and the Euro Area

As mentioned above, the convergence of business cycles in CESEE countries attracted increased interest in the literature in the early 2000s, just before the enlargement of the EU. The accession to the EU by 12 countries between 2004 and 2007 implied a path towards full monetary integration for those countries, although the year of the euro introduction differs across countries and is still open for some new member countries. Fidrmuc and Korhonen (2006) give a comprehensive literature overview on business cycle correlations between Central and Eastern European countries and the euro area and provide a meta analysis of 35 publications (between 1999 and 2005). They find that some of the more recent EU members already have comparably high, albeit mixed, correlations with the euro area business cycles.

The highest average business cycle correlation with the euro area is reported for Hungary, followed by Slovenia and Poland. The Czech Republic, Estonia and Latvia exhibit significantly lower correlations, but are still more synchronized than Bulgaria, Romania and Slovakia. For Lithuania, the meta analysis suggests even negative correlations with the euro area. Although the literature survey documents large differences among various publications, it suggests that the synchronization of business cycles in several CESEE countries matches or even exceeds the synchronization of business cycles of smaller, peripheral monetary union members. The results are basically in line with an earlier study by the same authors (Fidrmuc and Korhonen, 2004) where they assess the correlation of supply and demand shocks between the euro area and EU accession candidates from 1993 to 2002. Interestingly, however, the economic slowdown between 2000 and 2002 increased the heterogeneity between the two regions. Thus, an analysis of economic adjustments in the financial crisis after 2007 will show whether similar patterns of divergence have been emerging.

Darvas and Szapáry (2008) extend the analysis by including synchronization measures not only for GDP, but also for its components. They confirm the high degree of synchronization for Hungary, Poland and Slovenia (for GDP, industrial production and exports, but less so for consumption and services). The Czech Republic and Slovakia are less synchronized, while the Baltic states are hardly synchronized at all. Furthermore, as suggested by previous papers (see, e.g., Artis et al., 2005), the three leading new EU members indeed exhibit higher synchronization measures than peripheral euro area countries in the time period 1998–2002. This is basically confirmed by Eickmeier and Breitung (2006) who investigate the issue by calculating dynamic correlation and cohesion measures. However, in addition to the three new EU members mentioned above (Hungary, Poland, Slovenia) and contrary to other studies, they find that Estonia is also well prepared for joining the euro area.

While the findings by Artis et al. (2008) are consistent with previous results, their analysis of potential sources of business cycle synchronization suggests that EU integration might have ambiguous effects on the synchronization of business cycles. More precisely, fiscal shocks and labour market rigidities may counteract the positive effects associated with increased trade and financial flows. Benczúr and Rátfai (2010) show that business fluctuations in CESEE countries are generally more pronounced than in developed ones, being similar in size to those of other emerging market economies.

More recently, Savva et al. (2010), by allowing for the endogenous determination of the timing and the length of structural shifts in the degree of co-movement between the cyclical components of industrial production, find that CESEE countries generally experienced a sizeable increase in their business cycle synchronization with the euro area. Remarkably, all more recent EU members at least doubled their business cycle synchronization or changed from negative to positive correlations since the early

1990s, respectively. However, their results also show the great variety in the timing and speed of correlation shifts across the country sample, although most of the more recent EU members experienced a change around or after completion of their admission negotiations at the end of 2002.

On the other hand, Aslanidis (2010) reports a high synchronization of the Hungarian cycle, but less so for the Czech Republic and particularly for Poland, based on threshold seemingly unrelated regressions. In general, particularly when examining the business cycle synchronization of the more recent EU members, it should be highlighted that any analysis is necessarily backward-looking, which might be particularly relevant for transition economies (Eickmeier and Breitung, 2006), as they are undergoing a phase of structural change which could also change business cycle synchronization patterns. Therefore, an analysis of economic adjustment of those countries during the crisis seems particularly relevant to examine changing patterns in European business cycle convergence.

10.3   DATA AND METHODS

10.3.1   Dataset

Most previous studies for the euro area or CESEE countries focused on either GDP or industrial production to measure business cycle synchronization (de Haan et al., 2008). As GDP is clearly the most comprehensive output variable, we will use real GDP data (seasonally adjusted, 2005 price levels) from Q1 1999 to Q1 2012. The country sample includes the initial euro area countries (EA-12), the countries which joined the euro area between 2007 and 2011 (New EA-5), and the remaining non-euro area countries in the CESEE region, including Croatia (CESEE-8).[5] All data are extracted from Eurostat and are therefore comparable both in the cross-section and time series dimension.

10.3.2   Calculation of Business Cycles

The output gap is an important determinant for monetary policy, as it is usually a good measure of future inflation pressures. Therefore, the synchronization of business cycles (i.e. output gaps) across countries is commonly referred to as the most important criterion of an optimum currency area (OCA). To extract the trend from the cyclical component of the GDP time series, various filter techniques have been proposed in the literature (see Gächter et al., 2012, for a comprehensive discussion).

To increase comparability with other studies, we apply the widely used Hodrick–Prescott (Hodrick and Prescott, 1997) filter to calculate cyclical components.[6] The trend component is estimated by minimizing the deviation of the actual data points from this trend, with the smoothing parameter being determined *ex ante*. While the trend can be interpreted as potential output, the cyclical component corresponds to the output gap (i.e. fluctuation around the long-run trend).

10.3.3 Synchronization Measures

Subsequently, the cyclical components are used to calculate various measures of business cycle synchronization. Synchronous cycles imply that cyclical components of two countries (country aggregates) are moving up/down simultaneously and/or that the output gaps show similar values at a given point in time. The reason for diverging cycles can either be an asymmetric shock as such (i.e., concerning only one country, e.g., natural disasters) or a common shock (e.g. an increase of oil prices) which, however, affects countries in different ways. For a comprehensive analysis, we therefore need more than one synchronization measure. More precisely, we calculate both the dispersion (standard deviation) of cyclical components across countries at a given point in time; and the correlation between cyclical components in two-year rolling windows in various country samples, as described below.

Dispersion

Following Crespo-Cuaresma and Fernández-Amador (2010), the dispersion of the output gap at each point in time is measured by the standard deviation of cyclical components across the examined country sample. Thus, the dispersion can be used to assess whether business cycles are converging or diverging within a region. The main disadvantage of this measure is, however, that business cycles could exhibit similar output gaps (and therefore, low dispersion rates) even if they develop in different directions (i.e. one output gap is still increasing, while the other one is already decreasing).

Correlation

This drawback is offset by the second measure for synchronization, namely the correlation of two cycles. The correlation coefficient measures the strength of the linear relationship between two time series (i.e. cyclical components). Therefore, the absolute value of the output gap is not captured by a correlation analysis. Furthermore, the correlation cannot be measured at each point in time, but only for two time series (e.g. in rolling windows of two years). This synchronization measure is calculated either by the average bilateral cyclical correlations across a given country sample (e.g. euro area, CESEE etc.); or by the correlation coefficient between the corresponding country and the relevant country aggregate (e.g. euro area).

10.4 EMPIRICAL RESULTS

10.4.1 Cyclical Heterogeneity within the CESEE Region

First of all, we examine the development of business cycle synchronization within the CESEE region and the euro area, respectively. The top panel in Figure 10.2 shows the standard deviations of cyclical components for various country samples. The increase in the dispersion of cyclical components across all country aggregates since the end of 2006 clearly stands out.[7] Interestingly, this divergence starts approximately two years before the crisis in the corresponding boom period, while it somehow declines slightly in mid-2008 (when the cycles seem to move downward simultaneously). During the recovery phase in 2009, the standard deviation peaks the second time, before it starts to decline again in the light of the sovereign debt crisis that emerged in 2010, where economic activity weakens all over Europe. While this pattern is also observable for the EA-12 countries, it is much more pronounced for the CESEE-8 countries. Obviously, developments in CESEE economies during the crisis were much more heterogeneous than in the euro area. A large fraction of the observed divergence is attributable to the Baltic countries, which experienced unusually high growth in the mid-2000s at the price of increasing macroeconomic and financial imbalances leading to an unprecedented boom–bust cycle (see Figure 10.3).

For the group of more recent euro area member countries (New EA), it is theoretically ambiguous in which country aggregate they actually fit best. On the one hand, they belong to the group of new member countries which joined the EU in 2004, and therefore, should be classified as emerging market economies belonging to the CESEE aggregate. On the other hand, they fulfilled the convergence criteria very quickly and joined the currency union in recent years. Therefore, it is an empirical question whether the patterns point to an inclusion in the euro area or CESEE subsample, respectively. The two dashed lines in Figure 10.2 show the dispersion of cycles in the euro area and CESEE countries, in each case including the New EA-5 economies. While the standard deviation of the enlarged CESEE sample (13 countries) hardly deviates from its original values for the CESEE-8 countries, the dispersion of the euro area sample

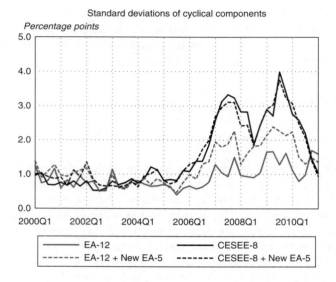

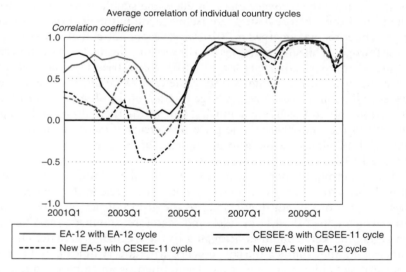

Source: Eurostat, authors' calculations.

Figure 10.2   Cyclical heterogeneity in the CESEE region and in the euro area

significantly increases when including the New EA-5 countries, at least for the period from 2006 to 2010. Thus, we conclude that the more recent euro area countries rather tend to follow the patterns of other (non-EMU) CESEE countries than the 12 (original) euro area countries.

Similar conclusions can be drawn from the bottom panel in Figure 10.2, where we report average correlations of the cyclical components with the EA-12 cycle and the CESEE-11 cycle in two-year rolling windows. For all country groups, the (comparatively small) recession in 2003–2004 led to a decrease in cyclical correlations, although the synchronization appears generally smaller in CESEE-8 than in the EA-12. At the beginning of the recovery, starting in Q1 2005, we observe a distinctive increase in cyclical correlations for all countries, which shows that the convergence process within the CESEE region is not only triggered by their accession to the EU, but also by other factors. At the cyclical peak in Q1 2008, there is a decline in synchronicity for a short period of time for all country groups, but to a much higher extent in CESEE economies than in euro area countries. In particular the New EA-5 countries seem to deviate substantially, which is likely caused by differing cyclical peaks among these countries (i.e. their cyclical peaks take place at different points in time).

A similar pattern can be observed in early 2010, during the most recent decrease in synchronization. However, contrary to 2008, the New EA countries closely mirror the behaviour of the other euro area countries, while the CESEE-8 countries record a slightly stronger decline in cyclical synchronization.

In brief, two main insights stand out: firstly, that the New EA-5 countries show a similar pattern as the CESEE-8 region, although they seem to converge towards the 12 initial euro area members at the end of the sample period; and secondly, while the dispersion of output gaps shows a significant increase in cyclical divergence since 2006, the pattern of cyclical correlations reflects an increase in synchronicity after the recession in 2004, although the end of the boom (Q1 2008) and the current crisis (since Q4 2009) are marked by declines, particularly in the CESEE-8 countries. Overall, we observe a higher heterogeneity among CESEE countries than within the euro area with respect to both the dispersion and correlation of business cycles, although the homogeneity seems to increase substantially towards the end of the sample period.

Figure 10.3 compares individual country cycles in the CESEE region and in the euro area, giving some insights into the economic adjustment of small and large economies. While the cyclical deviations are generally larger in the CESEE region as compared to the euro area (as indicated by the larger cyclical swings), the cyclical components are also smaller

Individual CESEE-11 country cycles

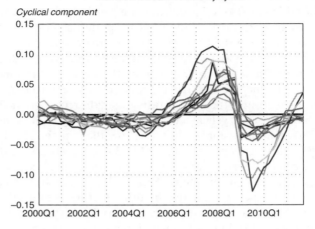

Individual euro area-12 country cycles

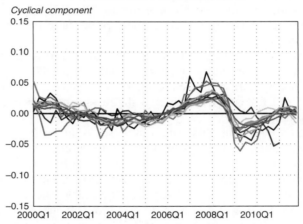

Note: BG = Bulgaria; CZ = Czech Republic; EE = Estonia; HR = Croatia; HU = Hungary; LT = Lithuania; LV = Latvia; PL = Poland; RO = Romania; SI = Slovenia; SK = Slovakia.

Source: Eurostat, authors' calculations.

Figure 10.3   Individual country cycles in the CESEE region and the euro area

Individual CESEE-11 country cycles: small economies

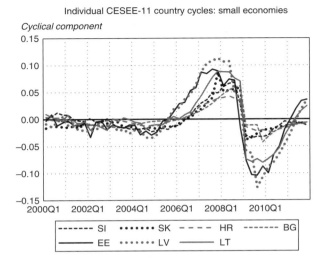

Individual CESEE-11 country cycles: large economies

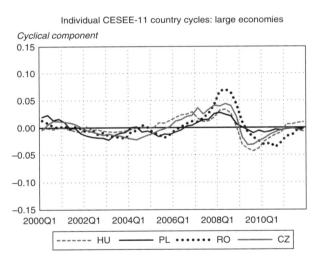

Figure 10.3 (continued)

in larger countries across the board, both in the euro area and in the CESEE region.[8] The largest cyclical swings (i.e. output gaps) during the crisis are reported for small open economies in CESEE, such as the Baltic countries, where the output gaps exceed 10 per cent of potential GDP in certain time periods. Poland, on the other hand, seems to have the most stable cycle, and thus, the lowest average output gap during the crisis in the CESEE region. Similarly, the remaining three large economies (Czech Republic, Romania, Hungary) also exhibit substantially lower cyclical swings than their smaller counterparts. However, as explained below, there is no obvious difference between large and small economies in terms of correlations.

The smaller swings of larger countries support the hypothesis that larger economies are less reliant on external markets, and thus, achieve more stable cycles. One obvious explanation is the relationship between the size and openness of an economy, as shown in Figure 10.4. Total trade – that is, the sum of exports and services (of goods and services) relative to GDP – tends to be lower in larger economies, which might imply smaller (more stable) cyclical swings and/or less dependence on external developments.[9] For the following analysis, where we examine the decoupling of CESEE from the euro area economy, we therefore divide our CESEE country sample into large (the Czech Republic, Hungary, Poland, Romania) and small economies (Bulgaria, Croatia, Estonia, Latvia, Lithuania, Slovenia, Slovakia). While the threshold between large and small economies is somehow arbitrarily set, the four larger countries also differ significantly in their economic policy. While the small economies either have already adopted the euro or exhibit a fixed exchange rate regime (currency board), the four large countries in our sample still feature floating exchange rates, which might enhance economic adjustment during the crisis significantly.

The following section focuses on a comparison of the euro area and the CESEE region and raises the question whether individual CESEE countries have decoupled or rather converged to the euro area cycle in recent years. As the New EA-5 countries show similar patterns to the CESEE region (as explained above), we include Slovenia, Slovakia and Estonia in the CESEE aggregate, summing up to a CESEE-11 sample. Next, due to their small size and geographical location, we subsequently exclude Malta and Cyprus from our samples. Furthermore, we will focus on the distinction between small and large countries in the CESEE region.

10.4.2 Decoupling of CESEE Countries from the Euro Area Cycle?

The top panel of Figure 10.5 shows the dispersion of cyclical deviations from the EA-12 cycle in the CESEE-11 region[10] as well as the results for two subsamples, namely small and large economies. As mentioned above, we include four CESEE countries in the large sample (Poland, Romania, the Czech Republic and Hungary), while the remaining seven CESEE countries are classified as small economies.

Once again, we observe a pronounced increase of cyclical deviations during the years 2006 and 2007, that is, in the boom phase before the

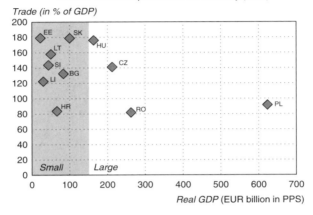

CESEE: size and openness of the economy (2011)

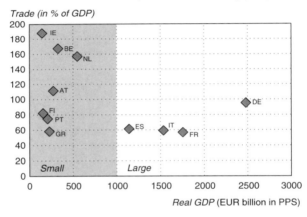

Euro area: size and openness of the economy (2011)

Note:　PPS = purchasing power standard.

Source:　European Commission (AMECO database), authors' calculations.

Figure 10.4　Size and openness of the economy in 2011

financial crisis. More importantly, however, we can interpret this figure as a substantial decoupling of the CESEE region from the euro area in terms of cyclical deviations. The decoupling starts at the beginning of 2006 and peaks twice in Q4 2007 and Q2 2009, before moving downwards again towards the end of the sample. While we also observe slightly elevated

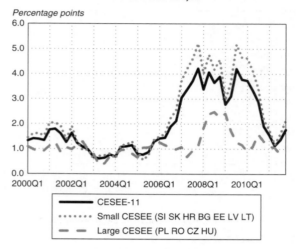

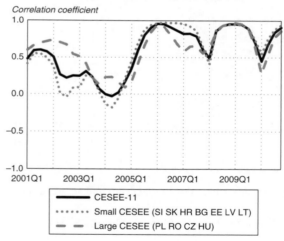

Note: BG = Bulgaria; CZ = Czech Republic; EA = Euro area; EE = Estonia; HR = Croatia; HU = Hungary; LV = Latvia; LT = Lithuania; PL = Poland; RO = Romania; SI =Slovenia; SK = Slovakia.

Source: Eurostat, authors' calculations.

Figure 10.5 Decoupling of the CESEE region from the euro area?

dispersions in the CESEE region at the start of the sample – that is, from 2000 to 2002, when the economies were moving towards the EU – the decoupling during the recent financial and economic crisis is considerably larger. Interestingly, this decoupling tendency is mainly driven by small CESEE countries, whereas the large economies show only some marginal deviation from the euro area cycle. This confirms that large (more closed) economies, where the size of the domestic market is significant, are less reliant on demand from advanced economies.

The bottom panel of Figure 10.5 shows average correlations between individual CESEE-11 cycles and the euro area-12 cycle, once again divided into small and large economies. It mainly reflects the pattern observed for the dispersion measure. The correlation with the euro area-12 cycle increases considerably after the small recession in 2004 – simultaneously with the increase of correlations within the euro area – but decreases remarkably during the boom and bust period around the onset of the financial crisis. The correlation coefficient decreases twice from around 0.95 to 0.5 in Q1 2008 and Q1 2010. Although a correlation coefficient of 0.5 is quite high compared to the period before 2005, the figure clearly shows a decoupling of CESEE countries from the euro area during this boom–bust period. Contrary to the dispersion of cyclical deviations explained above, the two declines in synchronization as measured by rolling-window correlations in 2008 and 2010 seem slightly more pronounced in larger economies. However, as the difference between small and large economies is quite small, the size of the economy does not seem to influence the co-movement of the cyclical component significantly.

Finally, it should be stressed again that the mean correlation coefficient after 2005 is much higher than in the period before. An analysis of two-year rolling window correlations of individual CESEE countries with the euro area-12 cycle[11] shows a pronounced increase in the synchronization of CESEE cycles after EU accession in 2004. Besides the already discussed declines in Q1 2008 and Q1 2010, only Hungary seems to have decoupled significantly from the euro area in 2006–2007, while the remaining CESEE economies exhibit high co-movement with the euro area cycle.

10.4.3   Implications for the Catching-up Process

While the previous two sections focused on business cycle synchronization from two different perspectives – dispersion and correlations of cyclical components – the following section examines economic adjustment not only in the short run, by investigating business cycles, but also in the long run, by examining the development of trend growth rates in the CESEE

Real GDP growth and trend growth rates

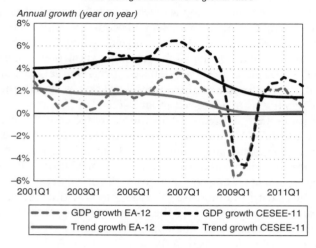

Growth differential: CESEE-11 vs. euro area-12

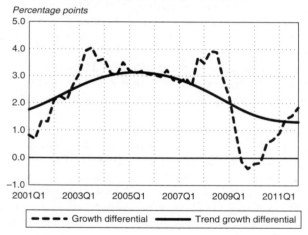

Source: Eurostat, authors' calculations.

Figure 10.6 The long-run perspective

region versus the euro area countries. The top panel in Figure 10.6 shows annual real GDP growth rates (on the same quarter of the previous year) for the EA-12 and the CESEE-11 aggregates as well as trend growth rates.[12] The bottom panel shows the growth differences (both for actual and trend growth) between the two regions. Several stylized facts stand out.

Firstly, the growth differential between the euro area and the CESEE region increased in the run-up to EU entry (until mid-2003) and stayed rather constant around 3 to 4 per cent until mid-2008. Subsequently, the growth differential even turned slightly negative during the Great Recession, but recovered towards 2 per cent again at the end of the sample. Secondly, trend growth rates have declined during the crisis both in CESEE and the euro area. Thirdly, the trend growth differential of the euro area and the CESEE region increased by more than one percentage point from 2001 to 2005–2006 and declined below two percentage points by end-2011, with trend growth in the euro area being estimated only slightly above zero.

Yet, what does that imply for the catching-up process? As shown in Figure 10.6, the catching-up process in the CESEE region even accelerated during the boom phase (as the growth differential increased), but slowed down significantly in the aftermath of the crisis. Hence, while the catching-up process is continuing, it is considerably slower than before the crisis. If one assumes that the growth differential stays constant at a rate of two percentage points, then the CESEE economies would exhibit the same per capita GDP levels as the euro area-12 economies by 2050 (Moder and Wörz, 2012).

To sum up, we gained three important empirical patterns in this section. Firstly, we observe a pronounced decoupling of trend growth rates between the euro area and the CESEE region until the onset of the financial crisis in 2008, which is in line with the evidence that global emerging market economies decoupled from industrialized economies. Secondly, trend growth rates started to decline during the crisis both in CESEE and the euro area and have converged ever since. Thirdly, the reduced growth differential of approximately 2 per cent since 2011 between the euro area and the CESEE region implies a decelerated catching-up process in the CESEE region.

10.5 CONCLUSIONS

In this chapter we analysed the empirical pattern of business cycle convergence/divergence in the EU, especially with regard to cyclical co-movements between the CESEE region and the euro area. In particular, we tested the decoupling versus convergence hypothesis for the CESEE region, as the impact of the catching-up process on business cycle synchronization is theoretically ambiguous. Moreover, in light of recent evidence,

showing a decoupling of global emerging market economies from industrialized economies, we explored the development of trend growth differentials between the CESEE region and the euro area. The most important
findings of our study can be summarized as follows.

Firstly, CESEE economies are still much more heterogeneous among
each other than the countries in the euro area, with respect to both cyclical dispersion and correlation. Secondly, we observe a pronounced business cycle decoupling of CESEE countries from the euro area starting
with the onset of the financial crisis in 2008, once again confirmed for
both the dispersion of output gaps and cyclical co-movement. The results
for the dispersion measure are mainly driven by smaller countries. This
can be explained by the fact that small economies seem to have larger
cyclical swings as they are more dependent on external demand, which
causes a decoupling in terms of higher output gap deviations from the
euro area cycle in times of economic crises. At the same time, this does
not necessarily affect business cycle synchronization as measured by
cyclical correlation, where the strength of the linear relationship of two
cycles is measured. In fact, there is some evidence for a more pronounced
decline in the co-movement of larger economies from the euro area
cycle. Despite the observed declines of correlation coefficients during
two particular time spans after 2007, the average cyclical correlation of
the CESEE economies with the euro area has risen significantly after
their EU accession in 2004. Furthermore, at the end of the sample, a
'recoupling' of the CESEE countries to the euro area economy can be
observed. Overall, the already high correlations of cyclical components
with the euro area cycle imply quite favourable conditions for a common
monetary policy in CESEE if the new member states in CESEE decide to
join the euro area.

Thirdly, we find a significant decoupling of trend growth rates
between the euro area and the CESEE region until the onset of the
financial crisis in 2008, which is in line with recent observations concerning the decoupling of global emerging market economies from industrialized economies. Moreover, trend growth rates have declined during
the crisis both in the CESEE region and the euro area, which resulted
in a considerable reduction of the growth differential between the two
regions from around four to approximately two percentage points. If
one assumes that the growth differential stays at two percentage points
from now on, the GDP levels would be aligned by 2050. Interestingly,
the growth differential between the euro area and the CESEE region
observed in the early 2010s is mainly driven by large CESEE economies,
with Poland's trend growth rate being the major driver of this gap.
Hence, from a long-run perspective, we conclude that the catching-up

process of the CESEE region has continued, but slowed down considerably during the crisis. At the same time, the lower growth differential might also be a rebalancing towards a more sustained and balanced growth in the region, hopefully leading to a more stable process of income convergence.

NOTES

1. Similar contributions (partly) by the same authors, albeit with a slightly different focus, had already been published earlier: see, for instance, Kose et al. (2003), Helbling et al. (2007) or Prasad et al. (2008).
2. The observed country sample includes the founding members of the euro area (EA-12), the five countries that have since joined the euro area (Cyprus, Estonia, Malta, Slovakia, Slovenia – the New EA-5) and the eight remaining CESEE EU member states (Bulgaria, Croatia, the Czech Republic, Hungary, Latvia, Lithuania, Poland and Romania – the CESEE-8). Croatia is included as it joins the EU in 2013. On the contrary, Denmark, Sweden and the United Kingdom are excluded as the issue of business cycle synchronization outside the currency union seems less important, and further, the focus of this study is on EU member states in the CESEE region.
3. See, for instance, Artis and Zhang (1997, 1999) or Inklaar and de Haan (2001).
4. Cyprus, the Czech Republic, Estonia, Hungary, Latvia, Lithuania, Malta, Poland, Slovakia, Slovenia.
5. As our study focuses on developments within the euro area and the CESEE region, Denmark, Sweden and the United Kingdom are not included in the following analysis.
6. Note that this estimation method might be subject to parameter instability at the end of the sample period. As was shown by Gächter et al. (2012) for the euro area, this parameter instability is most pronounced in the last four quarters and mainly affects the dispersion measure. Hence, results concerning the dispersion in 2011 exhibit considerable uncertainty.
7. For the euro area countries, this issue has been already discussed by Gächter et al. (2012).
8. This stylized fact is only shown for the CESEE region. However, the same applies to country cycles in the euro area, although the cyclical swings seem generally lower in high-income countries. This might be explained by the fact that the size of the government sector is higher in euro area countries, which is often found to be negatively related to output volatility.
9. However, while large economies are generally less open due to their large domestic markets, the relationship is less clear for small economies, where the degree of openness, *ceteris paribus*, spreads considerably.
10. Contrary to Figure 10.2 where we calculated standard deviations of cyclical components within the corresponding group of countries, Figure 10.5 shows the average dispersion of the individual CESEE cycles from the euro area-12 cycle. More precisely, we apply a slightly adapted standard deviation (i.e. deviation from the euro area cycle) across the corresponding groups, where we use the sum of squared deviations from the aggregated euro area-12 cycle (instead of the sum of squared deviations from the sample mean) to compute the corresponding measure.
11. Available from the authors upon request.
12. The trend growth rate is calculated as the annual growth rate (on the same quarter of the previous year) of the trend variable, as calculated by a standard Hodrick–Prescott (1997) filter. For simplicity, we calculate log differences to compute the corresponding growth rates.

REFERENCES

Artis, M.J., J. Fidrmuc and J. Scharler (2008), 'The transmission of business cycles: implications for EMU enlargement', *Economics of Transition*, **16** (3), 559–82.

Artis, M.J. and W. Zhang (1997), 'International business cycles and the ERM: is there a European business cycle?', *International Journal of Finance and Economics*, **2** (1), 1–16.

Artis, M., M. Marcellino and T. Proietti (2005), 'Business cycles in the new EU member countries and their conformity with the Euro Area', *Journal of Business Cycle Measurement and Analysis*, **2** (1), 7–32.

Artis, M. and W. Zhang (1999), 'Further evidence on the international business cycle and the ERM: is there a European business cycle?', *Oxford Economic Papers*, **51** (1), 120–32.

Aslanidis, N. (2010), 'Business cycle synchronization between the CEEC and the euro-area: evidence from threshold seemingly unrelated regressions', *Manchester School*, **78** (6), 538–55.

Barro, R.J. (1991), 'Economic growth in a cross section of countries', *Quarterly Journal of Economics*, **106** (2), 407–43.

Benczúr, P. and A. Rátfai (2010), 'Economic fluctuations in central and eastern Europe: the facts', *Applied Economics*, **42** (25), 3279–92.

Cavenaile, L. and D. Dubois (2011), 'An empirical analysis of income convergence in the European Union', *Applied Economics Letters*, **18** (17), 1705–8.

Crespo-Cuaresma, J. and O. Fernández-Amador (2010), 'Business cycle convergence in EMU: a first look at the second moment', Working Paper Series in Economics and Statistics, No. 2010–22, University of Innsbruck.

Darvas, Z. and G. Szapáry (2008), 'Business cycle synchronization in the enlarged EU', *Open Economies Review*, **19** (1), 1–19.

de Haan, J., R. Inklaar and R. Jong-A-Pin (2008), 'Will business cycles in the euro area converge? A critical survey of empirical research', *Journal of Economic Surveys*, **22** (2), 234–73.

Eickmeier, S. and J. Breitung (2006), 'How synchronized are new EU member states with the euro area? Evidence from a structural factor model', *Journal of Comparative Economics*, **34** (3), 538–63.

Fidrmuc, J. and I. Korhonen (2004), 'The euro goes east: implications of the 2000–2002 economic slowdown for synchronisation of business cycles between the euro area and CEECs', *Comparative Economic Studies*, **46** (1), 45–62.

Fidrmuc, J. and I. Korhonen (2006), 'Meta-analysis of the business cycle correlation between the euro area and the CEECs', *Journal of Comparative Economics*, **34** (3), 518–37.

Frankel, J.A. and A.K. Rose (1998), 'The endogeneity of the optimum currency area criteria', *Economic Journal*, **108** (449), 1009–25.

Gächter, M., A. Riedl and D. Ritzberger-Grünwald (2012), 'Business cycle synchronization in the euro area and the impact of the financial crisis', *Monetary Policy and the Economy*, **2**, 33–60.

Helbling, T., P. Berezin, A. Kose, M. Kumhof, D. Laxton and N. Spatafora (2007), 'Decoupling the train? Spillovers and cycles in the global economy', in IMF (ed.), *World Economic Outlook*, Washington, DC: International Monetary Fund, April, pp. 121–60.

Hodrick, R.J. and E.C. Prescott (1997), 'Postwar US business cycles: an empirical investigation', *Journal of Money, Credit and Banking*, **29** (1), 1–16.

IMF (2012), *World Economic Outlook: Coping with High Debt and Sluggish Growth*, Washington, DC: International Monetary Fund.

Inklaar, R. and J. de Haan (2001), 'Is there really a European business cycle? A comment', *Oxford Economic Papers*, **53** (2), 215–20.

Kenen, P. (1969), 'The optimum currency area: an eclectic view', in R. Mundell and A. Sowboda (eds), *Monetary Problems of the International Economy*, Chicago, IL: University of Chicago Press, pp. 41–60.

Kose, M.A., C. Otrok and E. Prasad (2008), 'Global business cycles: convergence or decoupling?', IZA Discussion Papers 3442, Institute for the Study of Labor (IZA).

Kose, M.A., C. Otrok and E. Prasad (2012), 'Global business cycles: Convergence or decoupling?', *International Economic Review*, **53** (2), 511–38.

Kose, M.A., E.S. Prasad and M.E. Terrones (2003), 'How does globalization affect the synchronization of business cycles?', *American Economic Review*, **93** (2), 57–62.

McKinnon, R.I. (1963), 'Optimum currency areas', *American Economic Review*, **53** (4), 717–25.

Moder, I. and J. Wörz (2012), 'CESEE-Konvergenzsimulationen', OENB AUSA mimeo.

Mundell, R.A. (1961), 'A theory of optimum currency areas', *American Economic Review*, **51** (4), 657–65.

Prasad, E., C. Otrok and M.A. Kose (2008), 'Dissecting the decoupling debate', *VOXeu*, 4 October, http://www.voxeu.org/article/dissecting-decoupling-debate.

Savva, C.S., K.C. Neanidis and D.R. Osborn (2010), 'Business cycle synchronization of the euro area with the new and negotiating member countries', *International Journal of Finance and Economics*, **15** (3), 288–306.

Solow, R.M. (1956), 'A contribution to the theory of economic growth', *Quarterly Journal of Economics*, **70** (1), 65–94.

Vojinovic, B. and M. Próchniak (2009), 'Divergence period in the European convergence process', *Transition Studies Review*, **15**, 685–700.

Wälti, S. (2010), 'No decoupling, more interdependence: business cycle comovements between advanced and emerging economies', MPRA Paper 20869, University Library of Munich, Germany.

11. South-Eastern Europe: impacts from the crisis, vulnerabilities and adjustments

Dimitar Bogov and Aneta Krstevska

11.1 INTRODUCTION

This chapter describes the impact that the world economic crisis which emerged in 2007–2008 and the sovereign debt crisis which hit individual euro area countries in 2010 has had on South-Eastern Europe (SEE), specifically the countries of Macedonia (abbreviated MKD in all figures), Albania (ALB), Bosnia and Herzegovina (B&H), Croatia (CRO), Montenegro (MNE) and Serbia (SRB); together referred to as SEE-6 in this chapter. Prior to the crisis, these countries all operated under broadly similar conditions; they all had robust growth rates and sound banking systems as well as macroeconomic imbalances of varying degrees. When the crisis occurred, the relatively low degree of integration in world financial markets helped the SEE-6 economies to maintain financial stability while advanced economies faced severe disorders. At the same time, the crisis affected the SEE-6 countries' growth perspectives, considering their traditional orientation towards the EU market; it put pressure on public finances; and it affected banks' sources of financing. During the crisis years, the main vulnerability areas of the region switched from the external sector and rapid credit expansion towards the fiscal sector and the worsened quality of the banking sector's credit portfolio. Looking ahead, the SEE-6 countries are facing the need to adjust their fiscal balances and to move towards medium-term sustainability, as well as the challenge of enhancing growth. In an uncertain global environment, the implementation of structural reforms should remain a priority in the SEE-6 countries that should lead towards long-term sustainable growth.

Section 11.2 of this chapter covers the pre-crisis conditions in the region, while section 11.3 assesses the impact of the crisis on the region, with a special focus on the Macedonian economy as well as a vulnerability analysis for the SEE-6 countries. Section 11.4 elaborates on the challenges of the region in the future, followed by the concluding section 11.5.

11.2   INITIAL CONDITIONS IN THE SEE-6 BEFORE THE CRISIS

In the period prior to the crisis, economic growth in the SEE-6 countries had accelerated significantly, with average gross domestic product (GDP) growth ranging from 4 to 6 per cent in the period from 2004 to 2008 (see Figure 11.1). Output growth was mostly driven by domestic demand, being supported by rapid credit growth and capital inflows from abroad (Angelovska Bezovska, 2012). Such circumstances resulted in the gradual build-up of external imbalances, especially in a deterioration of the current account deficits (see Figure 11.2). Strong credit expansion influenced both private and investment consumption, including imports from abroad. In addition, the massive capital inflows, mainly in the form of foreign direct investment (FDI), in the initial stage of the establishment of new entities, primarily fuelled the import of goods, especially imports of machines and equipment. The relatively high current account deficits run by some of the SEE-6 countries were financed also through an increase in external debt.

The banking systems in the SEE-6 countries were sound and stable,

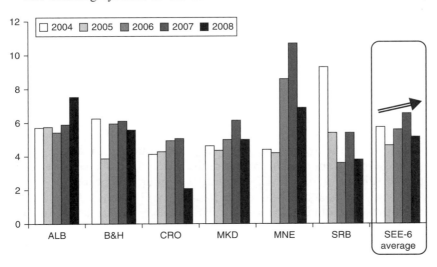

Source: IMF (WEO database, October 2012).

Figure 11.1   GDP growth rates before the crisis (in %)

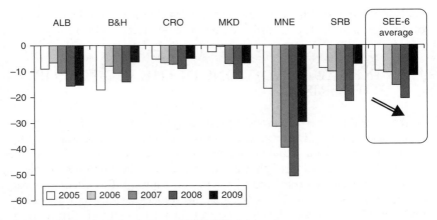

Source: Central banks' websites and IMF (IFS database).

Figure 11.2   Current account deficit (% of GDP)

well capitalized and liquid. The credit expansion in the period prior to the crisis was a common phenomenon in the region, although in some of the countries it started to intensify later (e.g. in Macedonia) than in others. The credit growth in these countries was mainly financed from domestic sources, although banks in some countries relied significantly on foreign sources of financing as well.

11.3   THE IMPACT OF THE CRISIS ON THE SEE-6 REGION

The latest global crisis affected the SEE-6 region through the sharp reversal of the macroeconomic trends. The crisis spillover effects were mainly due to the strong trade linkages with the European Union, which is the most important trading partner of the region. In 2009, with the exception of Albania, all other SEE-6 countries registered a decline of GDP. In 2011, only Albania and Macedonia had higher GDP levels than in 2008, while the other four countries were still below the pre-crisis levels. In 2012, the SEE-6 countries suffered a second blow from the crisis, with GDP growth rates re-entering negative territory in most of the countries and showing the pattern of a double dip recession (see Figure 11.3).

Considering trade linkages, the main channel of crisis spillovers to the SEE-6 countries was through the export decline, due to the slowdown in the external demand for their goods and services. Therefore, in 2009, all

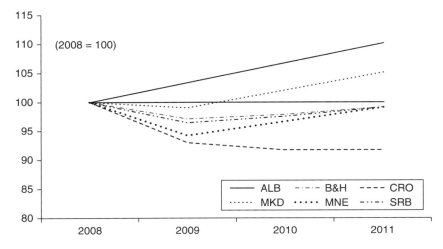

Source: IMF (WEO database, October 2012).

Figure 11.3   GDP levels before and during the crisis (2008 = 100)

SEE-6 countries experienced a decline in annual exports, followed by a moderate recovery in the next two years (see Figure 11.4).

In addition, one of the usual channels of crisis contagion was the drop in private capital inflows due to higher global uncertainty that negatively affected foreign investors' perceptions. In any case, it is worth mentioning that all SEE-6 countries registered positive net inflows of FDI during the crisis as well, although in the period from 2009 to 2011 those flows were rather smaller than in the previous years (see Figure 11.5). The fall in exports and the reduced capital inflows undermined the pre-crisis growth model of the SEE-6 countries.

The sound initial conditions in the banking systems contained direct spillovers during the early stage of the crisis. In this regard, the traditional banking operations and banks' low exposure to riskier financial instruments, as well as their moderate involvement in international financial flows, were important protective features against crisis contagion. Yet second-round effects through the worsened economic outlook were unavoidable. The deteriorated credit worthiness of the economic entities triggered a rise in non-performing loans (NPLs) and pushed credit markets into a bust cycle. The average NPL ratio in the SEE-6 countries was 6.6 per cent in 2008 while it jumped to 14.3 per cent in 2011 (see Figure 11.6) The worsening of the quality of the credit portfolio hit the profitability of the banking systems in the SEE-6 countries in the midstream of the crisis.

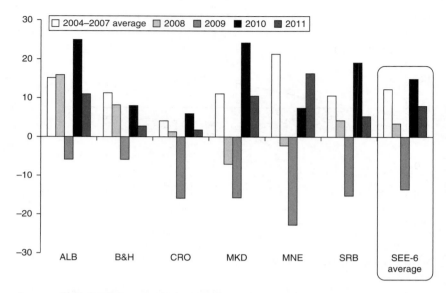

Source: IMF (WEO database, October 2012).

Figure 11.4   Exports of goods and services (year-on-year % change)

Overall, the financial stability in the region was not under threat. The sound capitalization of the banking systems with an average capital adequacy ratio of around 16 per cent during the crisis period (previously even higher) strongly contributed to the banking sector's resilience. In addition, banks' liquidity, although being affected at the beginning of the crisis, stabilized in the period after 2008 at reasonable levels (see Figures 11.7, 11.8 and 11.9).

On the other hand, public finances in the SEE-6 countries were under significant pressure during the crisis. The effect of the automatic stabilizers through lower budget revenues in the economic downturn as well as countercyclical expansionary spending led to larger budget deficit from around 2.5 per cent of GDP in 2008, on average for the SEE-6 countries, to around 4 per cent of GDP in the next two years (see Figure 11.10). The higher budget deficits drove public debt levels higher, although on average for the SEE-6 countries the debt ratio was still at a quite reasonable level of around 45 per cent of GDP in 2011, on average, but with an increasing tendency. In addition, external debt has also been on a rising track (from around 65 per cent in 2008 to around 78 per cent of GDP in 2011, on average for the region), partly due to the increased accumulation of foreign debt by the government (see Figure 11.11).

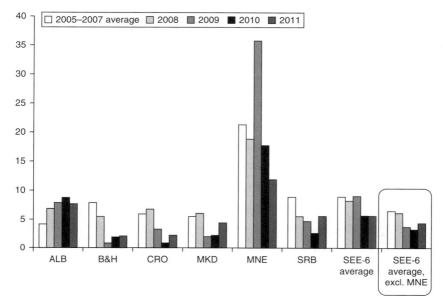

Source: Central banks' websites and IMF (WEO database).

Figure 11.5   FDI (% of GDP)

In general, central banks in emerging and developing countries responded to the crisis with measures that differed from those of advanced econo-mies in timing, type and magnitude. According to several studies explor-ing the crisis (Fujita et al., 2010; Ishi et al., 2009), these differences can be related to the varied degrees of financial stress and external vulner-ability in emerging and developing countries compared to advanced economies, as well as the varied macroeconomic context in these two groups of countries. The central banks in the SEE-6 economies moreo-ver generally started to implement anti-crisis measures later, and the measures were of a smaller magnitude compared to the advanced econo-mies and mainly focused on the foreign exchange market and banks' liquidity.

Monetary policy in the SEE-6 countries, as in many other parts of the world, has been implemented in a proactive manner during the crisis period. A range of conventional and unconventional measures have been undertaken, aiming at balancing the need for mitigating the crisis impact with the need to maintain a stable currency. Due to the relatively lower degree of financial integration in the global market, the first stage of the crisis, with financial turmoil hitting the advanced economies, had limited

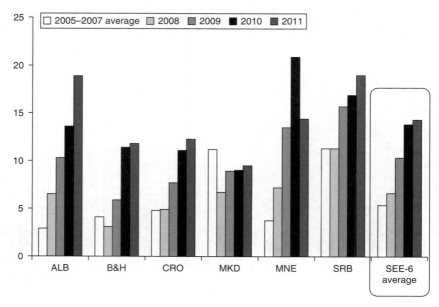

Source: Central banks' websites.

Figure 11.6   Non-performing loans (% of total loans)

effects on the SEE-6 countries. In such circumstances, in 2007 and 2008, the central banks in SEE-6 countries raised their policy rates in response to the inflationary pressures prevailing at that time (mainly due to supply-side factors; see Figure 11.12). However, after Lehman Brothers' bankruptcy, global liquidity dried up and crisis spillover extended. In order to mitigate the depreciation pressures on domestic currencies, the central banks in the SEE-6 countries largely focused on foreign exchange market interventions and liquidity measures. In this regard, stronger countercyclical responses were in place only in the countries with floating exchange rates, where currency depreciation was allowed in order to mitigate the impact of the crisis. On all accounts, central banks in many countries under observation experienced interventions on the foreign exchange market, while bolstering their foreign reserve level with external financing (International Monetary Fund support to part of the region). Reactions with interest rate cuts came later, when economic activity slumped and inflation expectations stabilized at large. Therefore, the main policy rates in the SEE-6 region at the end of 2011 were significantly lower than in the previous period. Still, the rates were cut cautiously and to a considerably lesser extent than in the advanced economies. Although monetary policy

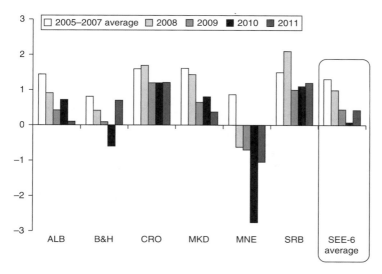

Source: Central banks' websites.

Figure 11.7   Return on assets (%)

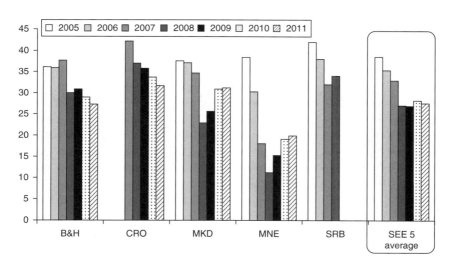

Source: Central banks' websites.

Figure 11.8   Liquid assets to total assets (%)

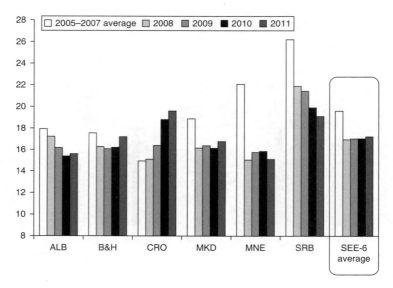

Source: Central banks' websites.

Figure 11.9   Capital adequacy ratio (in %)

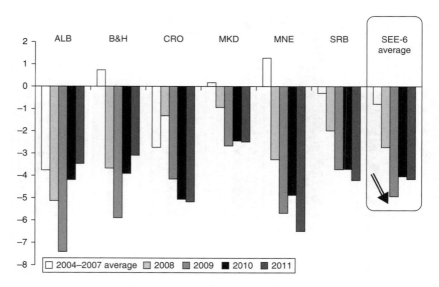

Source: IMF (WEO database, October 2012).

Figure 11.10   Fiscal balance (% of GDP)

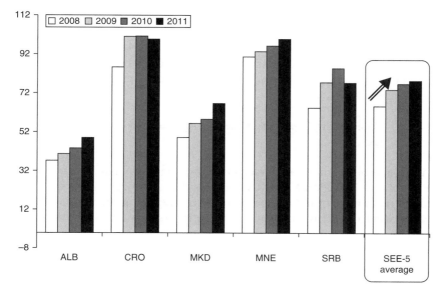

Source: Central banks, Eurostat, ECB, IMF (staff report 2012 on Montenegro, and World Economic Outlook, April 2012).

Figure 11.11 Gross external debt (% of GDP)

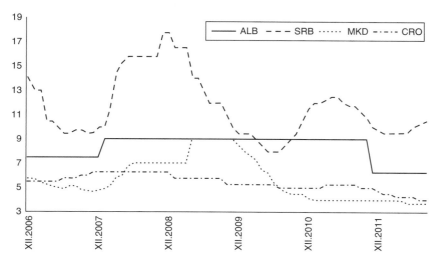

Source: Central banks' websites.

Figure 11.12 Central bank policy rate, end of period (%)

in the region was not constrained by a zero lower bound on interest rates, the central banks also adopted unconventional monetary policy tools, having in mind the potential risks of a repeated deterioration of the external imbalances and inflationary pressures (although coming mainly from the global oil and food prices, but with the risk of pass-through to core inflation).

11.3.1   Vulnerability Analysis of the SEE-6 Countries before and during the Crisis

A vulnerability analysis undertaken by the National Bank of the Republic of Macedonia (NBRM) reveals that significant shifts occurred in the main vulnerability areas of the SEE-6 region in the periods before and during the crisis, reflecting a sharp reversal in the main economic trends. The pre-crisis period was characterized by strong domestic demand, fuelled by the credit expansion and funds from abroad, which in turn caused the external sector balances to worsen. Thus, the vulnerability analysis shows the external sector (current account deficit and ratio of foreign assets to potential claims in foreign currency) and strong credit growth to have been the main vulnerabilities areas at the end of 2008. As previously explained, the widening of the current account deficit in the SEE-6 countries was partly affected by the strong FDI inflows that caused higher imports of machines and equipment at the early stage of setting up new entities as well as imports of raw materials from abroad for these entities, in most of the cases. Over a longer horizon, the overall net impact of their operations on external balances should turn positive. However, not all FDI undertakings had import components. Additionally, the relatively high level of domestic consumption in the pre-crisis period was also supported by intensive lending by domestic banks, which significantly contributed to the current account deficit deterioration as well. Thus, the pre-crisis deterioration of the external balances as well as strong credit growth were raising the issue of long-run sustainability. In addition, the slowdown of deposit growth relative to GDP has been also listed among the potential vulnerabilities, pointing out the first round of impact of the crisis, which was already present at the end of 2008 (see Figure 11.13).

During the crisis, vulnerabilities shifted to the government sector, non-performing loans and the banking sector's sources of financing. The lower budget revenues against the backdrop of the economic slump together with the increased countercyclical budget expenditures led to a widening of the budget deficit (in four of the SEE-6 countries) that was reflected in an increase of government debt in some of the countries.

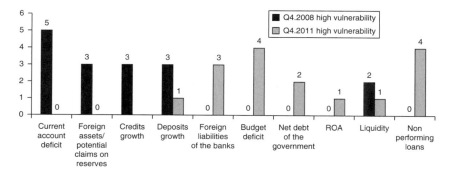

Note: This analysis is based on historical data, where thresholds are based on data variability and deviation from the historical mean value.

Source: Analysis of the National Bank of the Republic of Macedonia (NBRM).

Figure 11.13 Vulnerability in the SEE-6 countries before and during the crisis (in numbers of countries)

The banking systems of the SEE-6 countries were faced with numerous challenges during the crisis. The worsening quality of the credit portfolio seems to be the most pronounced challenge, being registered in four of the SEE-6 countries. The worsened economic outlook influenced the repayment ability of banks' credit clients which resulted in a continuous increase of non-performing loans. In some of the countries, these developments affected both banks' profitability and their liquidity. In addition, banks felt the force of the crisis through the more evident scarcity of sources of financing. The stronger impact was on the foreign liabilities of foreign-owned banks, which shrank significantly during the crisis due to liquidity and other budget constraints of the foreign (mainly European Union-based) parent banks. Deposit growth was initially affected by short episodes of deposit withdrawal during the first wave of the crisis due to uncertainty and the pressure of psychological factors. Later on, the deposit dynamics accommodated downward in line with the slowdown in economic growth.

11.3.2 The Macedonian Economy during the Crisis Period

The Macedonian economy broadly fits the framework of the regional profile during the crisis (see Figure 11.14). The GDP decline in 2009 (by 0.9 per cent), was followed by a moderate recovery in the next two years. Inflation was mainly driven by supply-side factors that enabled monetary

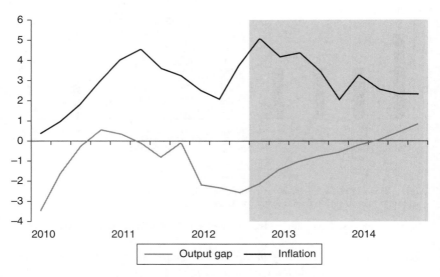

Source: NBRM and State Statistical Office (NBRM forecast for 2013 and 2014 from October 2012).

Figure 11.14   Output gap and inflation (%)

policy relaxation during the crisis, with the main policy rate being set at the historically lowest level (3.75 per cent, since May 2012).

New undertakings established on the back of FDI inflows before the crisis had a strong positive impact on economic recovery after 2009, by contributing, among other things, to a more diversified export structure. As a case in point, chemical products and machinery and transport equipment – that is, products with higher value-added – accounted for a significantly higher share of overall exports in 2011 than before the crisis. Regarding export destinations, Macedonian exports to neighbouring Greece declined, but exports to Germany increased at the same time. In addition, some new export destinations for Macedonian products were added during the crisis (mainly emerging and developing Asian countries), reflecting higher flexibility and some structural improvements, with a positive countercyclical effect (see Figures 11.15 and 11.16).

The current account deficit shrank mainly due to the smaller trade deficit (imports responded to lower exports and to reduced domestic demand) and strong private transfer inflows, being a traditional source of financing of the trade deficit. During the crisis, these inflows were stimulated by the uncertainty related to the euro zone crisis and the presence of non-residents visiting the country (mainly from neighbouring countries).

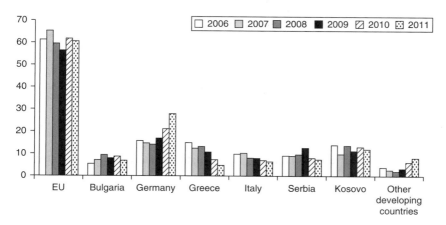

Source: State Statistical Office.

Figure 11.15   Macedonian export destinations (% of total exports)

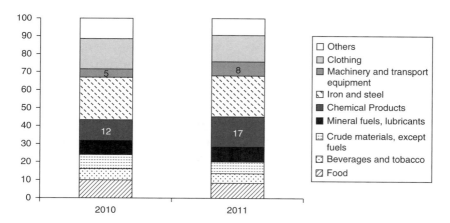

Source: State Statistical Office.

Figure 11.16   Export structure, by products (%)

FDI inflows were reduced but continuous, which combined with the bor-rowings from abroad resulted in an increase of foreign reserves. During the crisis, the budget deficit widened moderately to around 2.5 per cent of GDP in the period 2009–2011, which gradually drove up the public debt ratio, but not beyond 30 per cent of GDP.

Credit growth became moderate and the asset quality deteriorated only mildly (the NPL ratio reached around 10 per cent in mid-2012), which means that in this respect the Macedonian banking sector performs better than most of the countries in the region (where the NPL ratio is around 20 per cent). At any rate, higher loan loss provisions negatively affected banks' profitability. At the beginning of the crisis the liquidity ratios of the banking system registered a decline, therefore the NBRM introduced minimum liquidity requirements in mid-2009 which strengthened banks' liquidity further on. As before, the capital adequacy ratio remained at a reasonably high level of around 16 per cent during the crisis period, therefore presenting a strong buffer against increased risks in the business environment.

The main risks and challenges for the Macedonian economy in the future, in general, are broadly the same as those of the other countries in the region. Macedonia is faced with the need to enhance growth, maintain sound public finances, take care of the level of the external debt and stimulate credit growth, while maintaining banking sector soundness.

11.4   LOOKING AHEAD: CHALLENGES FOR THE SEE-6 COUNTRIES

All SEE-6 countries are facing a need for growth-enhancing models, but it seems that there is a limited space for policy manoeuvre in this direction. Fiscal consolidation is inevitable for medium-term fiscal sustainability, and according to the fiscal strategies of the countries it is expected to take place in the period from 2013 to 2015, when budget deficits should get back to their pre-crisis levels. Although the procyclical tightening in structural terms is already in place, the SEE-6 fiscal outlook is still characterized by numerous challenges. In addition, specific fiscal rules in some countries have already been embedded in the legislation (Croatia and Serbia). (See Figures 11.17 and 11.18.)

Buffers in foreign reserves need to be built further or maintained, especially in the countries with a fixed exchange rate, in order to counter external vulnerability risks. Therefore, the scope for countercyclical monetary policy in these countries will be rather narrowed. At the current juncture, when inflation pressures in the region and around the globe are building up, the scope for accommodative monetary policy might be limited even in countries with a flexible exchange rate.

Looking ahead, the role of the domestic banking system regarding growth support is also facing many challenges. Since the share of foreign financing, especially from the parent banks, is diminishing (see Figure 11.19), there should be a higher reliance on domestic sources of

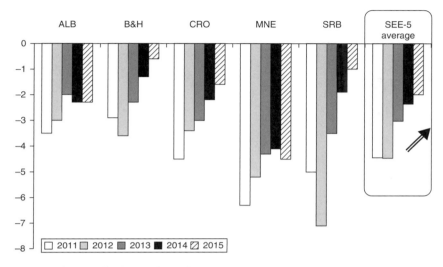

Source: Country fiscal strategies and IMF country reports.

Figure 11.17   Fiscal balance (in % of GDP; plan after 2011)

financing as well as available funds from the multilateral financial institutions. In most of the countries there is scope for additional financial
support of the economy. The credit-to-deposit ratio decreased from 122 in
2008 to 109 in 2011, on average, for the SEE-6 countries. The deteriorated
credit portfolio quality and generally weak economic outlook are serious
constraints for stronger credit growth in the near term. Additionally, a
potential risk to credit growth is related to deleveraging at the foreign
parent banks, which could impose additional constraints on subsidiaries
in the SEE-6 countries. (See Figure 11.20.)

Considering the features of the previous growth model that relied
heavily on external factors, the countries in the region should redefine
their economic growth model towards more balanced sources of growth.
In addition, the need for a growth-enhancing model requires further
efforts to deal with structural rigidities in the SEE-6 economies. Attracting
non-debt capital inflows in the tradable sector would be an important
prerequisite for increasing competitiveness. Having in mind the developments so far, FDI inflows to the region (see Figure 11.21) were broadly
concentrated in the non-tradable sector, with the exception of Albania and
Macedonia, which registered a more balanced FDI structure in the tradable and non-tradable sector (in Macedonia the balance has lately shifted
to the tradable sector).

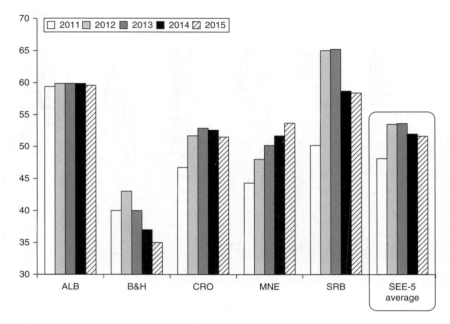

Source: Country fiscal strategies and IMF country reports.

Figure 11.18   Public debt (in % of GDP; plan after 2011)

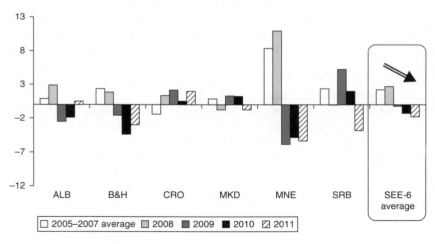

Source: Central banks' websites.

Figure 11.19   Banks' foreign liabilities (% of GDP, annual change)

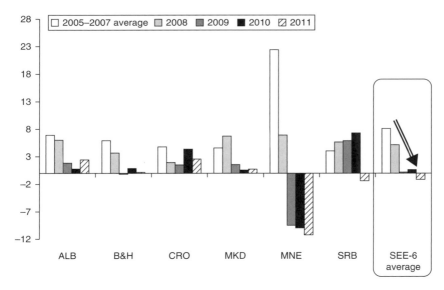

Source: Central banks' websites.

Figure 11.20   Banks' outstanding loans (% of GDP, annual change)

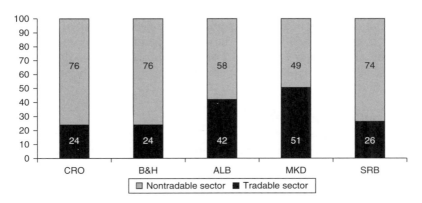

Note: Data refer to FDI stocks at the end of 2011 except for Albania (the latest available data were for end-2010) and Serbia (data on FDI flows).

Source: Central banks' websites.

Figure 11.21   FDI by sectors (%)

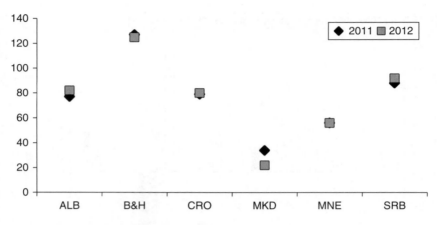

Source: World Bank (Doing Business database).

Figure 11.22   Doing Business ranking (1 is the best)

Structural reforms are necessary for income convergence and EU integration, for enhanced competiveness and removing bottlenecks in the investment climate. On a Doing Business ranking (see Figure 11.22), from among the analysed countries in 2012, Macedonia is the best-ranked country (22), while Bosnia and Herzegovina is the worst-ranked country (125), but obviously in all SEE-6 countries there is still room for structural improvements that will facilitate the conditions for doing business. In this view, the main issues to be addressed are: infrastructure enhancement, increase of institutional quality, increase of efficiency and innovations.

11.5   CONCLUSIONS

The SEE-6 countries experienced strong growth prior the crisis mostly driven by domestic demand, being supported by rapid credit growth and capital inflows from abroad. In the first wave of the crisis they remained quite stable, although being affected mainly through the export channel and reduced capital inflows that undermined their growth model.

Growth acceleration remains a main challenge for the SEE-6 region, yet the scope for growth-oriented macroeconomic policies is rather limited. The fiscal scope for a countercyclical response is rather narrow and the fiscal adjustment is expected to take place as a necessary precondition for medium-run sustainability. In addition, there are constraints on conventional monetary policy, although the unconventional measures can be undertaken in a countercyclical manner. The soundness of the banking system is considered to be one of the main strengths of the region, and there is room for the banking system to support growth further. Enhancing structural reforms, strengthening competitiveness and allocating or attracting capital in the tradable sector will be key priorities of the region in devising a new sustainable growth model.

REFERENCES

Angelovska Bezovska, A. (2012), 'South Eastern Europe: effects of the crisis and way forward', presentation, Belgrade, available at http://www.nbrm.mk/.

Fujita, K., K. Ishi and M. Stone (2010), 'Exiting from monetary crisis intervention measures', IMF Background Paper, available at http://www.imf.org/external/np/pp/eng/2010/012510.pdf.

Ishi, K., M. Stone and E.B. Yehoue (2009), 'Unconventional Central Bank measures for emerging economies', IMF Working Paper WP09/226, available at http://server6.kif.re.kr/KMFileDir/129004004614378750_IMF%20wp09226.pdf.

12. Economic adjustment in the Baltic countries

Ardo Hansson and Martti Randveer[1]

12.1 INTRODUCTION

Prior to the global financial crisis that emerged in 2008, Estonia, Latvia and Lithuania experienced several years of strong economic growth, followed by one of the deepest recessions in the world in 2008–2009. In a historical context, the cumulative output loss in the Baltic countries was almost twice as large as the gross domestic product (GDP) decline in the hardest-hit countries during the Asian crisis in 1997–1998. As compared to the euro area debt crisis, only the expected output loss in Greece is comparable to the GDP decline in the Baltics. In the other euro area countries, the recession in terms of a cumulative decline in output has been less pronounced.

After a severe recession, the Baltics have witnessed a relatively speedy recovery. As a result these countries have regained a significant part of the initial output losses and have seen a fall in unemployment levels. A swift reduction in several pre-existing imbalances and vulnerabilities was another prominent feature of the adjustment in the Baltics. Large current account deficits have been eliminated, credit growth is on a more sustainable path, and there has been a marked improvement in price and cost competitiveness. In addition, the Baltic countries have achieved a significant sectoral reorientation and managed to adjust their economies without a sharp increase in public and private indebtedness. Overall, the economic adjustment in the Baltics has been much faster than in the euro area economies most affected by the debt crisis.

Our analysis is motivated by the following three questions. Firstly, what explains the recent cyclical pattern of the Baltic economies? Secondly, what are the similarities and differences between the economic adjustment in the Baltics and the euro area countries most influenced by the recent crisis? And, finally, what are the advantages and disadvantages of fast versus gradual adjustment? In section 12.2, we outline the main developments in the Baltic countries in the period from 2000 to 2012. In section 12.3, we compare the adjustment in the Baltic countries with that in Ireland, Greece and Portugal. In section 12.4, we discuss the advantages and disadvantages of fast versus gradual economic adjustment. Section 12.5 concludes.

12.2 MAIN DEVELOPMENTS IN THE BALTICS DURING 2000–2012

12.2.1 Expansion (2000–2007)

The three Baltic economies experienced a strong expansion in the period from 2000 to 2007, when annual real growth averaged about 8 per cent (see Table 12.1).[2] To a large extent the robust growth was based on a rapid increase in the productive capacity of these economies. According to estimates by the European Commission, the potential output during that period expanded by 6 per cent annually. However, cyclical factors also played a significant role, especially during the latter part of the expansion. Although the Baltic countries entered the expansion with small negative output gaps, positive output gaps in all three countries exceeded an astonishing 10 per cent of their potential output near the peak of the cycle.

The primary driving force of the positive and reinforcing cyclical developments was the exceptionally high bank-intermediated capital inflow which led to a rapid credit expansion. From the supply side, these flows were generally supported by optimism regarding the growth prospects in the region and global factors such as low risk aversion and ample liquidity. Specifically to the Baltic countries, the very high relative level of these flows could be explained by the small size of these economies and by their proximity to the Nordic countries, where banks (especially the Swedish ones) had been among the first in Europe to start an active expansion of their retail banking activities abroad (Riksbank, 2007). In the process, the Nordic banks[3] opted for aggressive business strategies to gain market share and set nominal interest rates and other loan conditions at levels quite similar to their home markets.

The impact of these capital flows was magnified by several well-known channels. Firstly, the economic expansion and credit boom were amplified by the workings of the real interest rate channel. The credibility of the Baltic exchange rate regimes[4] and very optimistic credit risk assessments led to low nominal interest rates. This in turn accelerated output growth and inflation. As nominal interest rate dynamics were not affected by higher inflation, a strong positive feedback loop between decreasing real interest rates and accelerating growth and inflation took hold.

Table 12.1 Selected macroeconomic variables of the Baltic countries in 2000–2012

	2000–03	2004–07	2008	2009	2010	2011	2012
Real GDP growth (year on year, %)	7.4	8.8	−1.3	−15.6	1.1	6.3	3.2
Contribution of private consumption (percentage points)	4.6	7.4	−1.9	−12.6	−0.5	2.6	
Contribution of government consumption (percentage points)	0.4	0.6	0.4	−0.7	−0.4	0.2	
Contribution of investments (percentage points)	3.4	4.7	−5.8	−15.8	1.7	5.3	
Contribution of net exports (percentage points)	−1	−4	5.9	13.5	0.3	−1.7	
Share of manufacturing (% of GDP, constant prices)	16.1	16.3	15.5	14.3	16.3	17.5	
Share of construction (% of GDP, constant prices)	6.2	8.2	9.5	7	5.9	6.5	
Output gap (% of potential GDP)	−1	7.3	6.8	−10.1	−8.2	−2.2	−1
Inflation (year on year, %)	2.2	5.1	12.3	2.4	1	4.5	3.3
Unemployment rate (%)	13	7.5	6.3	14.8	17.9	14.7	13
Fiscal balance (% of GDP)	−1.4	−0.3	−4.4	−6.4	−4.7	−2.6	−2.2
Cyclically adjusted fiscal balance (% of GDP)	−1.1	−2	−5.5	−4.1	−2.6	−1.9	−1.7
General government gross debt (% of GDP)	13.8	11.2	12.4	23.1	28.2	27.4	28.5
Current account balance (% of GDP)	−6.9	−13.6	−11.9	5.6	2.5	−0.2	−0.7
Domestic investment (% of GDP)	25.3	32.7	29.5	16.6	18.6	23	23.8
National saving (% of GDP)	18.5	19.2	17.7	22.2	21.1	22.8	23.1

Share of world exports (5-year change)	26.7	44.8	34.6	21.3	8.9	20	−0.2
CPI-based REER (year on year, %)	1.3	1.4	7.6	4.6	−5.6	0.8	
Real unit labour costs (year on year, %)	−2	1.7	5.4	−0.6	−8.3	−4.1	
Nominal ULC-based REER (year on year, %)	0.7	8	10.1	−3.8	−8.8	0	
Private sector debt (% of GDP)	56.1	100.1	126.1	136.8	123.1	109.4	
Private sector credit flow (% of GDP)	11.2	26.9	12.2	−5	−6.2	1.2	
Gross external debt (% of GDP)	56.3	85.7	106	122.8	122.4	108	
Net international investment position (% of GDP)	−42	−63	−69.1	−74	−69.5	−61.2	
Real long-term interest rates (%)	4.8	−0.8	−4.3	9	6.6	1	
Residential property prices (year on year, %)	20.6	34.8	−3.8	−36.9	−5.6	12.9	

Note: CPI = index of consumer prices; REER = real exchange rate; ULC = unit labour costs.

Source: IMF (WEO database, October 2012), Eurostat, European Commission (AMECO database), Eesti Pank calculations.

Secondly, collateral and wealth effects played an important role. Rapidly increasing lending volumes increased the value of collateral by raising asset prices and increasing liquidity. This reduced reported loan losses and lowered the perceived credit risk of the borrowers, which in turn enabled the banks to continue extending credit. The positive financial loop between increasing collateral prices, loan volumes and economic activity was further magnified by the wealth effects from soaring asset prices.[5]

Thirdly, self-fulfilling expectations mattered. The relatively long period of high growth led to a gradual but quite significant rise in the estimates of the growth of potential output and long-run growth projections. Similarly the observed growth rates in several key economic and financial variables such as wages and property prices were often extrapolated to the future. All of this had a clear impact on investment and consumption decisions and thereby on economic activity. As a result, a strong reinforcing interplay between expectations and growth was formed.

In addition, the fiscal stance was slightly accommodative. Although the headline fiscal balances were quite close to zero in Latvia and Lithuania and in surplus in Estonia, the cyclically adjusted budget balances were slightly negative. The change in the fiscal stance was the largest between 2004 and 2007, when the cyclically adjusted budget balance deteriorated by two percentage points of GDP. In hindsight we can see that the fiscal policy did indeed act in a procyclical fashion.[6] However, it is hard to argue that a fiscal impulse of this size could have been a primary driver of the boom.

All of the above-mentioned factors – high capital flows via the financial sector, the feedback loops between the financial sector and the real economy, self-fulfilling expectations and an accommodative fiscal stance – contributed to a picture typical of foreign-financed credit booms. Real growth was increasingly based on the expansion of domestic demand; the current account deficit reached very high levels and high credit growth led to a rapid rise in private sector indebtedness. By the end of the expansion inflation accelerated and price and cost competitiveness indicators started to worsen. In addition to the build-up of financial and external imbalances, structural imbalances appeared. As a result of the credit boom, there was a rapid increase in the share of employment and value-added created in the construction and real estate sector.

In contrast, the developments in the competitiveness and export performance of the Baltic economies were not so clear-cut. The rapid expansion of the economy did lead to a clear increase in unit labour costs during the second half of the boom and to an increase in the consumer price-based real exchange rate by the end of the expansion. However, the worsening of the price and cost competitiveness indicators did not have a visible impact on exports, which continued to expand strongly until the end of 2008, when foreign trade collapsed globally. This is also evident in the dynamics of the share in world exports, which continued to grow throughout the expansionary phase.

12.2.2 Recession (2007–2008 and 2008–2009)

Recession did not hit the Baltic countries simultaneously. Both Estonia and Latvia, which had witnessed a stronger credit boom, entered the contractionary phase in the second half of 2007. In Lithuania, where rapid foreign-financed credit growth had started later, the expansion continued for longer and the economy started to shrink only in the third quarter of 2008.

In Estonia and Latvia, the recession can be divided into two distinct phases: (1) from the second half of 2007 to the intensification of the global financial crisis in autumn 2008; and (2) from autumn 2008 until the end of the recession by the end of 2009.[7] The first phase of the recession was relatively mild and can be characterized as a domestic-demand-led adjustment that was primarily related to deceleration of credit growth. By this stage the dependence of domestic demand on credit growth was such that even a relatively modest worsening in the credit risk and debt sustainability assessments of the Baltic economies by the Nordic banks had a significant impact. As a result domestic demand started to contract, mainly driven by a decline in investment. The recession was most visible in the real-estate sector, where prices fell and liquidity decreased. There was also an improvement in the current account balances. Still, the momentum of the expansion had been so strong that the impact of the correction in domestic demand did not have a clear effect on inflation and labour market variables. A stronger downturn was avoided due to export growth that continued until autumn 2008.

The second phase of the recession started with the deepening of the global financial crisis in September 2008 and was much more severe. Almost immediately there was a sharp reversal of foreign capital flows and steep fall in exports. The reversal was strongest for the capital flows via the domestic financial sector, reflecting both external and internal factors. With regard to external factors, rising global risk aversion and drying up of interbank markets caused significant liquidity and funding problems for the Nordic parent banks which had used these markets heavily to finance their activities in the Baltics. As a result, they were forced to retrench. Indeed, there is evidence that the Nordic banks that were more exposed to the interbank market were forced to deleverage more strongly in the Baltic countries (Dabušinskas and Randveer, 2011).

In addition, the reversal of capital flows reflected a sharp deterioration in the risk assessment of the Baltic economies. The global financial crisis clearly exposed the large external and financial vulnerabilities of these economies, increased the probability of the realization of tail risks (e.g. a sharp devaluation and systemic financial crisis) and created a strong incentive to rapidly reduce exposure to these countries. A good example is the rapid outflow of non-resident deposits from Latvia and the inability of several domestically owned Baltic banks to refinance their external liabilities. The severe liquidity and funding problems in one of the largest domestically owned Latvian banks and the subsequent request by the Latvian authorities for international financial assistance confirmed the seriousness of these risks.

In addition to the sudden stop and the subsequent outflow of capital, the small and open Baltic economies were greatly influenced by the huge negative shock to the world trade. The impact of the negative shock was stronger than average given that the Baltic economies trade intensively with each other and with Finland, Sweden and Russia, all of which recorded relatively large falls in their effective foreign demand. As a result the exports of goods and services in the Baltic economies fell by more than 15 per cent in 2009 as compared to the previous year.

The reversal in capital flows and the fall in exports resulted in a sharp and severe contraction in domestic demand. The brunt of the adjustment fell on investment (especially in the real-estate and construction sector), which halved in 2009, and on private consumption, which declined by one-fifth. The adjustment was by and large amplified via the same channels as during the expansion. Now the real interest channel operated in the opposite direction. The negative financial loop between falling asset prices, contracting loan volumes and economic activity further dampened demand via collateral and wealth effects. Finally, the self-fulfilling nature of expectations magnified the severity of the recession. As a result, the output gap turned strongly negative and the current account balance turned positive in 2009.

During the recession, the impact of fiscal policies on economic activity was moderate. There was a clear element of countercyclicality in 2008, when the cyclically adjusted budget balance deteriorated by 3.5 percentage points of GDP. However, by the end of the 2008 the headline fiscal balances were at a clear risk of becoming too high, especially given that access to international financial markets was limited for the Baltic countries. There were important country-specific factors as well: fiscal policy in Estonia was much influenced by the goal of achieving the convergence criteria and one of the main preconditions of the international assistance to Latvia was the strengthening of fiscal discipline. As a result, the fiscal impulse in 2009 was negative.

Despite the severity of the cumulative output losses, ranging from 16 per cent in Lithuania to 25 per cent in Latvia, the Baltic economies were relatively resilient. Although banks had contributed to the build-up of imbalances, disorderly deleveraging and bank failures were mostly avoided, displaying the importance of adequate capital buffers in the banking sector and recourse to liquidity via their parent banks. The flexibility of the Baltic economies also facilitated the necessary structural and macroeconomic adjustments.

12.2.3   Recovery (2009–2010)

The recovery of the Baltic economies started in the second half of 2009 and real annual growth averaged slightly above 3.5 per cent during 2010–2012. Initially the pick-up in economic activity was mostly based on strong export growth. The decline in export volume in 2009 was mostly offset in the next year, and by 2011 exports were markedly higher than pre-crisis levels. The contribution of domestic demand, especially investment, has gradually increased as well.

The reduction in various imbalances that started during the recession has continued during the recovery. The progress has been clear with respect to external and financial vulnerabilities. A significant improvement has been achieved with regard to the current accounts, which are now close to balance. During the recovery there has also been a significant deleveraging in the private sector. Together with the increases in nominal incomes this has led to a notable reduction in both domestic and external indebtedness.

In 2010 there were solid improvements in cost and price competitiveness indicators, which have been maintained in the following two years. Both Consumer Price Index (CPI)-based and unit labour cost-based real effective exchange rates have depreciated noticeably. The improvement in relative cost and price levels has also been accompanied by a sectoral reorientation from the construction and real-estate sectors to manufacturing. In addition there has been also been progress in fiscal consolidation.

12.3   COMPARISON OF THE ADJUSTMENT OF THE BALTIC ECONOMIES WITH IRELAND, GREECE AND PORTUGAL

The comparison of the adjustment in the Baltics with Ireland, Greece and Portugal (also referred to as the euro area-3 in the following), after the cyclical peak in 2007–2008 is valuable as there are many similarities

Table 12.2   Changes in real GDP since 2007 in the Baltics and Ireland, Greece and Portugal

	Change in GDP from cyclical peak to trough during 2007–09 crisis (%)	Change in GDP from cyclical peak in 2007/08 to current GDP level (Q2 2012) (%)	GDP level in Q2 2012 (2000 = 100)
Latvia	−24.6	−15.1	156.9
Estonia	−19.5	−6.3	157.5
Lithuania	−15.9	−6.4	166.9
Ireland	−10.7	−8.4	132.3
Portugal	−4.1	−6.4	102.0
Greece	−	−18.3	110.9
Cyprus	−3.0	−2.3	130.2
Spain	−4.9	−5.3	121.6
Italy	−7.1	−6.9	101.9
EU-27 average	−8.4	−3.6	130.2

Source: Eurostat, Eesti Pank calculations.

between these country groups. Firstly, an obvious advantage is that we are analysing the same time period, which enables us to control for some of the impact from the international economic environment. Secondly, both country groups showed significant vulnerabilities and imbalances prior to the crisis. Thirdly, from a country perspective all of the countries were unable (Ireland, Greece and Portugal) or unwilling (the Baltic countries) to adjust via changes in nominal exchange rates.

Indeed, from a qualitative point of view, there are many similarities in the economic adjustment of both country groups. All of the countries have witnessed severe recessions that have been characterized by exceptionally large cumulative declines in domestic demand and strong increases in unemployment (see Table 12.2 and Figure 12.1). After an initial significant deterioration in fiscal balances, these countries have embarked on a process of fiscal consolidation, which has resulted in a marked improvement in fiscal balances. As compared to the period prior to the crisis, current account balances and several price and cost competitiveness indicators have improved.

At the same time, there are also significant differences. The most obvious one is in the speed of adjustment. For almost all key macroeconomic variables, the adjustment in the Baltics was at least twice as fast. An important example is the correction in current account balances. The sharp reversal of capital inflows into the Baltics brought about a rapid improvement in current account balances. In Ireland, Greece and Portugal the adjustment has been much more protracted. As a flipside, the sharp improvement in the current account balances in the Baltics has enabled these economies to avoid a significant increase in indebtedness, while Ireland, Greece and Portugal have all witnessed a sharp increase in their public and private sector debts.

There are several explanations for the large difference in the speed of adjustment between the two country groups. In our view, the main reason is the ability of the countries to mitigate the impact of the sudden stop in private sector capital flows, which took place in all of the six economies during 2007–2009. As members of the euro area, Ireland, Greece and Portugal were able to draw on a very substantial central bank liquidity support, which to a large extent offset the very high private capital outflows. For the Baltics this option was not available.[8]

The variation in the speed of adjustment can also be explained by the differences in the conduct of fiscal policy, especially in the first phase of the cycle. As compared to the Baltics, the deepening of the financial crisis in autumn 2008 clearly had a weaker impact on Greece and Portugal. Therefore these economies were initially able to postpone fiscal consolidation. Later on, international financial assistance programmes enabled the three euro area countries to avoid a sharper fiscal consolidation. Among the Baltic countries, only Latvia applied for the EU and International Monetary Fund (IMF) financial assistance programme.

The two country groups offer two noticeably different experiences of adjustment. What can we learn about the advantages and disadvantages of 'fast' versus 'slow' adjustment from these episodes? We will turn to this question in the next section.

12.4 THE ADVANTAGES AND DISADVANTAGES OF FAST VERSUS GRADUAL ADJUSTMENT

In our view the disadvantages of a fast adjustment include: (1) the possibility of a costly overreaction; (2) political difficulties; and (3) the likelihood of mistakes in economic policy.

A sharp economic adjustment might result in an overreaction of certain variables. For instance, in the case of the Baltic countries, a relevant example would be the dynamics of current account balances, which fluctuated from a deficit of 18 per cent of GDP in 2007 to a surplus close to 6 per cent of GDP in 2009, and again to a small deficit in 2011. Under such conditions, a sharp tightening of financing conditions and large capital outflows could conceivably create severe liquidity problems for otherwise

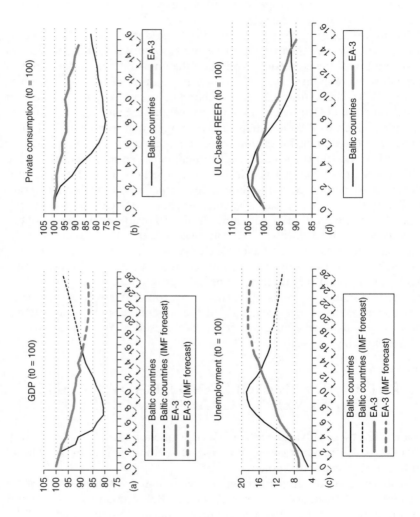

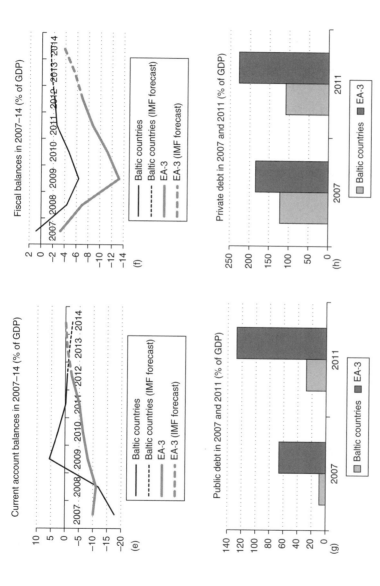

Note: Dashed lines are IMF forecasts until end-2014. EA-3 = Greece, Ireland and Portugal; REER = real exchange rate; ULC = unit labour costs.

Source: IMF (WEO database, October 2012), Eurostat, Eesti Pank calculations.

Figure 12.1 Macroeconomic variables for the Baltics and Greece, Ireland and Portugal compared

viable firms. If these firms were to be forced out of business, it might lead to losses in both physical and human capital. Policy-makers seeking to avoid such an outcome might seek to achieve a more gradual adjustment.

A significant economic adjustment is bound to create strong public resistance and thereby cause major political difficulties. This is likely to be especially relevant if the electorate is uninformed of the causes and the need for adjustment and very reluctant toward change. Under these circumstances, policy-makers might again opt for a more gradual adjustment.

In addition, as the quality of economic policy measures is crucial during the crisis, a very fast adjustment might leave too little time for the authorities to devise appropriate policy responses. Therefore, a very fast adjustment could lead to avoidable policy mistakes.

At the same time, there are also numerous clear advantages to a faster adjustment. Firstly, previous experience has shown that a successful implementation of the necessary measures, including fiscal consolidation and structural reforms, is dependent on avoiding reform fatigue. In this respect the fast adjustment in the Baltics has been quite successful.

Secondly, the comparison between the two country groups has demonstrated that the fast adjustment in the current account and fiscal balances in the Baltic countries has helped to avoid a significant increase in public and private sector indebtedness. As a result the starting position for the recovery has been much more favourable for the Baltic countries, as shown by the different growth performance and outlook.

Thirdly, the adjustment usually also entails the necessity to correct structural imbalances. A familiar example is the need to shift labour and capital from the non-tradable to the tradable sector. In this respect sharper adjustment helps to complete a faster closure of clearly unsustainable firms and thereby increase the growth of productive capacity in these economies.

Lastly, an adjustment is likely to create a great deal of uncertainty about the growth prospects of the economy, which is going to negatively affect aggregate demand, especially investment decisions. Again, if faster adjustment achieves an early return of confidence, this is bound to have a positive effect on growth prospects.

Although we can list the pros and cons of fast versus gradual correction, there is often not much of a choice about the speed of adjustment. For instance, the sharp adjustment in the Baltics was to a large extent inevitable. The Baltic economies had limited policy space when they were hit by a sharp reversal of capital flows and a very strong negative trade shock.

However, the impact of these shocks and the potential negative effects of the fast adjustment were mitigated by two factors. As discussed earlier, the Baltic economies were quite resilient despite the sharp downturn. They continued to have good long-run growth potential, and banking sectors were well capitalized and largely owned by strong foreign banks with good access to central bank liquidity assistance in their home markets. The fast adjustment was also facilitated by relatively flexible labour markets and large tradable sectors. In addition, the fast adjustment was made possible by reasonably high public acceptance of the necessary changes. There was an understanding that a part of the earlier growth, especially in the real-estate and construction sector, was unsustainable. The good performance prior to the crisis and the possibility of emigration also mattered.

Overall, the available evidence on the recovery, the correction of the macroeconomic and structural imbalances, and the good growth prospects allow us to conclude that the speedier resolution of the crisis and the fast adjustment has been a successful response in the Baltic economies.

12.5 CONCLUDING REMARKS

The recent cyclical pattern of the Baltic economies demonstrates that under a credible fixed exchange rate arrangement there are several channels (e.g. the real interest channel) that might strongly amplify the effects of various shocks. Therefore there is a need to address the build-up of imbalances and vulnerabilities early and decisively. The necessity of pre-emptive policy measures is also underscored by the lessons from the euro area debt crisis, which confirm that adjustment afterwards via wages and prices is likely to be protracted and painful.

The experience of the Baltic and euro area countries show that a strong external anchor in the form of a membership in a currency union or a credible fixed exchange rate regime might lead to policy complacency. The current financial and sovereign distress in the euro area is a good example that such an anchor cannot be a substitute for policy discipline in other areas. On the contrary, there is a need for stronger discipline in other economic policies.

The adjustment in the Baltic countries has provided a more solid foundation for future growth. The external and financial vulnerabilities have been reduced and a significant sectoral reorientation and elimination of unsustainable activities and businesses have been achieved. However, various shocks continue to pose a challenge. Therefore a more active use of fiscal and macro-prudential police measures is warranted. Also the resilience of the economies has to be maintained.

NOTES

1. We would like to thank Liina Kulu and Krista Talvis for excellent research assistance and Karsten Staehr and Märten Ross for discussions and helpful comments.
2. A comparative analysis of the Baltic countries prior to and after the onset of the global financial crisis is also provided by Bakker and Klingen (2012), European Commission (2010), Brixiova et al. (2009) and Gardo and Martin (2010).
3. Nordic banks dominated the banking sector in the Baltic countries. By 2007, the share of Nordic banks as measured by their share of assets of total banking sector assets exceeded 90 per cent in Estonia and Lithuania and 60 per cent in Latvia.
4. During this period, Estonia and Lithuania operated under a currency board arrangement (CBA). In Latvia a fixed exchange rate regime quite similar to a CBA was used.
5. The cumulative nominal house price growth in 2001–2007 was 310 per cent in Estonia, 335 per cent in Lithuania and 655 per cent in Latvia (ECB 2010, 2012).
6. The revisions to output gap estimates for the Baltic countries were much larger than for the large majority of other EU countries. For instance, in autumn 2007 the available estimates for the output gaps in the Baltics indicated positive output gaps in the range of 1 to 3 per cent of the potential output. According to the latest estimates, however, the positive output gaps amounted to an extraordinary 10 per cent of potential output.
   Some specific fiscal policy measures such as a reduction of tax deductibility of interest rate payments of mortgages were introduced. However, along with measures in prudential regulation that were focused on strengthening the capital base of the banks and increases in reserve requirement, they did not have a clear impact on overheating.
7. In the case of Lithuania, the first phase from the second half of 2007 to the intensification of the global financial crisis in autumn 2008 could better be described as an economic slowdown. However, the second phase of the recession (autumn 2008 until the end of 2009) was qualitatively quite similar in all of the Baltic countries.
8. Recourse to liquidity in the Baltic economies was mostly offered by the Nordic parent banks. The significance of this support is underscored by the fact that it was indeed the liquidity problem in the large domestically owned bank in Latvia that was one of the main triggers for the application for the international financial programme. However, the help from the Nordic banks was more akin to a liquidity backstop, and the Nordic banks have visibly reduced their exposure in their Baltic subsidiaries, thereby contributing to capital outflows.

REFERENCES

Bakker, B.B. and C. Klingen (eds) (2012), 'How emerging Europe came through the 2008/09 crisis: an account by the staff of the IMF's European department', Washington, DC: International Monetary Fund.

Brixiova, Z., L. Vartia and A. Worgötter (2009), 'Capital inflows, household debt and the boom-bust cycle in Estonia', OECD Economics Department Working Paper No. 700.

Dabušinskas, A. and M. Randveer (2011), 'The financial crisis and the baltic countries', in M. Beblavy, D. Cobham and L. Odor (eds), *The Euro Area and the Financial Crisis*, Cambridge: Cambridge University Press, pp. 97–128.

European Central Bank (2010), 'Convergence Report 2010'.

European Central Bank (2012), 'Convergence Report 2012'.

European Commission (2010), 'Cross-country study. Economic policy challenges in the Baltics', Occasional Paper no. 58.

Gardo, S. and R. Martin (2010), 'The impact of the global economic and financial crisis on Central, Eastern and South-Eastern Europe', ECB Occasional Paper No. 114.

Riksbank (2007), 'Financial Stability Report', 1, available at http://www.riksbank.se/Pagefolders/30482/nr24e.pdf.

PART V

A Practitioner's View

13. Basel III from a practitioner's perspective

Esa Tuomi and Eriks Plato

13.1 HISTORICAL CIRCUMSTANCES

Modern international financial cooperation can be said to have begun in 1930, with the establishment of the Bank for International Settlements (BIS). The BIS was initially set up to facilitate German World War I reparations, but effectively took over management of the Bretton Woods system of foreign exchange in 1945. In order to provide the Bretton Woods system with more tools for policy management, the International Monetary Fund (IMF) and the World Bank also were created at this time. This was the first time that a large number of nations (44 initially) had negotiated a fixed monetary and exchange rate regime.

The Bretton Woods system broke down in 1971 and this led to the threat of instability of large cross-border financial institutions speculating across many currencies and time zones. The focus then turned to regulating the institutions themselves rather than managing a fixed rigid system.

In 1974, the Basel Committee on Banking Supervision was created at the BIS. The culmination of cooperation in regulating banks came in 1988 with the adoption of the Basel I Accord. Originally 13 countries were party to the Accord, but more than 100 others eventually enacted the principles in their national regulatory framework.

The work of the Basel Committee is based on working groups focused on Standards Implementation, Policy Development, Accounting and Consultation. The Policy Development working group is the one that works out the actual regulatory proposals and its work is also divided into numerous subgroups. Each member country appoints its representatives to this work and generally they are central bankers, treasurers or other high-ranking policy-makers in their respective countries. It is important to realize that this is no anonymous, academic body, but rather an assembly of national policy-makers.

The main goal of Basel I was to introduce a standardized framework of banking supervision. It introduced five risk classes (weightings) and a universal 8 per cent capital requirement in a document consisting of 30 pages. It is important to note that the Basel Accords are only a cooperative framework and that the actual legislation is enacted at a national level. So, in fact, far more than 30 pages of regulations had to be complied with. The actual regulation that banks followed went into hundreds of pages (per country).

Given the success of Basel I, in terms of actually having negotiated a set of international regulatory standards, very soon work began on improvements to the framework. Simply put, Basel I was seen as being too simplistic. Actual risks within the individual asset classes might vary a lot. It was plain to anyone that a large manufacturer with a 100-year track record listed in the United Kingdom constituted a different credit risk than the start-up of a rural restaurant in Afghanistan. This had not been taken into account at all in the original Basel framework.

In the 1990s the committee, together with the banking industry, discussed a new, much more comprehensive and, supposedly, more realistic policy framework based on sound economic rationale. The proposal for a new framework came from the Committee in 1999 and it was finally worked out and adopted in 2004 with a number of subsequent revisions.

On 347 pages, the Basel II Accord outlines a regulatory framework based on three pillars:

- Pillar 1 outlines the capital requirements based on credit, operational and market risk.
- Pillar 2 outlines how the authorities should monitor the banks.
- Pillar 3 outlines the reporting requirements by the banks.

Once again, this is only the outline. The actual regulations are national. In the 27 member countries of the European Union (EU), it is the EU Banking Directive that legislates the overall Basel II framework, yet the actual regulations are adopted at a national level. Therefore, there are thousands of pages of regulations that a bank must comply with. Unfortunately, many countries such as the United States, China and Russia have not fully adopted Basel II and even in those that did adopt the new standards, most banks have yet to meet all of the requirements.

The core of Basel II is Pillar 1, which prescribes the actual capital requirements for credit, market and operational risk. For each one of these areas the following approaches are possible:

- Standardized approach: all parameters are external.
- Foundation internal ratings-based approach: customer ratings are internal (i.e. use the banks' historical data for probabilities of default).

- Advanced internal ratings-based approach: credit conversion factors, loss-given default and certain other parameters internalized.

Basel II is really quite theoretically sound, to the extent that it provides for credit risk differentiation-based company probabilities of default, empirically observed losses given default, and adjustments for products and maturities. In addition, it also provides for market and operational risk. Quite magnificent to be able to match regulations to real-life expected outcomes of financial transactions. Unfortunately, it did not work.

The events of 2008 provided ample evidence that the existing regulatory framework will not prevent the type of crisis that occurred. In fact, it can be argued as to whether bank regulation or deregulation (i.e. the repeal of the Glass–Steagal Act in the United States) had any impact at all. After all, Lehman Brothers did not fail because it engaged in retail banking nor did Washington Mutual fail because it engaged in investment banking. In fact, the entire United States (US) subprime crisis that precipitated the Great Recession did not arise due to inadequate regulation. The regulations on mortgage finance in the United States are quite comprehensive and seem quite reasonable. However, the regulations in place were obviously not adequately enforced.

It seems that another reason for the crisis was the lack of understanding of many bank decision-makers on the nature of the risks that they were undertaking. Once again, it is not so certain that you can entirely regulate away stupidity.

At the end of the day, banks alone had to write off US$3–4 trillion and the costs to the overall economy are difficult to ascertain. One anti-Wall Street non-governmental organization (NGO) calculated the cost to the US economy at roughly US$12 trillion in lost gross domestic product (GDP). Whatever the actual numbers, the impact was huge on banks, on governments and on societies.

There was a public outcry. 'Obviously someone has to pay.' Though nobody relevant has yet been prosecuted. 'Obviously, bankers are greedy.' Though banks have been bashed in the press, one must remember the old adage that 'sticks and stones may break my bones, but words will never hurt me'. Obviously, laws must be enacted so that this does not happen again. Unfortunately, here the public got its wish.

13.1.1 Policy Reaction

If 347 pages of regulation did not work, then what is the solution? Well, according to the Basel Committee, add another 616 pages and we can provide a much more stable regulatory environment. Remember, this again means thousands of extra pages in EU and local regulations.

In June 2011, the Basel III Accord was published and is expected to be implemented from 2013 to 2018. However, it is not clear which countries will follow it and whether the aforementioned timetable will not be extended. In fact, some parameters have yet to be established, but require a period of observation to ascertain the appropriate limits. In short, Basel III requires more capital and more liquidity in banks.

Not only will banks have to hold more capital, but a larger share of this capital will have to be in the form of common equity, which will form half of the required 9 per cent capital required. The amount of capital will go up to 13 per cent for most global systemically important financial institutions (another Basel III concept that includes 29 banks), due to the requirement to have an additional 2.5 per cent conservation buffer on top of all the other buffers. On top of this, some countries want even higher capital requirements, with Sweden in particular calling for a 14 per cent level.

In essence, capital requirements are still determined according to Basel II methodology, but then roughly another 40 to 50 per cent is added by the regulators as a buffer. It does make one wonder why all of the complicated calculations are needed in the first place.

In fact, 'complicated' is a severe understatement. Default probabilities are calculated based on a bank's own internal data using statistical cycles of up to 25 years. That is a lot of data on customers, products, individual collateral, and so on. Calculations for derivatives exposures are based on highly complex value-at-risk modelling. All in all, a bank may be using hundreds of formulas to calculate millions of parameters. The systems are so complex that no single individual is cognitively capable of mastering the entire framework. Plus, the more borders the bank crosses, the more complications arise.

Yet when it comes to operating risk, the situation is unfortunately exactly the opposite. The statistical database may not currently be sufficiently large in most banks to provide a meaningful degree of statistical confidence.

Of course, where statistics are not sufficiently available, the Basel framework allows banks to use the standardized approach, which is in principle much more akin to the Basel I approach. In essence, all parameters are externally standardized and no internal data are used. One point of criticism levelled at the Basel standardized approach is that it gives great weight to agency ratings, which have historically been shown not to be reliable in all situations.

Unfortunately, for smaller banks using the standardized approach, the amount of capital required will be significantly higher (maybe 20 to 40 per cent as opposed to using internalized data). It has yet to be seen what the impact will be on the competitiveness of smaller financial institutions.

Two more Basel III ratios, the liquidity ratio and the net stable funding ratio, were originally intended to provide so much liquidity reserves that the tenet of the central bank as a lender of last resort would be completely irrelevant. However, the central bankers need not fear for their jobs, because both of these ratios have been watered down substantially and their implementation postponed. The main driver was an estimated €1.8 trillion shortfall in the EU alone in liquidity under the original rules. The new rules would also have limited the use of mortgage-backed securities and sovereign debt for liquidity purposes. However, both will be eligible once again under the supervision of local regulatory authorities, which at times in certain countries have been quite flexible as to the types of instruments that are defined as eligible in both instances.

Basel III's most significant impact is in the requirement for more capital. This is necessary and has historically proven to be significant. The means of reaching this goal, however, add significant levels of compliance and reporting complexity that make this relatively simple principle absurdly Byzantine and costly to manage.

13.2 BANK REACTION

Banks have no choice. They must follow the law. Of course, banks lobby to make both rational, necessary changes in the law and some self-serving ones, but that is democracy. In fact, some argue that bank lobbying brought about many of the bizarre changes in Basel II and III that require substantial mental gymnastics to explain. Small companies fail more often than large ones. However, Basel II will argue that small companies fail due to idiosyncratic shocks (i.e. one-offs) rather than systemic shocks which influence larger companies. The research shows mixed results. What is clear, however, is that many European banks that depended highly on small and medium-sized enterprise (SME) business lobbied hard to ease the capital requirements for these companies, and it does seem that the current manifestation of this parameter is the result.

Some other aspects of Basel are not the result of lobbying but are nonetheless not immediately intuitive. For example, the effect of maturity on capital requirements. Better-rated companies have to hold more capital for long-term exposures than poorly rated ones. This may go against common sense, but the rating is only forward-looking for the next 12 months, so for any period after this there is a probability that the company could be downgraded requiring more capital. This is a typical example of the type of nuances in the models and formulas that banks have to deal with.

In any event, the banks have been forced to act. A higher level of capitalization is required, but given the amounts and the depressed economic environment, retained earnings will not be sufficient. It is also hard for European banks to raise capital, when the average return on investment is around 7 per cent. Though banks will try to do both, they must also look at better balance sheet management.

In other words, find more capital in the existing balance sheet through:

- better reporting of existing business with a view to enabling banks to fully use the Basel framework to lower capital requirements;
- implementation of the more advanced Basel approaches, which use more internal data;
- reducing the balance sheet through deleveraging;
- repricing;
- attempting to increase income through cost cutting and efficiency to retain more earnings and make the banks more attractive to investors.

Estimates vary, but McKinsey & Company (2012) believe that banks could add from 30 basis points to 160 basis points to their return on investment through technical means. This includes:

- more accurate reporting;
- improved risk management models;
- application of more advanced approaches to portfolios.

The problem is in the complexity. The circa 1000 pages of Basel II and III are filtered through EU Banking Directives into thousands of pages of local regulatory requirements. The exact wording of the requirements may also be slightly different in different EU countries and this may have an impact with regard to how they are implemented (mostly unintentionally). In this sense, banking regulatory compliance more resembles twelfth–thirteenth-century religious arguments over nuances of the Bible than following the law. There is so much detail that is at times written so ambiguously that it provides ample fodder for argument and discussion. Remember, more countries compound the number of pages.

However, the more advanced Basel approaches require a multitude of basic information. Each customer's rating (probability of default), various products and their usage, loan maturities, along with detailed information on collateral must all be sourced from all systems in the bank. Add to this the historical data and banks are dealing with tens of millions, if not hundreds of millions, of pieces of data on a monthly basis. If this entails numerous systems in various countries then these data must all be standardized and centralized for use.

This information and its eligibility are also strictly governed by the Basel rules. For example, not all collateral counts. In the foundation internal ratings-based approach, where product parameters are externalized, leasing is treated the same as a collateralized loan, while for factoring the external rating of the insurance company will determine collateral coverage. All reporting systems must reflect all of these rules (and there is a considerable amount) or the data will not be eligible.

Of course, the enticement is the promise of less capital. The more data, the more the advanced approach can be used. In the Basel framework, the approach used on any particular portfolio of credit risk will be approved by the local financial supervisory authority. The scope of the portfolio that the approach will apply to is also approved by the supervisory authorities.

In order to gain the capital benefits inherent in the more advanced approaches, those banks that have the data are applying to the supervisory authorities to use the more advanced approaches on as many portfolios as possible. This is not quite as easy as it sounds. The Bank must prove to the financial supervisory authority that:

- it has the relevant data;
- the data are systematically accurate (automation is crucial);
- the models that use the data are reliable and compliant with the framework.

These are not small projects but require much work and resources, and quite often substantial investments in information technology (IT). The supervisory authorities for their part are quite sophisticated and not easy to convince. After all, they are charged with safeguarding the public (not shareholder) interests.

Another technical initiative will be to review the current risk models in use. Banks will explore any adjustments to be made due to recent events to the actual formulas and weightings of parameters. Banks will seek to compare their own models and results with those of peers to see whether they have comparable models. Unfortunately, under Basel each bank works with its own specific models, which may be based on different weightings of the same parameters achieving substantial differences in ratings for the same corporate balance sheet. So it is quite possible that some of the differences in capital for some banks are due to a 'better model'. Of course, the supervisory authorities will be very cautious with any such initiative, but that is their job.

While all of this technical work is going on, the banks are also looking at cleaning up their business lines. Though no magic wand or truly 'capital light' business model exists, banks are rebalancing funding, reducing unnecessary credit lines and off-balance exposures, reducing exposures in certain industries such as real estate (that are capital intense, but with little possibility for other income generation), asking for more collateral, shorter maturities and trying to cherry pick the best-rated customers. Unfortunately, there are a lot of smart bankers out there and when they all try to cherry pick, the result is severe margin pressure for certain customers. This presents a conundrum.

In the years leading up to the current crisis, banks were not adequately charging for ratings-based capital allocations. Pricing due to competition was low in all ratings classes but the difference between best and mediocre was around 50 per cent, whereas it should be around 200 to 300 per cent and more. This is just to adequately charge for Basel II. (Strangely enough, the biggest impact from Basel III may not be to reduce banking sector risk, but to get all banks to fully implement Basel II as quickly as possible.) The problem with raising prices to an adequate degree is that in an environment of depressed demand with a substantial supply (one could argue the world has too many banks), competition is high. High competition reduces prices. Therefore, there is only one other avenue to take: cost-cutting.

Of course, as all companies during a prolonged boom, banks became very large and paid insufficient attention to efficiency. All over Europe, one can see banks closing branches, reducing staff, outsourcing some services and automating others. After these reductions, the remaining organization is optimized in terms of structure and management to try to reduce costs. Banks probably have to achieve around two-thirds of the net result increase through cost decreases. This is pretty dramatic by any stretch of the imagination.

Automation and IT are a constant mantra of consultants, but in reality what first needs to be redesigned are the underlying work processes. This is hard work. Processes should not only be efficient, but they should also be built so as to get the most benefit from Basel ('regulatory based reorganization'). One example could be as simple as harmonizing all collateral and product information at the point of sale to maximize regulatory impact. Products and collaterals can be grouped according to their regulatory classifications. Data relevant to the regulatory framework should already be prioritized in the front office.

Every manager should review key processes to reduce a signature here, a report there. In other words, what is nice to have versus what is critical to have. Given the bleak employment picture for bankers in the United States and the EU, managers are quite focused and ready to do their part. Now is the time to promote change.

Yet this leads to one complication. Banks are undertaking such a wide variety of initiatives, in reaction to the crisis in general and Basel in particular, that a distinct management risk arises. Too many change processes and projects are being undertaken at the same time.

13.3 IMPLICATIONS FOR THE CORPORATE CUSTOMER RELATIONSHIP

Corporate customer relations will certainly be impacted by Basel. The first thing most corporate customers noticed in 2008 and 2009 was that finance was no longer available to all. It started as a result of funding restrictions, but is now a matter of banks using their balance sheet very selectively for their best customers.

Secondly, what money is available is for shorter maturities. Paradoxically, banks want more high-rated customers, but the Basel advanced approach will require relatively more capital for longer maturities. Therefore, the market should tend to concentrate on maturities not exceeding 3–5 years. Tenors in excess of five years will be regarded as the exception amongst some commercial banks.

Thirdly, many customers will face higher pricing. This is an objective necessity of pricing for more capital. The increases in capital costs are so large that only some of the price increase will remain as profit. More will have to come from cost-cutting.

That leads to the fourth major impact: reduced quality and availability of service. With the closure of branches and reductions in staff, service quality can drop. However, this will also force banks to become more efficient and rely on more e-banking and automated solutions. At the end of the process, the customers will receive better service than before the crisis.

Finally, one must expect other terms and conditions for credit to change. Collateral will be a high priority and one should also expect more Basel-related covenants (i.e. tied to parameters that impact upon a particular bank's internal rating system such as equity, interest coverage, liquidity ratios, etc.)

Beyond these features of immediate change, there will be other more gradual changes. It is quite possible that completely universal banks will no longer be the norm. As Basel is not based on any particular bank's historical portfolio data, some banks may have ratios that favour certain industries as opposed to others. This may lead some banks to concentrate on some industries while shunning others.

This thinking may also be extended to geography. For a while, the markets priced the EU as one country. Unfortunately, we now see how different the countries actually are in terms of development, credit and market risk. Banks engaged in cross-border banking will be taking a hard look at all of the geographic markets they are in and assessing whether they should be there in the first place. There have already been quite a few European banks that have withdrawn from certain markets, which is also a possibility to deleverage some assets that are not deemed core.

One thing is certain: almost all banks will require ancillary business in conjunction with credits. Cross-selling will be an increasingly important theme, especially as concerns cash management (i.e. transactional banking). For those banks for which funding is important or even critical, when the European Central Bank (ECB) reduces its life-supporting liquidity facilities, current account balances will become a must for any credit. One would expect that most banks will automatically require a proportion of a customer's account turnover relative to credit exposure.

Because of the continuing counterparty risks, corporate customers will increasingly view the banks from a risk perspective. It is clear that banks that are not sufficiently large will have a clear disadvantage under Basel compared to those banks that require less capital, because they can use more advanced approaches. Of course, banks with an ownership less concerned by return on investment (such as cooperatives or state-owned institutions) may ignore Basel pricing adjustments and gain a competitive advantage in terms of market share. However, those banks whose owners care about capital will be increasing prices and decreasing costs, but not all will do so. That is just the nature of a market economy. Customers know this and will be cautious. There is, of course, one final risk for everyone involved: too much regulation. A positive is that this should create more space for bond financing and new players will enter the corporate finance market.

13.4   UNINTENDED CONSEQUENCES

As Basel III is driving the implementation of Basel II, banks are seriously reviewing everything through the eyes of the regulatory framework. This is a consideration when choosing customers, developing pricing policy, reorganizing, reducing staff, structuring products and transactions, and choosing which countries to work in. In other words, Basel is driving real-life business decisions to a greater degree than anything seen in banking before.

Unfortunately, Basel is a regulatory framework: a model. As yet, no human model has ever fully been able to fully model complex real-world events. The Basel models also have not worked. Look at 2008. Basel II did not work. Basel III is adding complexity without any real assurance that the final implemented version will have any real chance of preventing the next crisis. (Is that even a realistic objective?) The real tangible benefit of Basel III will be to increase the capital that banks hold. This is good, but the complexity is adding costs and hidden risks.

It is arguably easier to circumvent very complex regulations than very simple ones. Indeed, this has been put forward as one of the reasons that no bankers have yet been prosecuted for not following the rules and regulations already in force in 2008–2009. Loopholes can be found in any set of regulations, but the complexity of Basel will ensure that any circumvention will be even more complex. Therefore, the stability of the entire system may actually be reduced through the creation of ever more incomprehensible investment vehicles and financial legal structures.

More complexity leads to one certainty. Banks will need substantially more people and resources working on compliance issues, while society will need ever more and more sophisticated regulators.

As banks emulate the world of Basel in real life, we could see more reliance on product profitability rather than customer profitability. The basic premise of relationship banking could be under threat, in order to achieve short-term financial results. The ownership of banks is also likely to change. It is hard to see many of the current owners of banks being satisfied with 8 to 10 per cent long-term return on investment levels.

The market distortion of Basel, together with the market distortion of policy-makers' support for banks during the crisis, ensure that many banks that should have failed will live, while others that would have lived will die. This is a dramatic compounding of the moral hazard that has been a common thread throughout this crisis. This will most certainly decrease the public faith in the banking industry.

Once the die-off has occurred and competition is reduced, the remaining banks may adjust their pricing according to regulatory models that do not reflect business or economic rationale. This would make the banks less efficient as businesses. Basel is already leading banks to terminate some long-term customer relationships, in order to manage short-term requirements. To the people involved on both sides, this is a pity.

Yet the most striking, but little-mentioned, consequence of the Basel framework is that it makes the banking system much less transparent.

Given that risks are modelled by internal data for each portfolio, it is not possible to fully compare any two portfolios, let alone any two banks. This is further compounded by the use of different approaches, which are also not comparable. Given that so many business processes and decisions are impacted upon by Basel, this lack of Basel transparency also shrouds everything else the bank is doing. There is no way for a bank analyst to be able to see a particular business or strategic decision as related to regulatory impact, if that information is not made explicitly public. The risk-adjusted return on capital at risk for any particular bank has no analytical relevance outside of the financial institution. By definition, these returns cannot be compared across banks.

Unfortunately, Basel has not altered the real-life fact that markets with more information are more efficient than markets with less information. Of course, there could be other positive consequences. The drive towards efficiency, if managed correctly, should substantially improve the level of service quality and the long-term financial stability of the surviving banks. In other words, society will have better banks.

If Basel were to force a change of ownership to those investors looking for lower risk at lower rates of return, then once again society could benefit. Less profit maximization in the financial industry should lead to less unhealthy risk-taking.

13.5   CONCLUSION

Whatever the ultimate consequences of Basel III, it is here and it is here to stay. It will add to complexity, cost and provide work to regulatory specialists. Will it reduce instability and provide for a more resilient banking system? Inasmuch as it calls for recapitalizing the banks, yes. What is questionable though is the complexity through which this is achieved. This will certainly make for a more costly banking system.

After Basel I, the banking industry wanted a more fair model that would attribute capital according to risk. Which reminds one of the saying: 'Be careful what you wish for'.

BIBLIOGRAPHY

Bank for International Settlements (BIS) (n.d.), 'History – overview', available at http://www.bis.org/about/history.htm.
Bank for International Settlements (BIS) (2009), 'History of the Basel Committee and its membership', available at http://www.bis.org/bcbs/history.htm.

Ferguson, Niall (2012), *The Great Degeneration: how Institutions Decay and Economies Die*, Harmondsworth: Penguin Books.

Haldane, A.G. and V. Madouros (2012), 'The dog and the frisbee', available at http://www.bankofengland.co.uk/publications/Documents/speeches/2012/spe ech596.pdf.

McKinsey & Company (2012), 'Day of reckoning for European retail banking', available at http://www.mckinsey.com/client_service/risk/latest_thinking.

PricewaterhouseCoopers (2012), 'Banking industry reform: a new equilibrium', available at http://www.pwc.com/gx/en/banking-capital-markets/publications/ banking-industry-reform.jhtml.

Wikipedia (n.d.), 'Basel I', available at http://en.wikipedia.org/wiki/Basel_I.

14. Banks' challenges in Central and Eastern Europe

Radovan Jelašić

The banking sector in Central and Eastern Europe (CEE) is facing historical challenges on several fronts. First of all, not only has banker-bashing by politicians become a daily exercise, but fiscal measures such as a banking tax or a financial transactions tax are endangering the basic business model of the entire financial sector. Moreover, these actions have come on top of the constantly increasing regulatory requirements imposed by local and European Union (EU) lawmakers since the outbreak of the recent financial crisis in 2008. Secondly, macroeconomic uncertainties are posing a substantial challenge, especially in countries with traditionally unbalanced growth dynamics reflected in excessive foreign currency borrowing, high levels of public debt or lending booms financed mainly by foreign funding. Therefore, countries with a relatively low inflation rate, low budget deficits and low public spending have not undergone major gross domestic product (GDP) downward adjustments. Thirdly, investors are able to clearly differentiate among the countries of CEE, an expression that today is only a geographical phrase as the countries of this region are more different than ever due to their divergent macroeconomic developments. Last but not least, the honeymoon between the commercial banks and their clients is definitely over as clients have become well-informed, critical and selective when using financial services, and they are conscious of their rights. All of these reasons contributed to fundamentally reshaping the set-up of the banks in all aspects compared to what they used to be before the beginning of the financial crisis:

- Employee structure: the ratio of people employed in the sales network has decreased substantially compared to the number of staff employed at headquarters; risk-related jobs due to an explosion of non-performing loans have more than doubled or even tripled; the number of employees involved in internal audit, compliance, reporting requirements and dealing with supervisory-related tasks has grown at a disproportionally high rate, making management of operating cost a substantial challenge.

- Financing: due to substantial deleveraging, the importance of local funding has increased tremendously while intra-group funding has been reduced substantially; the importance of funding provided by international financial institutions such as the EBRD (European Bank for Reconstruction and Development), EIB (European Investment Bank), KfW (Kreditanstalt für Wiederaufbau – German development bank) group of German promotional banks and the IFC (International Finance Corporation, a member of the World Bank group) has become significant; government guarantee schemes have gained in importance as well; cross-border financing has become reserved to just a limited number of top-rated clients.
- Activity focuses: rather than continuing to hire and increase the branch network, banks have been cutting staff and closing down banking offices; despite valuations below book value, the interest in acquisition is close to zero; rather than enhancing scope and moving out of core business areas, everybody is going back to basic banking.
- Profitability: non-performing loans have become main profit drivers; return on equity has been falling also partly due to increased capital requirements; double-digit returns on equity have become a real exception.

While in good times before the collapse of Lehman Brothers even mediocre banks were able to show significant profits, the banking market today is far more competitive. For the move to this new reality, traditional remedies such as efficiency increases, pricing adjustments and scope revision, by the time they have been implemented, are too little and too late. Hoping to grow out of the existing problems is hardly possible either, as in most CEE countries banks' non-performing loans are reducing the size of interest-bearing assets day by day; the volume of amortized loans is much higher than the volume of newly extended loans; deposit gathering is very competitive and pricy; the repricing of existing loans even due to substantially increasing administrative or funding costs is challenged by supervisors; and non-business-related expenses are increasing continuously. Last but not least it is not only the banks but clients as well that are deleveraging, while GDP growth is in the best case a meagre 1 to 2 per cent per annum. Under such circumstances, which are not expected to change soon, one definitely has to pose a question: what to do next? There is a lot of work to be done by all participants.

Banks need to reinvent themselves and prepare for the new reality in all aspects. Banks need to focus on their core services in which they are the best rather than on areas that might look most profitable or are currently in vogue. Moreover, instead of focusing on transactions, when the pricing of stand-alone transactions can hardly cover costs, they need to focus on relationship banking based on maintaining salary accounts. In order to become a one-stop shop for financial services in general, banks need to offer not only their own products but also services offered by other financial service providers. The previous strategy of offering all services to all clients definitely failed due to lack of exclusive knowledge in all areas and the absence of economies of scale. Efficiency needs to be boosted substantially as well, almost like in car manufacturing during the last decades, in order to be able to deliver services that are customer-tailored and exactly on time.

Supervisors more than ever need daily contact with the industry as their measures can substantially impact upon the banking sector. No mistakes are allowed, as both parties should be fully aware of the responsibilities they have for the entire macroeconomic stability. Supervision has become more costly not only for the institutions that carry out supervisory tasks but also for the objects of supervision, as the number of supervisors has been constantly increasing and as the number of regulations has been growing exponentially in the same way as reporting requirements. The establishment of new regulatory measures and institutions should not be the end of it; if the set-up changes, it should become normal procedure to also remove an institution or regulation in the process.

Governments are also playing a key role in achieving a stable and active banking sector by securing macroeconomic stability and providing a maximal level of medium-term and long-term predictability. Supporting the existing banking sector, even if that is not politically opportunistic, is much more beneficial than trying to build up a new financial sector with more state ownership. The need for some state involvement at the beginning of the financial crisis should not be used today to take away the benefits of strategic owners in the banking sector created in the 1990s and the 2000s in the CEE countries.

International financial institutions also need to readjust their strategy in the region and refocus away from privatization and cross-border lending towards the development of local currency money markets, working out non-performing loans and providing partial guaranties for certain industries. The market must be allowed to clean up the existing banking system by mergers, takeovers or partial sales, soon.

As the set-up of the new supervisory framework in the EU has not been optimal by far, several countries have used it as an excuse to intervene on a local basis, thereby further segmenting the delicately balanced banking sector. In addition to the different macroeconomic perspectives, the 'me first' syndrome practised by some countries has also contributed to the fact that in many cases the valuation of subsidiaries on a stand-alone basis is much higher than the value of an entire group. It is entirely opposite to what took place just a couple of years ago.

The banking sector was an engine of the transition process in CEE since its very beginning and if that is fixed soon, it can become a driving force once again. Therefore, instead of replacing the banking sector, one must fine-tune and adjust it as there is neither the time nor the need to build up a new one.

15. Banking in CEE: less growth, more balance

Gianfranco Bisagni, Matteo Ferrazzi and Pia Pumberger

15.1 CENTRAL EASTERN EUROPE AND THE ECONOMIC ENVIRONMENT

Central Eastern European (CEE[1]) economies are no longer at the centre of the financial storm as it was the case in 2008–2009, when many CEE countries were under the fire of rating agencies and had to ask for the support of the International Monetary Fund (IMF).[2] Growth has regained some strength, too. However, the recovery has been more sluggish in many of the CEE economies than in other emerging markets;[3] moreover, the CEE countries are, at least indirectly, exposed to the sovereign debt crisis in the euro area: they feel the effect of the financial stress (and economic slowdown) spilling over from the western part of Europe.

Following the recent economic and financial crisis, Western Europe experienced a weakening of growth momentum and an increase of market pressure related to the debt vulnerabilities in the so-called 'peripheries'. The country picture is highly heterogeneous: while Germany and France showed a positive gross domestic product (GDP) development (following the relevant drop in 2009), Italy and Spain are facing severe recessions. Crisis countries (such as Italy and Spain) as well as 'programme countries' (Greece, Ireland, Portugal) are taking measures to reduce their deficits, but this is having an impact in terms of growth for the whole euro area. However, the developments in 2012 led to an increased strengthening of the euro area, credibly indicating the authorities' determination to avoid a break-up of the European Monetary Union (EMU), especially following the European Central Bank (ECB)'s Outright Monetary Transactions (OMT) initiative. The renewed market optimism during 2012 and the reduced financial stress will have a positive impact on EMU-wide real economy.

This said, CEE GDP growth forecasts have been progressively marked

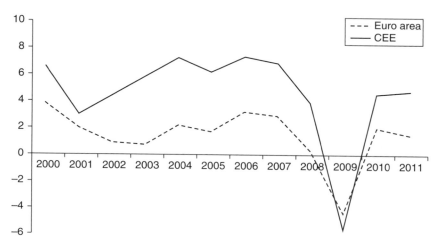

Source: Central banks, UniCredit.

Figure 15.1 *Economic performance in the euro area and CEE (real GDP growth in %)*

down due to weakening momentum in Western Europe, but the financial conditions were more relaxed during the second half of 2012. It is not only the trade channel (via exports) or the financial market sentiment which is having an impact on CEE economies, but also the linkages with the Western European banking sector (the top financial players operating in CEE are from Austria, Italy and France). Still, CEE is set to significantly outperform EMU. Convergence will continue, but at a lower pace than in the first part of the 2000s (see Figure 15.1). What is also different from before is the increased heterogeneity in the economic performance: it is crucial not to consider the CEE region as a uniform bloc. Hungary, the Czech Republic and Romania were in technical recession during 2012; Poland, Slovakia, Ukraine and Russia all displayed steady growth in 2010 and 2011, even if they gradually lost steam in 2012.[4] In general, the larger and less open economies (Turkey, Russia and Poland) with a greater reliance on domestic markets show resilience in the face of global headwinds.

The size of the shock observed during the peak of the crisis, as well as the performance of the CEE region in the post-crisis period, stem from structural differences among the different economies. The Commonwealth of Independent States (CIS), and Russia in particular, are very much dependent on the commodity cycle; Central European economies are more stable, structurally solid, but exposed to German demand and Western European's manufacturing cycle; South-Eastern Europe (SEE) is more vulnerable and dependent on foreign refinancing, given the high foreign debt levels. The different country risk profiles should continue to drive significant divergence in banking sectors' performance also in the years to come. Over the medium to long term, banks in CEE should maintain enough potential to generate a growth higher than average in the EU, in terms of both volumes and profitability. One of the drivers of growth is the still relevant difference in the financial penetration rate compared to Western Europe. The ratio of banking assets in per cent of GDP is as yet half as big as the correspondent ratio of the euro area. If we compare the banking penetration of CEE with that of other emerging markets, the potential is also clear. On the consumer side, retail volumes in CEE correspond to around 100 per cent of disposable income, while they exceed 390 per cent of disposable income in Western Europe, Asia and North America (only Latin America having a lower ratio than CEE). On the corporate side, corporate volumes are less than 60 per cent of GDP in CEE and Latin America, and close to 100 per cent or higher in the Middle East, Western Europe and Asia, according to the estimates of McKinsey Global Banking Pools.

15.1.1   Impact on CEE from EMU Bank Deleveraging is a Manageable Drag

The severity of the sovereign debt crisis in the euro area that started in 2010 contributed to the rising fears that capital needs and funding pressures faced by Western European banks may heighten pressure to deleverage in Central and Eastern Europe. Multiple capital linkages among CEE and Western European banks have exposed the region to knock-on effects from the current crisis in the euro area. For many years some banking sectors in CEE have been relying strongly on foreign funding (mainly parent funding) and foreign liabilities currently account for a significant part of their assets.

Still, concerns about a credit crunch and a widespread deleveraging of Austrian, Italian or French banks that belong to the most active players in the CEE region, did not materialize. On the contrary, overall exposure to the region increased. The CEE business of Austrian banks has been a major source of revenue and growth for instance.[5]

In the mid-term a less favourable macroeconomic environment and persistent regulatory pressure may force some Western European banks to implement more rebalanced (towards self-funding) business models in their CEE subsidiaries. The group of the most exposed countries includes

Bulgaria, Croatia, Romania and Serbia. This is related to the fact that their banking systems are highly penetrated by foreign players,[6] which in the past heavily funded their local subsidiaries and in some cases might be exposed to heightened pressures. On the other hand there is a group of countries (e.g. Russia and Turkey) that does not face any risk of deleveraging related to parent banks' problems.

Regarding most recent mergers and acquisitions activity in the region, Russian banks dominated the scene both locally and abroad. VTB acquired Bank of Moscow (number six in terms of assets in the Russian market) while Sberbank entered the CEE market via Volksbank International. The market consolidation in Russia is also witnessing an increasing role of state banks. The banking sector in CEE was also affected by the consolidation of the Greek banking sector at home: the National Bank of Greece and Eurobank EFG, both having a relevant presence in SEE countries, merged. In Slovenia, some banks need to be recapitalized and some potential buyers are from Russia. Some additional opportunities are deriving from the need to divest by Hypo Alpe Adria, which is expected to sell some subsidiaries in Central Eastern Europe, and by the Belgian KBC.[7] Turkey is confirmed to be one of the most attractive markets: banks from the Middle East and Russia as well as global players are looking to increase their presence (Sberbank acquired DenizBank, for instance). The role of domestic owners in CEE is increasing, but foreign players continue to play an important role. Foreign players account on average for more than 60 per cent of total banking assets in the region (excluding Russia). In the Czech Republic, Latvia, Bosnia and Herzegovina, Estonia, Croatia, Hungary and Slovakia, foreign banks account for nearly or more than 90 per cent. Overall, top foreign banking players in CEE recorded an increase in CEE assets out of their group assets in 2011 and 2012.

15.2   CEE BANKING SECTOR

In 2010–2012 wide divergences in lending performance persisted, but larger economies and those with lower funding gaps see generally higher growth (with exceptions; see Figure 15.2). Comparable trends could remain in place also in 2013 and 2014.

The crisis had an influence on credit demand and investment activity in CEE. Still, the evolution of corporate loans showed an accelerating trend in 2012 (versus 2011) with a year-on-year (YOY) growth higher than 10 per cent in the CEE region. With 2009 being the only negative year for the banking sector, with deleveraging activity done regarding corporate

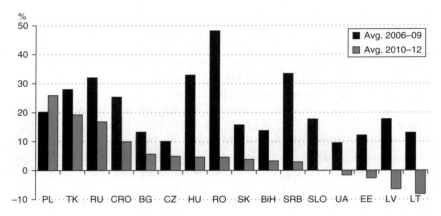

Source: Central banks, UniCredit.

Figure 15.2   Average growth in lending in CEE countries

lending in most CEE countries, a credit crunch only took place in the Baltics and in Hungary for a short period of time. In general, the forecast growth of corporate lending for 2013–2015 is around 10 per cent, whereas especially Turkey and the former CIS countries (Russia, Ukraine and Kazakhstan) show a stronger upturn. However, corporate lending growth levels as experienced before the crisis are not expected to return in the near future. The 'golden age' of the credit boom has finished, and it is not a negative development per se: less growth will be accompanied by a more balanced and sustainable approach, which will be beneficial in some cases for the stability of the economies in the region and their banking sectors (many CEE economies were clearly overheated before the Lehman Brothers collapse in September 2008 – Estonia, Latvia, Lithuania, Romania, Ukraine are the best examples – and the macroeconomic imbalances brought them to a difficult situation).

Looking at the deposit side, a key variable in the current environment, the CEE banking sector experienced a significant slowdown during the peak of the crisis; only Turkey and former CIS countries remained in positive territory in terms of annual growth. In 2012, further acceleration in deposit growth happened; again Turkey and former CIS countries outperformed growth levels of the other CEE countries.

This said, the loan-to-deposit ratio (see Figures 15.3 and 15.4) – a good indication for the long-term sustainability of funding – across the whole banking sector in CEE region is remaining broadly stable; structural imbalances in the Baltics are offset by low loan-to-deposits ratios in

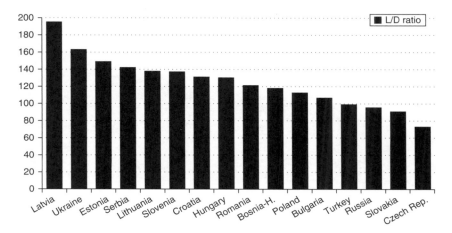

Source: Central banks, UniCredit.

Figure 15.3   Loan-to-deposit ratio in 2011

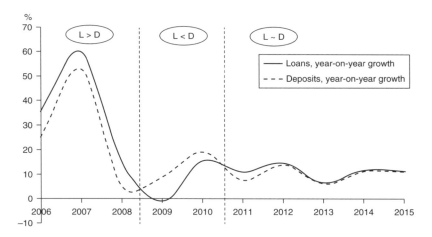

Source: Central banks, UniCredit.

Figure 15.4   Growth in loans and deposits in CEE

former CIS states, Turkey and some Central European countries such as the Czech Republic and Slovakia.

Banks' clients suffered from the crisis and had problems, in some cases, repaying the money they had borrowed; the crisis of 2008–2009 had a

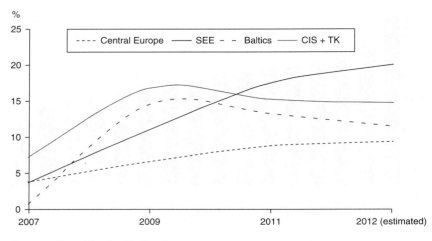

Source: Central banks, UniCredit.

Figure 15.5   Credit quality in CEE (impaired loans in % of gross loans)

strong impact on the quality of assets also within the CEE area. Especially Ukraine, Romania and Hungary were and still are countries with a much higher percentage of impaired loans (in per cent of gross lending; see Figure 15.5) than countries such as Turkey, the Czech Republic and Slovakia, where the quality of assets has been preserved quite well. The CEE average of impaired loans of gross loans is expected to decrease slowly but steadily.

In this respect provisions for non-performing loans (NPLs) saw a heavy increase in 2008–2009, but started to decrease significantly in 2010–2011. In the future they are expected to decline further. Slow volume growth, lower revenues, deterioration in credit quality, all forced banks to put in place various restructuring measures. Both costs and revenues were reduced. In the past, the expansion of banks drove costs to increase faster than revenues. However, this trend was reverted after a successful restructuring within the banking industry following cost rationalization, balance sheet restructuring and efficiency increases. For the next few years the cost-to-income ratio is expected to remain rather stable (see Figure 15.6).

The profitability of the banking sector in CEE as a whole suffered a very relevant deceleration in 2009 (see Figure 15.7), but it did not become a loss (losses, however, were registered in the banking sectors of various countries, such as Romania, Bosnia-Herzegovina, Ukraine, Latvia and Lithuania). Profit before tax was of course hit by the strong increase in provisions during 2008–2009. A reduction of provisions and cost-cutting

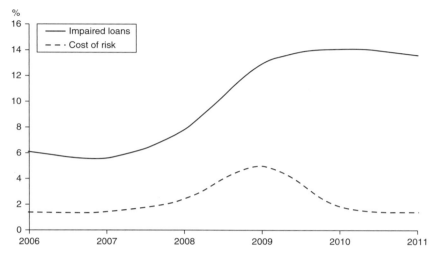

Source: Central banks, UniCredit.

Figure 15.6   Impaired loans and cost of risk (per cent of lending) in CEE

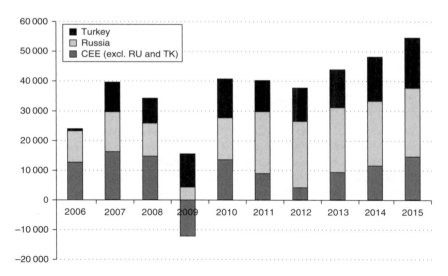

Source: Central banks, UniCredit.

Figure 15.7   Banking sector profitability

led to a strong increase in profit starting in 2010. Profitability is expected to improve in 2012–15. The next few years will also witness a positive (even if moderate) development of revenues, with special focus on non-interest income due to strong efforts on cross-selling,[8] and more or less stable operating costs and provisions. Emerging priorities for banks are also the reduction of unproductive assets from non-profitable segments and geographies, and a stronger focus on core business areas to improve efficiency.[9]

15.3   MAJOR CHALLENGES FACED BY BANKS

Since the start of the financial crisis in 2008 the CEE region has been witnessing an increase in the regulatory pressure on banks (starting from the increase in the level of guaranteed deposits, early repayment schemes, fine-tuning of reserve requirements, etc.), with the aim of improving the stability of the financial sector. Later, specific regulations on foreign exchange (FX) lending[10] (in Hungary, Croatia, Serbia, Ukraine, Turkey) were also applied, as well as banks' levies (in Hungary, Slovakia, Slovenia, Romania). On top of this, the Basel III reforms were finalized and will enter into force during the next few years.

There is still much uncertainty about the new regulatory framework[11] in the euro area, which will also impact upon CEE countries. However, one thing is clear: politicians want banks to take less risk and to continue to stimulate the real economy. In such a context, over-regulation remains a risk for the banking sector and could make it harder to capitalize on growth opportunities.

15.3.1   Cross-border Regulatory Challenges

In November 2011, the Austrian central bank and the Austrian Financial Market Authority announced that subsidiaries of the three largest Austrian banks (Erste Group Bank, Raiffeisen Bank International and UniCredit Bank Austria) have to ensure that the loans to local stable funding ratio (LLSFR) of new loans to local refinancing does not exceed 110 per cent.

Convergence toward a much healthier funding structure is clearly a highly desirable target.

The LLSFR will affect lending in countries where the loan-to-deposit (L/D) ratio is already high (for example Ukraine, the Baltics, Serbia). In countries that are characterized by huge funding gaps a stronger focus will be placed on funding strategies, with the most successful ones helping banks diversify properly between stable funding sources. On the back of that, the role of domestic funding resources (especially deposits) will continue to increase in importance. Similarly, the increased use of supranational funding will help banks achieve a greater diversification of funding. In this respect there is also some risk that a few smaller CEE countries could be affected more strongly, especially if their home-country supervisors start implementing their own regulations as well.

The role of non-bank financial intermediaries
Local capital markets remain a fairly shallow source of financing in the region (see Figure 15.8). Only a number of countries have been able to actively develop their markets, with the size of the bond market exceeding the level of 25 per cent as a share of GDP (as in the case of Turkey, Poland, Hungary and the Czech Republic, as well as Slovakia and Slovenia). In a similar vein the local equity markets are also small, with only Poland, Russia, Turkey, Croatia and the Czech Republic exceeding the 15 per cent of GDP mark. From this perspective the role of non-bank financial intermediaries remains in the developing stage in most countries of the region, and both the crisis and recent pressures on liquidity and funding make any substantial development quite unlikely in the foreseeable future.

15.3.2   Basel III and Capital Requirements Directive (CRD IV)

Basel III is the new global regulatory standard on bank capital adequacy, stress testing and market liquidity risk agreed upon by the members of the Basel Committee[12] on Banking Supervision in 2010 to 2011. Different from Basel II (which concentrated on credit, market and operational risk), the main focus of Basel III is on: (1) capital requirements; (2) liquidity requirements; (3) the leverage ratio of banks; and (4) a substantial strengthening and unification of the supervision of the financial sector. Basel III also reinforced the rules covering market risk, particularly the ones that deal with counterparty risk management and created a new category of financial institutions, the systemically important financial institutions (SIFIs, 'the ones too big to fail'). However, the rules regarding operational risk remained unchanged from Basel II:

1.   Basel III will require banks to increase their capital:
     - Tier 1 capital will have to be increased from 4 per cent (Basel II) to 6 per cent of risk weighted assets while the list of eligible tier 2 capital instruments will be reduced.
     - Basel III will introduce a mandatory capital buffer of 2.5 per cent – in effect requiring banks to add this percentage to their total capital.

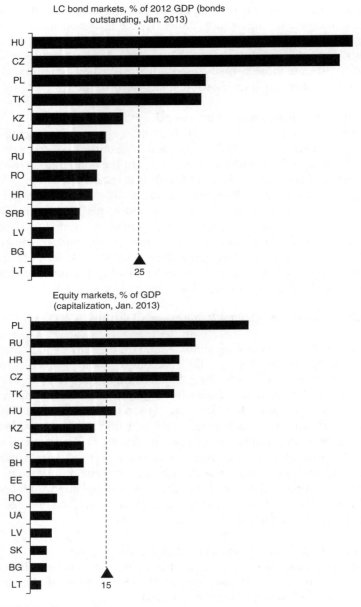

Source: Bloomberg, UniCredit

Figure 15.8   Local capital markets in % of 2011 GDP

- In addition the local regulator may add a discretionary counter-cyclical buffer of up to 2.5 per cent of capital during periods of high credit growth.

All this will raise the total capital to be held against risk-weighted assets to 10.5 per cent against 8.0 per cent at the time of writing.

2. Basel III will introduce minimum liquidity standards:

   - A short-term (30 days) liquidity coverage ratio (LCR) is a ratio designed to ensure that financial institutions have the necessary liquid assets on hand to ride out short-term liquidity disruptions. Banks are required to hold an amount of highly liquid assets, such as cash or Treasury bonds, equal to or greater than their net cash outflow over a 30-day period.
   - A longer-term structural liquidity ratio called net stable funding ratio (NSFR) that measures how much stable funding a bank has to tolerate a year-long liquidity crisis. This funding ratio seeks to ensure that long-term assets are funded by long-term, stable liabilities.

3. Introduction of a leverage ratio to limit the amount of maximum leverage: the sum of on-balance sheet and off-balance sheet assets may not be greater than 33 times the bank's capital.

4. Further tightening of counterparty risk management requirements:

   - Introduction of credit valuation adjustment (CVA) indicators, measuring the risk due to the deterioration in a counterparty's credit rating.
   - Strengthening of the capital requirements for counterparty credit exposures to large regulated financial entities and to unregulated financial entities arising from banks' derivatives, repo and securities financing transactions.

All of the above-mentioned measures will add to the cost base of banks and will either force some of them to shift these costs or reduce those types of businesses which will be especially affected by the new rules (mainly market-related transactions). So far the impact on the economic growth perspectives in the CEE region has not been adequately assessed. Still, the Basel III regulatory requirements could prove to be a challenge for banks active in CEE. While the quantitatively and qualitatively tighter capital requirements under Basel III should not pose significant challenges for the CEE subsidiaries of foreign banks (CEE banking sectors are generally overcapitalized), they obviously require the further build-up of high-quality capital at the group level during the gradual phasing-in of Basel III.

The new requirements regarding liquidity coverage and net stable funding ratios, however, could represent a major challenge for CEE banks. In view of the fact that the new rules will force banks to reconsider their present funding policies and to substantially adjust their portfolios of funding products, the Basel Committee has since decided to postpone the implementation of these liquidity requirements until the end of 2018. This should give all banks concerned more time to adjust their business strategies to the tighter regulatory environment.

15.4 SUMMARY AND CONCLUSIONS

Overall the CEE region's performance is expected to remain positive in the coming years, despite challenges ahead. CEE growth should move in line with global trends, still outperforming Western Europe: taking into consideration the past as well as current developments, it is anticipated that the CEE banking sector will continue to generate above-EU average growth in banking volumes and profitability. But the divergence among segments and countries will remain relevant. Besides the macroeconomic environment, changes in regulatory requirements such as cross-border regulatory changes and Basel III (the latter focusing on capital adequacy, liquidity management and derivative products), pose challenges in the future. Banks will have to focus on various areas to mitigate the effects of the new regulations on their profitability; among those, product redesign (especially to fulfil the liquidity requirements) and a different customer segmentation[13] (their capital must be allocated to higher-return clients to be sure to allocate the capital to high-return customers).

NOTES

1. CEE includes Bosnia and Herzegovina, Bulgaria, Croatia, Czech Republic, Estonia, Hungary, Kazakhstan, Latvia, Lithuania, Poland, Romania, Russia, Serbia, Slovakia, Slovenia, Turkey and Ukraine.
2. Before the Greek package, three-quarters of the money that the IMF spent to support various countries around the world in 2008–2009 was devoted to Central Eastern Europe. Ukraine, Latvia, Hungary, Belarus, Serbia, Romania and Bosnia-Herzegovina received support from the IMF.
3. See EBRD (2010).
4. See Vienna Institute for International Economic Studies (wiiw) (2012); UniCredit (2013).
5. Source: OeNB (2012).
6. See De Haas and van Lelyveld (2006).
7. KBC is one of the largest international players in CEE, after UniCredit, Raiffeisen, Erste and Société Générale (which reported €140 billion, €87 billion and €72 billion of total assets, respectively, in mid-2012).

8. Companies in general work hard to persuade existing customers to buy additional products. Banks are trying to obtain revenues from non-lending products, which are very often more profitable and less RWA (risk weighted assets)-consuming. For an analysis of the positive and negative sides of cross-selling, see Shah and Kumar (2012).
9. See Capgemini (2012).
10. See Beckmann et al. (2012).
11. For a comprehensive overview of regulatory reform, see Dayal et al. (2012).
12. At the time of writing (early 2013) the final deadline for Basel III implementation in the different European countries is not yet clear, nor the final text is ready. In Europe, the trilogue (European Commission, Council, European Parliament) has been ongoing since May 2012 and progress was slow in some cases because of the complexity of the files and interdependencies on other dossiers (Banking Union and the single supervisory mechanism, Crisis Management Directive, etc.).
13. See Capgemini (2012).

REFERENCES

Beckmann, E., J. Fidrmuc and H. Stix (2012), 'Foreign currency loans and loan arrears of households in Central and Eastern Europe', OeNB Working Paper 181, November.

Capgemini (2012), 'Trends in the global banking industry'.

Dayal, R., G. Grasshoff, D. Jackson, P. Morel, P. Neu and T. Pfuhler (2012), 'An inflection point in global banking', Boston Consulting Group.

De Haas, R. and I. van Lelyveld (2006), 'Foreign banks and credit stability in Central and Eastern Europe: a panel data analysis', *Journal of Banking and Finance*, **30**, 1927–52.

EBRD (2010), 'Transition Report 2010: Recovery and reform', London.

OeNB (Oesterreichische Nationalbank) (2012), 'Financial Stability Report', n. 24, December.

Shah, D. and V. Kumar (2012), 'The dark side of cross-selling', *Harvard Business Review*, December, available at http://hbr.org/2012/12/the-dark-side-of-cross-selling/ar/1.

UniCredit (2013), 'CEE Quarterly Q1'.

Vienna Institute for International Economic Studies (wiiw) (2012), 'Current analyses and forecasts', July.

Index

Acemoglu, D. 117
Africa 93
  North 94, 99
  sub-Saharan 95, 99
Albania 63, 66, 170, 172, 185
Angelovska Bezovska, A. 171
Artis, M.J. 152
Asia 49–59, 93, 94, 228
  emerging markets in 49
Aslanidis, N. 153
Association of Southeast Asian
    Nations (ASEAN)
  +3 countries: offer of multilateral
    FX backstop 52, 54
Austria 21, 40, 227
  and Austrian Financial Market
    Authority 234
  banks in 228, 234

Baba, C. 103
Bakker, B. 4, 5
balance of payments (BoP) 92–3,
  98–103 , 105–6, 108
  shortcomings of traditional
    framework of 101–2
Balassa–Samuelson effect 22
Baltic countries 5, 25, 26, 29, 31, 101,
  114, 155, 159, 190–205, 230–31, 234
  economic adjustment in, *see*
    economic adjustment in the
    Baltic countries
Banerjee, A.V. 10
bank lending survey (EIB) 64–81
banking in the CEE (and) 226–39
  Basel III and Capital Requirements
    Directive (CRD IV) 235, 237–8
  the CEE banking sector 229–34, 238
  the economic environment 226
  impact from EMU bank
    deleveraging as manageable
    drag 228–9

major challenges 234–5
  cross-border regulatory changes
    234–5
  role of non-bank financial
    intermediaries 235
Banking Regulation and Supervision
    Agency (BRSA) 126, 136, 141
banks' challenges in CEE countries
  222–5
  activity focuses 223
  employee structure 222–3
  financing 223
  government support 224
  preparation for the new reality
    223–4
  profitability 223
  readjustment of strategy 224
  supervision 224
banks/banking
  Austrian 228, 234
    Central Bank 234
    Erste Group Bank 234
    Raiffeisen Bank International
      234
    UniCredit Bank 234
  Bank for International Settlements
    (BIS) 81, 209
  Bank of Moscow 229
  Basel capital requirements for 13
  Central Bank of the Republic of
    Turkey (CBRT) 126–7, 132–3
  challenges for, *see* banks' challenges
    in CEE countries
  Eurobank EFG 229
  European Bank for Reconstruction
    and Development (EBRD) 135,
    142, 223
    Transition Indicator 31
  European banking union 44
  European Central Bank (ECB) 42,
    106, 218, 226

and Outright Monetary
    Transactions (OMT) initiative
    226
survey on lending 64–81
European Investment Bank (EIB)
    223
and bank lending survey for
    CESEE region 61, 64–80
Greek 68, 82, 229
KfW German development bank
    223
National Bank of Greece 229
National Bank of the Republic of
    Macedonia (NBRM) 180–84
Nordic 191, 195, 204
Oesterreichische Nationalbank
    (OeNB) 5
and OeNB–BOF projections 10
simulations and growth
    differential 7
Riksbank 191
Russian Central Bank 120
in SEE-6 economies 175–81
Washington Mutual 211
see also CESEE banks: deleveraging
    or rebalancing?
Barro, R.J. 149
Basel I Accord 209–10, 212, 220
Basel II Accord 14, 210–14, 218–19,
    235
and core of Pillar I 210–11
regulatory framework of 210
Basel III 14, 209–21
bank(s) reaction to 213–17
capital adequacy/liquidity
    requirements for banks 13, 14
and Capital Requirements Directive
    235, 237
as driving implementation of Basel
    II 218–19
historical circumstances of 209–11
and implications for corporate
    customer relationship 217
policy reaction 211–13
ratios 213
reforms 234
and unintended consequences
    218–20
Basel III from a practitioner's
    perspective, *see* Basel III

Basel capital requirements for banks 13
Basel Committee on Banking
    Supervision 17, 211–12, 235, 238
Standards Implementation, Policy
    Development, Accounting and
    Consultation 209
Belgium 21, 229
Benczúr, P. 152
Biroli, P. 44
Bosnia 170, 188, 229
Bosnia-Herzegovina 66, 232
Brazil 113
Breitung, J. 152, 153
Bretton Woods system of foreign
    exchange 151, 209
BRIC (Brazil, Russia, India, China)
    countries 113
Bulgaria 21, 22, 26, 27, 28, 31, 66, 95,
    101, 151, 160, 229
business conditions, indicators of 30–31
Ease of Doing Business ranking
    30–31
EBRD Transition Indicator 31
business cycle convergence or
    decoupling (and) 147–69
data and methods 153–5
calculation of business cycles
    153–4
correlation 154–5
dataset 153
dispersion 154
synchronization measures 154
empirical results 155–63
cyclical heterogeneity within
    CESEE region 155–60
decoupling of CESEE countries
    from Euro area cycle? 160–63
implications for the catching-up
    process 163–5
literature: business cycle convergence
    between CESEE region and
    euro area 151–3
literature: income vs. business cycle
    convergence 148–51

capital flows (and) 92–110
ability of countries to influence size
    and direction of private 103–5
capital mobility and monetary policy
    105–7

changes in current account balance
98–9
free and turbulent 92–7
free capital movement and current
account imbalances 99–103
capital flows in a globalized economy,
see capital flows
the Caribbean 94, 98–9
Cavenaile, L. 149
Central and Eastern European (CEE)
countries/economies 19–35
banking in, *see* banking in the
CEE
banks' challenges in, *see* banks'
challenges in CEE countries
cost competitiveness of 23–4
fiscal balances of 26–7
joining the EU (2004) 21
non-euro 22
movement in real GDP over time in
21–2
vs. other countries 19–34
see also restarting growth in
Europe
Central, Eastern and South-Eastern
European (CESEE) economy 49
Central Europe 5, 31, 227–8, 231–2
CESEE banks: deleveraging or
rebalancing? (and) 60–81
background to unique bank lending
survey (EIB) 64–71
banking in CESEE 62–4
non-performing loans (NPL) 61,
63–4, 75–7
results from subsidiary level section
of EIB survey 71–8
statistical exercise using bank
lending survey results 78–80
CESEE countries/economies 3–10,
123, 138, 141
affected by surge in NPLs 75–6
economic adjustment of 147–69
see also business cycle convergence
or decoupling
EU member states 6–7, 147, 149
lessons for 49–59
see also managing stop–go capital
flows in Asian emerging
markets
CESEE-8 countries 153, 155–7

changes in banking in run-up to the
crisis (and) 12–18
comparison with other structural
proposals 17
lack of restraint from regulation,
supervision and market
discipline 13
public reaction to crisis/need to
rebuild trust 14
regulatory response, *see* regulatory
response to global financial
crisis
role of banks in financing the
European economy 18
Chen, S. 50, 107
Chiang Mai Initiative 52, 54
China 4, 93, 107, 113, 119, 120, 210
and increasing share in CEE exports
33
Commonwealth of Independent States
(CIS) 94–6, 227
economies 99
former countries of 230–31
cost competitiveness 21, 22–4, 190,
194–5, 198
Crespo-Cuaresma, J. 154
Croatia 66, 153, 160, 170, 184, 229,
234, 235
Cyprus 160
Czech Republic 21, 22, 24, 27, 28, 33,
66, 151, 153, 160, 227, 229, 231,
232, 235

Dabrowski, M. 101
Dabušinskas, A. 195
Darvas, Z. 152
de Haan, J. 153
Denmark 30
Dubois, D. 149
Duflo, E. 10

EA (new) countries 155, 157
EA-3 countries 198, 200, 201
EA-5 countries 153, 155–7, 160, 167
EA-12 countries 153, 156, 160, 164,
167
East Asia 119
Eastern Europe 10, 119
economic adjustment in the Baltic
countries (and) 190–205

advantages/disadvantages of fast vs.
  gradual adjustment 199–203
comparison with Ireland, Greece
  and Portugal 197–9
expansion (2000–2007) 191–5
recession (2007–2008 and
  2008–2009) 195–7
recovery (2009–2010) 197
Economic Co-operation and
  Development, Organisation for
  (OECD)
  Code of Liberalization of Capital
    Movements 103
  data 30
  'Going for Growth' report 122
  index of employment protection 30
economic freedom, Hermitage
  Foundation index of 118
Eichengreen, B. 36
Eickmeier, S. 152, 153
emerging market economies (EMEs)
  49, 58, 92–3, 101, 107, 122–3, 132,
  139, 141–2, 147–9, 152, 155, 165–6
  as drivers of global growth 122
  HSBC report on 122
Enikolopov, R. 119
Estonia 21, 23, 32, 151, 152, 160, 190,
  194–6, 229, 230
European Banking Authority (EBA)
  16
European Commission (EC) 14, 44, 60
  proposal to use bail-in instruments
    16
European Council 44
  and European banking union 44
European debt crisis and stable design
  of EMU (and) 36–46
  competitiveness problems 39–41
  credit growth 38–9
  government finances 42
  house prices 39
  imbalances 42
  rules governing EMU 36
    see also European Monetary
      Union (EMU)
  Stability and Growth Pact 36, 38, 42
    see also subject entry
  a stable design of EMU 44–5
  strengthening the Macroeconomic
    Imbalances Procedure 44

European High-Level Expert Group
  recommendation of European
    Commission evaluation 17
  and reform of structure of EU
    banking sector 15, 16, 17
European Monetary Union (EMU) 42,
  44–5, 226–7
  bank deleveraging 228–9
  CESEE member states of 147
  rules governing 36
  stable design of, see European debt
    crisis and stable design of
    EMU
  as trading partner of SEE-6 region
    172
European Union (EU) 19, 101, 129,
  210, 222
  accession by ten countries (2004)
    151
  acquis 103
  -based banks 181
  fiscal balances of countries in 26–7
  regulatory reforms 14

Fed, *see* United States (US)
Feldstein, M. 100
Fernández-Amador, O. 154
Fidrmuc, J. 151–2
Filardo, A. 52, 58
financial crisis (2008–2009) 19, 120; *see
  also* Great Recession
Finland 21, 30, 40, 41, 196
fiscal policy 26, 104, 126, 138, 151, 194,
  199
  in Estonia 196
France 21, 36, 226, 227
Frankel, J.A. 147
Fujita, K. 175

G-20 107
Gächter, M. 7, 153
Georgia 95
Germany 21, 36, 39, 40, 41, 45, 182,
  223, 226, 228
Gershenkron, A. 116
Ghosh, A.R. 106
GIIPS (Greece, Ireland, Italy, Portugal,
  Spain) 21, 22–5, 27, 28–9, 32, 34
Global Competitiveness Index of
  World Economic Forum 41

global financial crisis 12, 19, 21, 34, 66, 93–4, 122, 132, 138, 142, 190, 195–6 138; *see also* Great Recession
Great Depression 92
Great Recession 19, 21, 25, 32, 34, 60, 75, 165, 211; *see also* restarting growth in Europe
Greece 21, 38–41, 42, 182, 190, 191, 197–8, 199, 226, 229
banks in 68
Grenville, S. 58
Guriev, S. 115

Halter, D. 10
Helbling, T. 148
Herzegovina 170, 188, 229
Hodrick, R.J. 154
Hong Kong 50–52
Horioka, C. 100
Hungary 21, 22, 27, 28, 31, 33, 66, 138, 160, 151, 152, 153, 160, 163, 227, 229, 230, 232, 234, 235

Independent Commission on Banking 17
India 4, 107, 113
inflation 50, 93, 99, 105, 114–15, 125–7, 153, 176, 180–81, 191, 194, 195, 222
and cost competitiveness 22–4
International Finance Corporation (IFC) 223
International Monetary Fund (IMF) 60, 176, 199, 209, 226, 238
Multilateral Consultation framework of 107
Ireland 21, 30, 38–40, 41, 42, 45, 191, 197–8, 199, 226
Ishi, K. 175
Italy 21, 31, 38–41, 42, 226, 227

Janský, P. 33
Jaumotte, F. 41
Joint Action Plan of international financial institutions 61

Kazakhstan 101, 114, 230
Kenen, P. 149
Klingen, C. 4, 5

Kokenyne, A. 103
Korhonen, I. 151–2
Kose, M.A. 147, 148
Krugman, P. 101

Latin America 93, 94, 98–9, 228
Latvia 21, 23, 32, 33, 151, 160, 190, 194, 195, 197, 229, 230, 232
and financial assistance from EU and IMF 199
legislation
and Basel Accords 210
Glass–Steagall Act (US) 12, 211
on specific fiscal rules 184
Lehman Brothers 5, 101, 114, 132, 138, 176, 211, 223
Lithuania 21, 23, 33, 151–2, 160, 190, 194, 195–6, 197, 230, 232
loan-to-deposit (LTD) ratio 63–4, 80

Macedonia 66, 95, 170–84, 185
as best-ranked country on Doing Business ranking (2012) 188
and its economy during crisis period 181–4
see also SEE-6 countries
McKinnon, R.I. 149
McKinsey & Company 214
McKinsey Global Banking Pools 228
Macroeconomic Imbalances Procedure 44
Malta 160
managing stop–go capital flows in Asian emerging markets (and) 49–59
capital flows and reality 50–54
lessons for CESEE economies 58–9
risks and policy space 54–8
Mayer, T. 101
Mexico 119–20
Middle East 94, 99, 228, 229
Moder, I. 165
Moldova 95
Montenegro 170
Morsy, H. 41
Mundell, R.A. 149

Netherlands 21, 30, 39, 40, 41, 45
non-performing loans (NPL) 61, 66, 72, 73, 79, 81, 138, 173, 180–81, 184, 222–4, 232

definitions of 63–4
  surge in 75–6
Nordic countries 30, 191
North, D. 117
North Africa 94, 99

OECD, *see* Economic Co-operation
  and Development, Organisation
  for (OECD)
Oechslin, M. 10
openness 31–3
Ostry, J. 106

Pisani-Ferry, J. 38
Poland 7, 21, 22, 23, 24, 27, 28, 30, 31,
  32, 151, 152, 153, 159–60, 166,
  227, 235
Portugal 21, 31, 38–41, 42, 191, 197–8,
  199, 226
Prescott, E.C. 154
*Proceedings of the National Academy
  of Sciences* 119
Próchniak, M. 149
Putin, President 118–19; *see also*
  Russia

quantitative easing in the US 50, 133

Randveer, M. 195
rankings
  Doing Business 118, 188
  Ease of Doing Business 30–31
  Global Competitive Index (WEF) 41
Rátfai, A. 152
regulatory response to global financial
  crisis (and) 14–17
  additional separation conditional on
    recovery and resolution plan 16
  capital requirements on trading
    assets and real estate-related
    instruments 16–17
  facilitating use of bail-in instruments
    16
  proposal and rationale for separation
    15
restarting growth in Europe (and)
  19–35
  convergence and growth 20–22
  the future: openness and integration
    31–3

and evolution in quality of
    exports 33
  imbalances: external, public and
    private 24–8
  inflation and cost competitiveness
    22–4
  unemployment and structural
    aspects 28–31
  and indicators of business
    conditions 30–31
  product market regulation 30
Riedl, A. 7
risk-sharing 45
risk-taking 14, 126, 220
Ritzberger-Grünwald, D. 7
Robinson, J. 117
Romania 21, 22, 23, 25, 28, 31, 32, 66,
  151, 160, 227, 229, 230, 232, 234
Rose, A.K. 147
Rostowski, J. 104
Roubinim, B. 101
Russia (and) 101, 113–21, 196, 210,
  227, 229, 230, 235
  Communist regimes 120
  economic freedom (Hermitage
    Foundation index) 118
  fast-growing economy of 113–14
  privatization 120
  ranking in World Bank Doing
    Business index 118
  reduction of food consumption in
    115
  reforms 120
  Russian Central Bank 120
  South Korea 115–18
  as WTO member 120

Savva, C.S. 152
SEE, *see* South-Eastern Europe (SEE)
SEE-6 countries/economies 170–89
  growth acceleration as challenge for
    188–9
Serbia 63, 66, 170, 184, 229, 234
Setser, B. 101
Single Market basic freedoms 103
  acquis communitaire 103
Sinn, H.-W. 101
Slovak Republic 21
Slovakia 33, 66, 151, 152, 160, 227,
  229, 231, 232, 234, 235

Slovenia 21, 31, 33, 63, 66, 95, 151, 152, 160, 229, 234, 235
small and medium-sized enterprises (SMEs) 18, 72–5, 213
Solow, R.M. 149
South Korea 115–18
    post-1998 crisis 116
South-Eastern Europe (SEE) 5, 228
South-Eastern Europe: impacts from the crisis, vulnerabilities and adjustments (and) 170–89
    challenges for the SEE-6 countries 184–8
    impact of crisis on SEE-6 region 172–80
    initial conditions in the SEE-6 before the crisis 171–2
    Macedonian economy during crisis period 181–4
    vulnerability analysis of SEE-6 countries before and during the crisis 180–81
Southern Europe 31, 40–42
Soviet Union 21, 119
Spain 21, 38–41, 42, 45, 226
Stability and Growth Pact 36, 38, 42, 44
    strengthening of the 147–8
Summers, L.H. 100
survey on bank lending (EIB) 64–81
sustainable growth and continued income divergence in Europe (and) 3–11
    balanced growth as important issue 3–4
    characteristics of sustainable growth model 4–5
    impact of crisis on income convergence 5–10
sustaining growth in emerging markets, *see* Turkey
Sweden 30, 191, 196, 212
Szapáry, G. 152

trust, rebuilding 14
Turkey (and) 114, 122–43, 227, 229, 230, 231, 232, 234, 235
    assessing growth experience of 123–32

before 2001 crisis 124–5
    after 2001 crisis 125–32
Banking Regulation and Supervision Agency (BRSA) 126, 136, 141
Central Bank of the Republic of Turkey (CBRT) 126–7, 132–7
    its economy vs. CESEE economies 138–41
    monetary policy stance after Lehman crisis 132–3
    recovery and growth 133–7
    Reserve Option Mechanism 135
    'Strengthening the Turkish Economy' reform programme 126

Ukraine 63, 66, 95, 227, 230, 232, 234
United Kingdom (UK) 15, 167, 210
United States (US) 12, 15, 96–7, 133, 210, 211
    Federal Reserve Board (Fed) 105–6
    jurisdiction 15
    legislation: Glass–Steagall Act 12, 211
    quantitative easing in 50, 133
    Volcker Rule 17
    Washington Mutual Bank 211
USSR, former 92

Van Rompuy, H. 44
Vickers, J. 117
Vienna Initiative 60, 61
Vienna Initiative 2 61, 64, 81
Vietnam 93
Voitchovsky, S. 10
Vojinovic, B. 149
Volcker Rule 17

Wälti, S. 147
Ward, K. 122
Western Europe 4, 7, 10, 228
World Bank 209, 223
    Doing Business index 118
World Trade Organization (WTO) 120
Wörz, J. 7, 165
Wyplosz, C. 36

Yetman, J. 58

Zhuravskaya, E. 115